Occasional Papers in the Study of Islam, No. 9 (2021)

I0223219

Perspectives on Islam and Politics

Edited by
Ruth J. Nicholls

Arthur Jeffery Centre for the Study of Islam
Melbourne School of Theology

An affiliated college of the Australian College of Theology

mst press
Melbourne School of Theology

Occasional Papers No 9, 2021 *Perspectives on Islam and Politics*
ISSN 1836-9782
ISBN 978-0-9876401-2-3

Editor Ruth Nicholls
Series Editor Peter Riddell

Production and Cover Design
Ho-yuin Chan

Publishing Services
Thanks to Richard Shumack for his publishing services.

Arthur Jeffery Centre for the Study of Islam,
Melbourne School of Theology
5 Burwood Highway, Wantirna, Victoria 3152, Australia
PO Box 6257, Vermont South, Victoria 3133, Australia
Ph: +61 3 9881 7800
info@jefferycentre.mst.edu.au

People involved in the field of Muslim-Christian relations are welcome to submit related items to the Editor for consideration for publishing in the Arthur Jeffery Centre Occasional Papers.

ARTHUR JEFFERY CENTRE FOR THE STUDY OF ISLAM,
Melbourne School of Theology, Australia

Formerly known as the Centre for the Study of Islam and Other Faiths it was renamed the Arthur Jeffery Centre for the Study of Islam in 2016. Arthur Jeffery was an Australian Methodist missionary who first went to India and ultimately developed proficiency in 19 languages. A contemporary of Samuel Zwemer, Jeffery was invited to join the staff of the American University in Cairo, also becoming a recognized scholar of Islam. His book, "The Foreign Vocabulary of the Qur'an" which was first printed in 1938, still stands as the standard text in the field.

The Arthur Jeffery Centre for the Study of Islam is the only such Centre in Australia. Through its team of expert scholars and teachers of Islam it provides a variety of resources at both academic and public levels for those involved in or desiring to be involved in loving and meaningful engagement with Muslims.

The Centre is responsible for designing, preparing and teaching subjects approved by the Australian College of Theology at undergraduate and postgraduate levels relating to Islam. The Centre also aims for academic excellence through its publications which include not only scholarly works but also information for those who desire to increase their understanding of Islam. As part of its public engagement the Centre also holds open seminars and events, often joining with others sharing a similar vision and ethos. Staff are also available to speak at public programmes.

In 2018 the Centre celebrated 10 years of operation and has established itself as a major centre for postgraduate studies in Islam.

For further information about the Centre and its activities, as well as opportunities to study Islam in a Christian context at both undergraduate and postgraduate levels, email info@JefferyCentre.mst.edu.au

TABLE OF CONTENTS

EDITORIAL

School teacher beheaded! Paris, France: 16 October 2020.[1]

Two people killed and a woman beheaded! Nice Church, France: 30 October 2020[2]

Four people killed in terrorist attack! Vienna, Austria: 2 November 2020[3]

Each of the perpetrators of these killings has been identified as a Muslim, with each one reportedly calling out *Allah hu Akbar* as they killed their victims. Each one was given the freedom to enter the country, enjoy what it had to offer, but in return killed its citizens!

Once again, the world has witnessed violent expressions of Islam.

How is one to understand these terrorist attacks of brutal violence? Are they to be understood only from a political point of view or is there also a religious perspective? The reaction from the Muslim Scholars Association as expressed by Muhammad Abd Al-Karim, the Secretary-General after discussing the issue of the teacher showing his class cartoons of the Prophet Muhammad, as reported on Turkish TV, was:

> ...the main crime had been the insults against the Prophet Muhammad. Arguing that the killing was a natural reaction to provocation, Abd Al-Karim criticized French President Emmanuel Macron for "encouraging" insults against Islam and the Prophet Muhammad. He said that if France wanted to stop such reactions, then it should stop offending Islam and its symbols, such as Prophet Muhammad. Abd Al-Karim

---

[1] https://news.com.au/world/europe/2277cfd2fe5a4e25a96aa723fc22d179, cited November 16, 2020.

[2] https://news.com.au/world/europe/640c94fbf77f678b30517c595e6c44c1, cited November 16, 2020.

[3]https://news.com.au/world/europe/640c94fbf77f678b30517c595e6c44c1,cited November 16, 2020.

1

said that Macron encourages offence to Islam in the name of free speech…[4]

On the other hand, the implications are certainly political with political leaders in the Muslim world appearing to be divided on their response.[5]

> Several leaders of Muslim-majority countries including Pakistani Prime Minister Imran Khan and Turkish President Recep Tayyip Erdoğan have accused Macron of Islamophobia for his reactions to the beheading of the French schoolteacher Samuel Paty.
>
> Turkey has, however, led the response of Muslim countries in condemning the Nice attack. "We stand in solidarity with the people of France against terror and violence," a statement by the Turkish foreign ministry said.
>
> However, in recent weeks, Turkey has been extremely critical of Macron's remarks on Muslims and Islam.
>
> Erdogan has not only spearheaded calls for a boycott of French goods, but suggested that Macron should get his head examined.
>
> Meanwhile, Iran's foreign minister Javad Zarif described the knife attack in Nice as a "terrorist attack." He tweeted, "We strongly condemn today's terrorist attack in #Nice. This escalating vicious cycle — hate speech, provocations & violence — must be replaced by reason & sanity."
>
> Zarif said "peace cannot be achieved with ugly provocations."
>
> Jordan's Foreign Ministry said this was a "terrorist crime" and condemned crimes that "aim to destabilize security and stability and are inconsistent with religious and humanitarian values and principles."

Not surprisingly, Macron, the President of France, has been taking a harder approach towards these acts, but by so doing has been maligned as being Islamophobic. Jason Thomas writes,

---

[4] Channel 9/Qanat TV (Turkey): https://memri.org/tv/sudanese-scholar-abd-karim-beheading-french-teacher-offensive-cartoons-real-crime-natural-reaction, cited November 16, 2020.
[5] https://timesnownews.com/international/article/how-the-muslim-world-is-reacting-to-terror-attacks-in-france-and-macron-s-remarks/675167, cited November 16, 2020.

The Islamist global insurgency has been turning our system against us for some time… the weakness of the West is fertile ground… Our freedoms, laws, and human rights are being exploited to attack us. Then those freedoms are used to defend the same terrorists.[6]

The heading of another article in the same newspaper also captures Thomas' sentiment:

Enlightenment Is Under Siege as Islamists Remain Hostile to the West: Conflict Inevitable when the Values of Liberal Democracy Meet Theocratic Islam.[7]

The Muslim religion and at least democratic politics collide! According to the World Atlas,

The Muslim World can be used to mean three different aspects related to those who practice Islam: religious, cultural, and geographical. This term is sometimes also stated as the Islamic World. On the religious level, the Muslim World refers to Muslims, or individuals who practice Islam. Culturally, the term refers to Islamic civilization. In the geographic sense, which is perhaps the most commonly used, it refers to the countries and other political regions where Muslims make up the majority of the population.[8]

However, even in that geographical sense, it is further nuanced. There are Islamic States where Islam is not only the state religion but Shari'a law is also implemented to varying degrees. These include Iran, Pakistan, Saudi Arabia, Afghanistan, Mauritania, and Yemen. Then there are countries which acknowledge Islam as their state religion and where Muslims are the majority of the population but they do not exclusively operate on Shari'a law. They include Egypt, Jordan, Iraq, Kuwait, Algeria, Malaysia, Maldives, Morocco, Libya, Tunisia, United Arab Emirates, Somalia, and Brunei. In some countries such as Niger, Indonesia, Sudan, Bosnia and Herzegovina, Sierra Leone, and Djibouti, there are significant Muslim populations,

---

[6] Jason Thomas, "Islamist Killers Work on West's Weaknesses," *The Australian*, published October 30, 2020.

[7] Jennifer Oriel, "Enlightenment Is Under Siege as Islamists Remain Hostile to the West: Conflict Inevitable when the Values of Liberal Democracy Meet Theocratic Islam," *The Australian*, published November 2, 2020.

[8] https://www.worldatlas.com/articles/islamic-countries-in-the-world.html, cited November 16, 2020. Note that a significant section of this paragraph has been adopted from this cite.

but Islam has not been declared the state religion. The Atlas also goes on to identify what it has termed 'Secular Muslim States.'

> In secular Muslim majority countries, the majority of the population identifies as followers of Islam. The government, however, has declared a separation of religion and state. This declaration means that religion should neither interfere nor influence civil and political affairs. These countries include Albania, Azerbaijan, Bangladesh, Burkina Faso, Chad, The Gambia, Guinea, Kazakhstan, Kosovo, Kyrgyzstan, Mali, Northern Cyprus, Nigeria, Senegal, Syria, Lebanon, Tajikistan, Turkmenistan, Turkey, and Uzbekistan.

Nevertheless, even in countries where Islam is not declared the state religion, the influence and execution of Islamic principles is strong and non-Muslims endure varying degrees of *dhimmi* status.

So the Muslim/Islamic world in terms of geographical and parliamentary politics is extremely diverse. Given Islam's history, that is not surprising. Firstly, the Prophet operated within a tribal context and would appear to have followed tribal 'political' practices at a time when formalised forms of Government, such as those evidenced in the Roman Empire and in the flowering of Greek democracy, were still emerging. In the context of Arabia, each of the tribes operated as a 'political unit' in the sense that each tribe managed affairs within its own group, maintaining the group as an identity and in terms of its relationships with other Arabian tribes. Within the tribal context, there was minimal formalisation of responsibilities for managing the affairs of the tribe. Nevertheless, within the Qureshi tribe of which Mohammad was a member, there was some division of responsibility. One of the clans (which was the Prophet's own clan) was responsible for the Ka'ba and its related events, and one of the members was a 'custodian' of the key to the building. Within Mecca, it would appear that there were individuals who were responsible for making decisions for the tribe and leading it into war should that be the case.

Further, the Apostle of Islam began his career as a religious teacher, prophet, and 'reformer.' His initial ten years were spent within a hostile tribal context in a culture where personal, then clan, then tribal relationships were the basis of life and living. However, among his followers, he not only related to them 'tribally,' but he was also their religious leader who validated his calling through divine

4

revelations. Such revelations with their 'other than human' validation would have commanded awe and respect, elevating the status of the Prophet and giving an 'authority' to his pronouncements. Subsequently, the Prophet of Islam has virtually assumed a 'divine persona' which is therefore above reproach, criticism, or trivialising, hence the accusation of the Secretary-General of the Muslim Scholars Association.[9] Anything less than absolute devotion is considered 'hate' and therefore reprehensible.

Ultimately, the Prophet regarded these religious revelations as superseding tribal affiliations, so creating a community *ummah* whose foundations, though religious, like the tribe, also included political implications. Using Thomas Messick's term (following Heck), the Prophet had "authoritative knowledge" in that he had divine revelations which, within the context of Islam, makes it 'superior' to other knowledge and which simultaneously demands 'obedience' and 'submission.'[10] Even in Mecca, the Prophet was forced into making 'political' decisions. He arranged with the King of Abyssinia to send some of his beleaguered followers there for their protection. Choosing to refrain from 'revenge' for his mistreatment and that of his followers during the Meccan period could also be viewed as a political decision. The Prophet's move to Medina, certainly in the eyes of the Khazraj who first approached him, was more political than religious, though they were willing to accept the religious teaching that was associated with the Prophet.

In moving to Medina, the Prophet, while having his religious role, increasingly assumed a political one which was infused with, directed by, and validated through his revelations from Allah. Indeed, as Nicholls points out, for the furthering of Islam, at least from Ibn Ishaq's account, 'striving for God' became the war cry as 'war' after 'war' and 'raid' after 'raid' extended the impact of Islam.[11] Any opposition, it would appear, was dealt with harshly – assassination, extermination, and even what today would be called ethnic-cleansing. It was during the Medinan period that many of the practices associated with Islamic war or *jihad*—such as dying in the

---

[9] At a popular level, it would seem that 'Allah' and 'Mohammad' have "equal veneration," for their names were usually written in equal positions in the public transport in which I travelled when I was living in Pakistan. Also, the co-relation of Muhammad as 'light' also carries with it divine overtones.

[10] Messick, p151 (this volume)

[11] Nicholls, p40 (this volume)

cause of Allah becoming a promotion to Paradise, killing the men, taking the women and children as slaves, claiming of and distribution of the booty, the institution of dhimmi status, and using traps and deception—were woven into the fabric of Islamic practice.

When the Prophet died, he left no formal political organisation, at least in terms of what would be understood in these days as 'government organisation,' nor any formal governmental type structure such as a 'parliament.' Essentially, like a tribal leader, he operated under tribal practices. He made no provision for a successor, which has had consequential implications for those practising the religion and is at the basis of the significant difference in approaches of the Sunnis and the Shi'ites. Even the question of what is an 'Islamic State' lacks definition, and consequently, Muslim scholars have often been at variance with one another in their definitions of what an Islamic State means and how it should operate.

Following the death of the Prophet, the spread of Islam was mainly spearheaded by military advance with Muslim rulers exercising their powers in a variety of ways over a significant number of diverse peoples, most of whom were not Muslims. The *dhimmi* status, which was first introduced by the Prophet in Medina, became increasingly defined by Muslim scholars and became the *operandus modi* by which Muslims treated subjugated non-Muslims.

As the West advanced through education and industrialisation and the extension of trade and colonisation, Islamic influence was weakened. Many areas which were under Muslim control became subject to foreign powers. Not surprisingly, Islam has reacted. Islam, as a political expression, has become increasingly active not only in demanding independence from the imposition of foreign powers in their domains, but in their desire to expand what for them is 'the best religion' and so follow Allah's revelation to the Prophet to bring the world under Allah's rule. However, it was the terrorist attack of September 11, 2001, on the World Trade Centre in New York City that rudely awakened the world, especially the Western world, to the political side of religious Islam. While there had been many significant terrorist attacks prior to September 11, it was the magnitude, the audacity, and the brazenness of this particular event that has had ongoing repercussions. Political Islam (politicisation of Islam), Islamism, and military Islam have become the words which endeavour to encapsulate and explore these violent expressions of

Islam. At the same time, these explorations in the West earn the accusation from the Muslim world of being Islamophobic.

The focus of this edition of the Occasional Papers (vol. 9) of the Arthur Jeffery Centre for the Study of Islam is "Islam and Politics." Politics is an incredibly difficult word to define and, like a ball covered with minute mosaic mirrors, it has multiple facets which reflect the varied aspects of the topic. Those invited to contribute to this volume were free to choose how they interpreted the topic. Not surprisingly, then, this edition includes both theoretical comments, explorative papers, analytical evaluations, as well as an examination of Islam in a number of modern geographical contexts. It is in those countries where Islam is being shaped to a large degree by that very context which is very different from that in which the Prophet lived and exercised his leadership. At the same time, many of these countries are trying to create in a 'modern environment' a 'true to the text' Islam that has largely been undefined and which found its origin in a tribal context, with tribal patterns of operation in times that have long since past. In many of these geographical contexts, it is the power of the conservative and orthodox expressions of Islam that are desiring to install an Islam that reflects the world of the Prophet's tribal Arabia and exert its power as the world's 'best religion.' So, the contents of this volume are varied in the foci taken, though the analyses are thorough and scholarly.

The first section of the volume deals with some of the more theoretical aspects of Islam in its political expressions. Given that Islam is a religion, what form does that political expression take? Is it a theocracy – a state governed by God (Allah)? The first paper explores Shabir Akhtar's philosophical justification of political Islam as a 'nomocracy' – a rule by divine law in which there is no division or separation between the sacred and the secular. Theoretically, nomocracy can be supported by various schools of legal thought. However, as Richard Shumack has pointed out, developing the practical expressions of that is anything but straightforward, especially when the Islamic legal schools are in disagreement with each other. Shumack's paper examines Akhtar's "four positions or degrees of political engagement that he sees as the only viable options available for any faith community."[12] Shumack's assessment of Akhtar's position is a Christian one, and from that perspective, he

---

[12] Shumack, p20 (this volume)

finds Akhtar's arguments, "while philosophically plausible," "pragmatically questionable," and "religio-politically unimaginative."[13] In conclusion, Shumack writes,

> Akhtar has persuasively shown [nomocracy] to be a philosophically plausible theistic model that has created liveable societies that many have found satisfying. [...] Akhtar has not... provide[d] strong arguments that Islamic nomocracy is either a true religio-political account or a preferable model to Christian alternatives.[14]

The next article by Ruth Nicholls, "Striving for God: Expanding Islam in Peninsular Arabia," acknowledges that, although the primal root for the word Islam is derived from the Arabic root which means peace, wellness, and wholeness, wars and raids significantly characterised Islam's expansion within peninsular Arabia. She examines the justification for war in the expansion of Islam which was modelled by the Prophet and validated by divine revelation and command. Thus 'war,' 'jihad,' and 'striving in the cause of Allah' are divinely sanctioned, and therefore foundational in the religious commitment of Muslims in their submission to Allah. For some, it is the sixth pillar. To Ibn Ishaq, the earliest of the extant historians of the Prophet's life, the retelling of these wars formed a significant part of the history of the Prophet's endeavours to expand the impact of the religion for which he was the Apostle. Not surprisingly, the outcomes of these models and the subsequent revelations associated with and resulting from these wars have a continuing impact on the operation of Islam and its desire to expand today.

This is followed by an exploration into the Qur'anic use of the words associated with the "Caliphate" by Bernie Power. Those who would advocate for a return to 'pure' Islam or 'original' Islam, as in the case of ISIS, consider the re-establishment of the Caliphate essential to positing Islam not only as the 'best religion' but the one which is designed to rule the world. Power's article shows that this claim, at least from a Qur'anic base, is fraught with difficulties and is not as straightforward as the claimants would suggest. Kirmanj, in an article "Challenging the Islamist Politicization of Islam: The Non-Islamic Origins of Muslim Concepts," comments:

---

[13] Shumack p28–32 (this volume)
[14] Shumach p33 (this volume)

It is important to note that the theory of the caliphate was first formalized during the Abbasid era, not by the early Muslims of Mecca and Medina.[15]

Even during the Prophet's lifetime, his relationships with Jews and Christians soured to the extent that both were considered enemies of Islam with the added dimension of divine sanctions to treat them as such (Q5:51, 57; 9:29). Following the wars with various Jewish tribes in the Medina area, the practice of the 'dhimmi' was instituted. Mark Durie, in his article, "The Dhimmitude of the West: A New Trajectory," examines the development of this Islamic political policy of dealing with those over whom Muslim rulers are exercising power but who refuse to submit to Islam. Durie notes that, for those under 'dhimmi' status, it is a sad story. Durie shows how Christian values play into this psychological, though very real practice of one of the Islamic forms of submission, emphasising their victim status and making them vulnerable to attack. Sadly, the continued violent terrorist attacks, as well as the separatist agendas of Muslims in the West, are beginning to turn attitudes against Muslims. Macron of France, at least, is beginning to take a hard line.

Following on from Durie's article is one by the international religious liberty analyst and advocate Elizabeth Kendal. Her article, "Islam and Geopolitics," reflects some of the sentiment that Durie expressed in his article: the art of Islam in playing its hand to extract what it wants from the West and how it has achieved its goal. That is, Muslim leaders make skillful use of asymmetric conflict and information dominance. Kendal's article is very broad in its geographical scope and is filled with many examples, and in some instances reveals the West's duplicity in its handling of issues that have an Islamic flavour, even sacrificing Christians in order to appease the Muslims. Kendal's article is a revelation of how Islam does its politics and uses its religious foundations as a means of justifying its actions and supporting its claims. The Prophet of Islam sanctioned the use of deception, lies, and trickery, and these are still valid 'weapons' in Islam's armory.

---

[15] Sherko Kirmanj, "Challenging the Islamist Politicization of Islam: The Non-Islamic Origins of Muslim Concepts," in *Political Islam from Muhammad to Ahmadinejad: Defenders, Detractors, and Definitions*, ed Joseph Morrison (Santa Barbara, ABC-CLIO, LLC, 2010), 38.

The second section of the volume considers 'Islam and Politics' as it occurs in a range of geographical areas: the North Caucasus, Turkey, the Middle East, Iran, Pakistan, and Malaysia.

The first of the articles by Denis Savelyev examines the current interplay of Islam and Russian politics in several of the North Caucasus republics which though largely Muslim are within the Russian Federation. These republics have had a long historical association with Islam and as Savelyev demonstrates express their Islam which, has not only been contextualized but also, (not surprisingly) in a number of cases diverges from Russian Federal law. A fact which the Russian Government chooses to ignore. The next paper focuses on Turkey – that land at the crossroads of Europe and Asia but also a land where Islam and the modern world collide. It is a collision which is still being worked out in daily life and where activists attempt to impact the direction of change. Thomas Messick explores the life of one such early activist, Bediüzzaman Said Nursi, a "politico-religious opponent of the Early Turkish State." In other words, he was opposing Mustafa Kemal's attempt "to reform and subjugate the religion of Islam to the *devlet*."[16] Interestingly, this was a conflict essentially between a modernist Muslim (who wasn't considered to be very devout) and a Muslim whose foundations and thinking were determined by the "classical" interpretation of Islam and how it should operate. Nursi's story provides an interesting exploration into the life of one man whose Islamic political beliefs and practices informed his "fight" and "his method of warfare."

It was after the Prophet's death that Islam, for some 400 years or so, extended its sphere of influence through military expansion. After that initial burst into the world scene, Islam's military prowess faded, but that original triumph has been understood by Muslims as an example of the glory of Islam. Under colonization by many of the Western powers, Muslims became the subjects of the infidel, and visions of the past have filled their imagination and longings. The muddled and muddied politics of the Middle East, where Islam had its seat of power and glory for many years, has seen in recent times the rise of ISIS—Islamic State of Iraq and Syria—or the Islamic State Caliphate. Amirul-Mu'uminin Abu Bakr al Husayni al-Qurashi al Baghdadi claimed by force, horrifying many Muslims in the process, to be the Caliph of the newly created Caliphate. Anthony McRoy

---

[16] Messick, p148, 154 (this volume)

skillfully examines the development of the Caliphate concept and practice. He then outlines the context in which al-Baghdadi rose to power and how this new Caliphate understood shari'a, determined its citizenship, and expressed its 'foreign policy' in terms of jihad. While that Caliphate only had a short life, there were many Muslims who understood al-Baghdadi's position to be the true expression of Islam and are still working, longingly, though somewhat currently indirectly, wherever they have dispersed, to make Islam the world's religion.

Just across the border, so to speak, is the Islamic Republic of Iran, which is the focus of Anthony McRoy's next article, "A State of 'Unrealised Eschatology': Shi'ism, Iranian Constitutionalism, Regency and Khomeini's theory of the *Vilayet-i-Faqih*." Iran presents an interesting case in that its political theory is grounded in Shi'ite theology and interpretation of the Muslim state. Using the Christian concept of unrealised eschatology and applying a British historical practice of 'regency,' McRoy outlines Iran's political history from the early days of Muslim rule to the present. Shi'ite Islam rejects the caliphate, choosing instead to be led by a divinely designated Imam, belonging to the *Ahl-ul-Bayt*. McRoy points out that even in Iran the political expression of Shi'a Islam has had a checked history. In these recent times, especially since Khomeini, there has been the attempt to create a religiously viable state operating under the direction of divinely inspired Shari'a while waiting for the Mahdi to return and resume the rightful rule of a truly Islamic leader. The extent to which this model has created a successful vibrant growing state is surely open to question.

Sharing part of its border with Iran is Pakistan, the Islamic Republic of Pakistan. As Ruth Nicholls notes in her article, "Islam and Politics, Politics and Islam: Pakistan's Ongoing Conundrum," it is the struggle between Islam as a religion and its undefined but very real political foci that lie at the very heart of Pakistan's instability and its inability to make genuine progress as a nation. Pakistan is full of religious parties wielding varying degrees of political power while being essentially at war with each other since they represent different legal schools of Islam. Consequently, they not only have different understandings of the nature of an 'Islamic state,' but also disagree with each other in how that state should operate. Given the frequent allegations of 'shirk' and 'bida' against each other, these religious parties express their opposition in various forms of violence which the government is powerless to manage because the perpetrators claim religious validation through the Qur'an and its exegesis for their actions. While the government is theoretically elected, it is the religious parties that essentially hold the Prime Minister in their power since the balance of power and the ability to form a government depends on the support of the religious parties.

Further east is Malaysia, which includes the Malay Peninsula, North Borneo, and Sarawak, resulting in a multi-ethnic and multi-cultural community, with Malays constituting about 60% of the population, Malaysian Chinese about 23%, and Malaysian Indians about 7%. About 61% of the population are classified as Muslims. In the remaining percentage, Buddhists, Hindus, and Christians are also represented. Since the formation of Malaysia, there has been a continued thrust to implement shari'a related laws and extend Islamic policies in the country. Peter Riddell's article, "Islam and Politics in Malaysia: The First 60 Years of Statehood," outlines the various trajectories of Islamisation in that country, the challenges that the non-Muslim minorities have faced, and how they, in turn, have responded.

Islam and politics! Firstly, it must be recognised that Islam is a total system – that is, it assumes authority and power over every aspect of people's lives. In other words, it is both a religious and political as well as an economic and relational system. Indeed, it embraces every dimension of life and living. To focus on Islam as only political or only religious is to ignore the reality of its very nature. Yet, while Islam claims to be a unity, expressing the oneness of Allah, that position is illusional. Islam is deeply divided. Its four legal schools which essentially determine the practice of Islam differ, at times significantly, on their understanding of what constitutes an 'Islamic State' and how Islamic politics should operate. Not surprisingly, there is great diversity within the Islamic geo-political world and even within a single Islamic geo-political unit. At the same time, each would claim Allah's sanction while claiming that any other interpretation is *bida* and therefore can be subject to violent opposition. Added to that is the Islamic nomocratic validation of the use of force and violence not only within the *ummah* but also against those who are not members of their *ummah* or refuse to become members. Islam justifies violence as a religiously validated means of exercising its political authority.

This small volume can only provide a very limited insight into 'Islam and Politics,' but it does add to the current scholarship that is focusing on this very varied, extremely diverse, and multi-faceted subject. Nevertheless, it is our hope that this volume will provide insights and encourage your further explorations into the subject.

Finally, in the preparation of this volume, I am grateful to Yvonne Ritchie and Margaret Rickard for checking the manuscript, and to Ernie Laskaris for making sure the volume met with the 17th edition of the Chicago Manual of Style.

Ruth Nicholls
Editor

SECTION I

ISLAM and POLITICS

GENERAL PERSPECTIVES

Chapter I

NORMATIVE NOMOCRACY?
Shabbir Akhtar on the Grounds for Political Islamism

Richard Shumack[1]

Introduction

Traditional Islam views political power as an inherently religious feature of human community. It holds that it is necessary for government institutions to wield coercive power in the service of creating a safe and just society in line with God's revealed law. Muslim philosopher Shabbir Akhtar sees this nomocratic model as religio-politically normative, claiming that "Islam, a paradigmatically political religion, embraces power as a means of securing social justice and corporate amelioration."[2]

This paper considers Akhtar's philosophical arguments in support of this normativity against a brief background of Islamic thought and offers a Christian critique. I hope to show that, while Akhtar's arguments succeed in defending Islamic nomocracy as a plausible religio-political model, they fall short of establishing either its truth or its normativity.

Islamic Nomocracy in Islamic Thought

Traditional Islam sees religio-politically executed divine law as the means through which God exercises his power in shaping society for good. Seyyed Hossein Nasr identifies this model of divine and political power as a 'nomocracy' and explains it like this:

---

[1] Dr. Richard Shumack is the Director of the Arthur Jeffery Centre for the Study of Islam at Melbourne School of Theology, and adjunct faculty at Queensland Theological College and Sydney Missionary and Bible College. He is also pastor of Trinity Chapel at Macquarie University. Richard specialized in Philosophy of Religion and missiology

[2] S. Akhtar, *Islam as Political Religion: The Future of an Imperial Faith* (New York: Routledge, 2011), 120.

17

Technically speaking, the Islamic ideal is that of a nomocracy, that is, the rule of Divine Law. It is true that all power, including political power, belongs ultimately to God, as the Quran states, "The command rests with none but God" (Q6:57; 12:40). But in the case of Islam, the rule of God was never associated with the rule of the priestly class; rather, it was associated with that of the Shari'ah... Today the one principle that remains clear to all Muslims is that sovereignty belongs ultimately to God as expressed in the Divine Law and an Islamic society is one in which this sovereignty is accepted.[3]

This idea of nomocracy—a society ruled by divine law—is hard to define precisely, and scholars debate both its meaning and appropriateness in the case of Islam.[4] Nevertheless, the idea does seem to broadly capture the dominant traditional Islamic conception of human society – that is, belonging to God, set up by him to operate, at every level, in the good way described by, and prescribed by, his revealed law and not in the evil ways proscribed by that law.

Some form of nomocracy is clearly what most Muslim philosophers of the classical period had in mind when they considered the question of politics.[5] Al-Farabi, for example, blended the concept with Platonic political thinking by recasting Plato's ruling philosopher-king in terms of Muhammad's role as a divinely inspired prophet-king who legislated, in the Shari'a, an ideally functioning community in which humans might flourish.

...the idea of the philosopher, supreme ruler, prince, legislator, and Imam is but a single idea. No matter which one of these words you take, if you proceed to look at what each of them signifies among the majority of those who speak our language, you will find that they all finally agree by signifying one and the same idea.[6]

---

[3] S. H. Nasr, *The Heart of Islam* (San Francisco, CA: Harper One, 2004), 148–150.

[4] For more on this, see Majid Khadduri, "Nature of the Islamic State," *Islamic Culture* 21 (1947): 327–331.

[5] Black puts it like this: "The Islamic Philosophers never adopted the idea of a universal, intercultural moral language for all humankind, or of rights and duties pertaining to human beings as such. Rather, all humans should adhere to the one true moral Code, the Muslim Shari'a." Antony Black, *The History of Islamic Political Thought* (New York: Routledge, 2001), 59.

[6] *Tahsil al-sa'ada*, 43–44.

For al-Farabi, the prime purpose of any political system is the instilling in their citizens of the knowledge and practice of Islam.[7] Daniel Frank writes:

> For Islamic political philosophers, the divine law (*shari'a*) revealed to Muhammad was a necessary and sufficient condition for bringing about human felicity.[8]

The more recent, and highly influential, political thinker Abul Ala Maududi also had nomocracy in mind when he wrote:

> The chief characteristic of Islam is that it makes no distinction between the spiritual and the secular in life. Its aim is to shape both individual lives as well as society as a whole in ways that will ensure that the Kingdom of Allah may really be established on earth and that peace, contentment and well-being may fill the world.[9]

Islamic nomocracy need not involve a wooden, legalistic, or strict traditionalist approach that attempts to imitate the particular application of Shari'a in the time of Muhammad. The concept of nomocracy can incorporate a wide range of interpretations of the Shari'a (as seen in the variety of Islamic schools of legal thought and in the idea of *ijtihad* – i.e. the independent interpretation of the law) and the political models suitable for implementing it. This was argued by al-Ghazali. His sensible idea was that the application of Islamic law under any sort of judicial system unavoidably required reasoning and theological interpretation, and in *Asas al-Qiyas*, he attempted to spell out the various principles involved. Thus, Islamic nomocracy can be conceived in a variety of ways so long as it

---

[7] Black, *The History*, 66.
[8] While it is generally agreed that some sort of nomocratic ideal was the model of religious political engagement envisaged by classical philosophers, there were dissenting voices. Ibn Tamiyya was one. Ovamir Anjum, a modern-day revisionist, argues that the dominant Sunni account fails to reflect early Islam in which the caliphs were political leaders rather than jurists. Drawing on the thought of Ibn Tamiyya, he develops an Islamic political theory that argues that *fitrah*—i.e. the inherent Islamic nature of all humans—can undergird political thinking in a way that allows human political reasoning freed from the constraints of a rigid judicial approach to Shari'a. Ovamir Anjum, *Politics, Law, and Community in Islamic Thought* (Cambridge: Cambridge University Press, 2012).
[9] Abul Ala Maududi, "The Islamic Concept of Life," n.d., http://www.islam101.com/sociology/conceptLife.htm, accessed March 25, 2021.

achieves the goal of sanctifying political power by subsuming it within religious authority.

Outlining just how this nomocratic ideal should be implemented in any particular national or social setting is controversial within Islamic political theology. Debates rage over fraught political questions like the relationships between Islam and democracy; Islam and nationalism; Islam, pan-nationalism and the caliphate; Islam and secularisation; Islam and Westernisation; Islam and globalisation; Islam and the legacy of colonialism; Islam and Western militarism and imperialism; as well as (just to make it really messy) Islam and the state of Israel. This paper does not propose to address any of these sorts of concerns. They are, to my mind, largely practical questions that can only be addressed once the underlying concept of Islam as a political religion (as nomocracy) can be established as reasonable and normative. This prior question is our concern here, and it is precisely the question that Shabbir Akhtar is seeking to explore.

Akhtar's case for Islamic Nomocracy

Shabbir Akhtar's thought is distinctive for its commendable determination to offer non-question-begging arguments in support of his Islamic positions. So, in *The Qur'an and the Secular Mind* and *Islam as Political Religion*, he presents a range of different arguments in defence of the notion of Islamic nomocracy.[10] Four are central to his thinking: the first is political, the second is anthropological, the third is meta-ethical, and the fourth is comparative.

1. An argument to do with political necessity

Akhtar recognizes that any religion in which adherents participate meaningfully in society necessarily adopts a political posture and theology – either implicitly or explicitly. From this plainly sensible presupposition (which, for sake of argument, we will assume without discussion) he identifies four positions, or degrees, of political engagement that he sees as the only viable options available to any faith community.[11]

1. Everyday dealings with the political establishment as citizens.

---

[10] S. Akhtar, *The Qur'an and the Secular Mind: A Philosophy of Islam* (New York: Routledge, 2008).
[11] Ibid., 90–91.

2. Agitation against unjust political and economic structures.

3. The absorption of politics into religion.

4. The establishing of religion as an imperial power.

Akhtar claims that every faith must unavoidably do (1) and has a moral obligation to also do (2). He then suggests that Islam, uniquely, seeks to do both (3) and (4) – that is, "the Qur'an seeks to absorb politics into religion and thus sanctify it."[12] (A note about terminology here. When Akhtar speaks of imperial power, he is not using the term to simply mean military power. He understands Islamic imperialism – both historically and ideally – as encompassing a whole range of missionary activities including evangelism, social service, economic influence, as well as governmental military activity where appropriate.)

Although, in describing this typology, Akhtar does not use the term nomocracy, it is clear that this is broadly what he has in mind by *absorption*. He states:

> Islamic political ambition is typically embodied in the drive to establish an Islamic caliphal state whose power exceeds the merely social pressure of communal cohesion. Private piety is publicly and forcibly enforced through paternalistic legislation. The state, which upholds the Shari'ah, seeks to extend its power into private lives.[13]

Akhtar sums up his political argument thus:

> All faiths, including apolitical ones, must interact with the powerful institutions of their day... What makes Islam remarkable is its decision to absorb political community in order to sanctify it.[14]

The straightforward idea here is that, unavoidably and necessarily, there just are religio-political norms in any society and Islam's nomocratic model is sensibly—indeed to Muslims appealingly—the best set of norms among those on offer. The second and third of

---

[12] Ibid., 91.
[13] Ibid., 91.
[14] Ibid., 100. When he speaks here of sanctification, he does not mean it in the Christian sense that includes the concept of salvation. Instead, he uses it in a similar way to the term 'sacred' – that is, completely devoted to God.

Akhtar's arguments are in defence of why the Islamic option is preferable.

2. A pragmatic argument from human nature

The second plank in Akhtar's case is that much of the reasonableness and appeal of Islamic nomocracy stems from the way it accounts for human moral nature. In this regard, he offers a pragmatic anthropological argument that humans flourish best under enforced Shari'ah. In short, Akhtar holds that:

- all humans have some sort of inbuilt knowledge of, and inclination towards obeying Islam – that is, divine law (*fitrah*);

- all humans are born into a world of weakness and are vulnerable to forgetfulness of, and disobedience to, divine law;

- this weakness is not innate or binding, so all that humans require is reminders of, and education concerning divine law.

Akhtar's full account of human nature is beyond the scope of this paper, but its key features can be identified in the following passages in which he contrasts Islamic anthropology with the Christian doctrine of original sin.

> The Islamic position is morally and doctrinally opposed to this proposed external rescue from the plight of sin. We are not innately deviant or crooked or unsound although we are easily misled into temptation. Divine education therefore suffices. We need mentors who can guide us out of our heedlessness.[15]

> For Muslims, since human beings are not inherently corrupt or fallen, every resource and facility is to be harnessed in the service of a comprehensive lordship... Muslims feel religiously obliged to establish a just order governed by a sacred law.[16]

Roughly speaking, the idea here is that since all humans are innately (if unconsciously) Muslim, politics need only be an exercise in instruction in the societal elements of divine law.

---

[15] Ibid., 277.
[16] Ibid., 271.

Important in Akhtar's account is the recognition that divine education *alone* does not suffice to create a just and prosperous (Muslim) society. He thinks that despite education and the doctrine of *fitrah*, many humans remain recalcitrant and disobedient to divine law. His solution is to recognise that some form of legitimate governmental enforcement of divine law is required in any society. Indeed, it is not merely required, but mandated: if government has the potential to create a just society through the enforcement of divine law, then it should do so by all means available. Although political enforcement of the law upon the unwilling or unbelieving is unfortunate, it is nevertheless legitimate because social evil, and/or the social effects of personal evil, cannot be ignored wherever there are political tools available that "enable one to eradicate the social consequences."[17] So, Akhtar suggests that

> It is our moral duty to legitimize the employment of power by qualifying force: making it authoritative, rational, constrained and discriminating, limited in scope and accountable to an electorate... part of the religious arsenal.[18]

In short, the government should implement divine law by force, if required, for the greater good.[19] And force *is* periodically required in an imperfect society.[20]

Obviously, the persuasiveness of this argument from human nature rests upon the success of Islam in creating good societies. If Islam's anthropology—especially the doctrine of *fitrah*—is accurate, then surely societies adopting some form of Islamic nomocracy should, all things being equal, display greater degrees of flourishing. Do they? We will return to address this question shortly.

3. A meta-ethical 'divine command' argument

In addition to pragmatic credibility, Akhtar desires his political theology to find metaphysical and, therefore, meta-ethical support. Straightforwardly, his account rests on a 'divine command' meta-ethic in which the God of theism exists, and human political norms and obligations consist in obedience to God's revealed commands. He puts it this way:

---

[17] Ibid., 107.
[18] Ibid., 122.
[19] Ibid., 103.
[20] Ibid., 144.

The Islamic State is a manifestation and an instrument of power, the power of Shari'ah. It is a theo-nomocracy with God as King and Sovereign (*malik*; Q 59:23; 62:1).[21]

The philosophical route taken by Akhtar to justify this meta-ethic is indirect, subtle, and, at points, technical. Nevertheless, we can, I think fairly, summarise it in three main ideas.

First, and unusually among Muslim scholars, Akhtar does not believe that irrefutable, or even conclusive, arguments can be offered in support of such an Islamic meta-ethic. Instead, he recognizes that various secular meta-ethics are, prima facie, plausible candidates for undergirding a flourishing society. He generously concedes:

Secular humanism, with its defensible intellectual foundations, is potentially universal in its appeal. Some atheist humanists boast that the most successful cultures in the modern world—cultures with workable institutional structures—are atheist in all but name, while the most dysfunctional cultures are the religious autocracies and theocracies located in the Islamic belt from Indonesia to Morocco... Could a totally secular ethic, grounded in atheism, undergird a morally healthy society? Yes... Aristotle and the Stoics have left us enduring moral legacies. Spinoza created an original ethical scheme and presented it in a geometric model. Kant and (John Stuart) Mill constructed ethical systems, deontologies and utilitarianism respectively, with little or no regard for Christian values.[22]

Akhtar's recognition of the existence of plausible philosophical arguments in favour of even atheistic meta-ethics stem, in part, from his recognition that significant epistemic barriers are raised by the so-called problem of the 'hiddenness of God.' In a nutshell, with mainstream analytical philosophy, he recognises the apparent ordinary hiddenness of God as a genuine philosophical problem that renders reasonable religious claims ultimately unprovable. He claims that "the silence of God is a fact both undeniable and religiously disturbing."[23] Thus, he sensibly believes that all humans are left in the philosophical situation wherein there is

---

[21] Ibid., 149.
[22] Ibid., 107ff.
[23] S. Akhtar, *A Faith for All Seasons* (Chicago, IL: Ivan R. Dee, 1990), 85.

24

no uncontroversially accepted criteria which could effectively provide a decision-procedure... Moreover, religious assertions are not publicly testable, and perhaps not even putatively factual.[24]

Indeed, these strong consequences of God's hiddenness lead Akhtar to even concede a rough epistemic parity of theistic ethics with plausible non-theistic meta-ethics:

> It seems to me, however, that in justifying the ways of the Almighty to the modern questioning mentality... the current silence of God takes a place at least as prominent as the more time-honoured problem of the calamity of natural and moral evil... My own view is that the religious perplexity about God's radical inaccessibility and essential elusiveness could, in the decades to come, become for modern sensibilities an even richer source of argumentative material in favour of a reluctant agnosticism if not outright atheism.[25]

So, Akhtar's first, seemingly backward, step is to concede epistemic parity between agnosticism and theism. While this (perhaps) surprising move might make Muslims seeking high degrees of certainty uncomfortable, it allows him the philosophical space to argue for the reasonableness of Islamic theism via teleological arguments.

Secondly, then, Akhtar argues that natural theology offers fruitful grounds for establishing the reasonableness, if not the necessity, of theism. He puts it that:

> The natural order is the visible token of an invisible grace which suffuses nature with a sacramental quality. The earth's beauty and bounty disguise God's presence... (These) signs of God *rationally* attest to God's sovereignty. Application of reason leads to faith, the basis of the design argument (see Q50:6–11; 89:17–21). Natural events supply evidence of divine craftsmanship, not of undirected biological evolution. God is continuously evident in routine but dynamic processes in nature and society. He is not merely a dramatically interventionist or capricious deity. Natural order implies the existence of the merciful one (*Al-Rahman*), not merely of an abstract deity (see e.g. Q43:45; 67:3–4). One

---

[24] Akhtar, *The Quran,* 331.
[25] Ibid., 83–84.

Quranic surah opens with this moral attribute of the creator (Q55:1). Only philosophers have "demoralized" God to a first efficient cause in a physical system and then sought to prove the existence of such an anaemic and irrelevant being.[26]

This passage reveals the heart of Akhtar's meta-ethical argument: the creation can reasonably (again if not conclusively) be taken to be morally purposive in such a way that is best explained by a moral God. This idea, while plausible, is merely posited by Akhtar though not argued for in detail in any of his writings. Despite this limitation, however, the support found for this idea in the philosophical literature renders it a plausible premise in the wider argument.

Thirdly, Akhtar offers a very similar teleological argument for the divine origin of the Qur'an. He observes that:

The Qur'an arises out of the desert, out of nowhere... Unlike Jesus or the Hebrew prophets, Muhammad did not belong to a tradition of revealed wisdom or prophecy. Born and raised among pagans, there is little in his environment to explain the event of the Arabic Qur'an... While biblical scholars have satisfactorily accounted for the two biblical testaments... the Qur'an's origins still defy adequate naturalistic (secular) explanation.[27]

The various features of the Qur'an that Akhtar views as best explained supernaturally are the standard within Islamic thought – in particular, its inimitable linguistic features, remarkable content, and extraordinary historical influence.[28] Here, again, Akhtar is at pains to clarify that any supporting teleological case for the divine origin of the Qur'an is probabilistic, and not deductive: all its relevant features suffer alternative explanations. Therefore, the claim here is that belief in the divine origin of the Qur'an is entirely *reasonable* due to these features.

Noting that "the Qur'an... [is] a complete amalgam of metaphysics, ethics and ontology," reasonable belief in its divine origin straightforwardly allows Akhtar to draw on it as a precisely the right sort of revelation upon which to resource an Islamic

---

[26] Ibid., 196.
[27] Ibid., 135.
[28] Ibid., 117–214.

nomocracy.[29] That is, the Qur'an, for Akhtar, richly sets out theory and proper practice of political Islam.

We can sum up this meta-ethical argument as follows:

- Natural theology provides good, but not conclusive reasons for believing in theism.

- On theism, divine command meta-ethics are sensible.

- The extraordinary nature of the Quran provides good reason for believing Islam to be the truest revelation of divine law.

4. A comparative argument.

Akhtar's arguments, thus far, are not conclusive in favour of Islamic nomocracy: they are merely for its reasonableness and plausibility. His next move, then, is to offer an argument favourably comparing the religio-political credentials of Islamic nomocracy versus what he sees as its most viable alternative – Christian political theology. In this regard, he views the Islamic idea that religion subsumes and sanctifies politics as one of Islam's prime, and most appealing, strengths. So, he claims that,

> The virtue of political religion—a cardinal virtue characteristic of Islam—is its honesty about the periodic need for force in a constituency imperfectly malleable to just demands.[30]

The sensible idea here is that theistic religion includes the belief in some sort of divine law, and any plain and honest assessment of society reveals the need for the enforcement of these good laws in order to flourish.

Akhtar believes that the historical Christian notion of church-state separation denies this apparently virtuous position. He argues that Jesus' command to "therefore render to Caesar the things that are Caesar's, and to God the things that are God's" (Matt. 22:21) contains an unrealistic, indeed culpable, command to withdraw from the world:

---

[29] Ibid., 325.
[30] Ibid., 144.

> Islam's laudable realism removes the necessity for that false
> antithesis of rendering unto Caesar the things that belong to
> Caesar at the expense of the things that rightfully belong to
> God.[31]

Akhtar sees two problems here: the impossibility of separating religion from politics and a moral failing to address situations of injustice in the world – "private piety is futile if one cannot dismantle the structures of evil."[32]

It is unclear here just which Christian religio-political version of church-state separation Akhtar is referring to and he neglects to engage with the various models on offer in either historical or contemporary Christian political theology. As a result, we are left with Akhtar comparing a politically engaged Islam with a crudely disengaged Christian position.

Drawing these four arguments together, then, Akhtar's philosophical case for Islamic nomocracy is that any religion is inherently political; any theism sensibly recognizes a divine command meta-ethic; among the main theistic religions, only Islam properly integrates such a meta-ethic into its political theology; and this theology appears to align nicely with human nature and so produce good results.

A Christian Assessment of Akhtar's Islamic Nomocracy

I commence a Christian assessment of Akhtar's case with praise for the uncommon modesty and generosity of both the content and style of his arguments. His work is no exercise in philosophical bluster and his desire to avoid question begging is genuine. Further, the modesty of his core claim—essentially that Islam's religio-political theology is most sensible—allows it to be held with philosophical integrity. Nevertheless, I remain unconvinced by his arguments. Three points are worth making in explaining why.

1. Akhtar's case is philosophically plausible.

It is easy for the Christian philosopher to concede that Akhtar's religio-political model is entirely plausible on its own general terms. So, prima facie, and in philosophical (not theological or historical) terms, the classical Islamic theistic metaphysic/meta-ethic is

---

[31] Ibid., 124.
[32] Ibid., 240.

plausible. Moreover, if the Islamic account of divine/human interaction, revelation, and human nature is correct, then some form of nomocracy is reasonable. If true human religion centres on obeying universal divine law, then it is (philosophically) straightforward enough to think that the role of human government is to simply mandate and enforce the social elements of Islamic law. This is reasonable – and simple too, because Islam, like government, is legislative by nature: Islam consists of teaching and enforcing laws, and so does government. It is also reasonable to think that enforcement of Islamic law on the unwilling and/or unbelieving might not be immoral if the laws were good laws and if it achieved the greater good of creating a just and prosperous society. Surely this principle is central to any meaningful concept of societal law. It makes sense in the same way that enforcing tax law makes sense: I may not believe in paying tax or I may be unwilling to pay tax even if I believe in it, but it is legitimate for the government to tax me—and/or punish me for evading paying tax—so that it can use tax revenue to benefit society by building roads, hospitals, schools, and so on.

Furthermore, it also the case that the Christian philosopher can (relatively) uncontroversially agree with many of the premises and presuppositions undergirding Akhtar's framework *on Christian terms*. So, Christians and Muslims can both reasonably suppose that divine laws (including moral, social, and liturgical laws) exist which are universal – that is, they are necessarily true for all people to whom they are relevant, regardless of whether those people acknowledge it. We can further suppose that humans are able to follow those rules that are relevant to them. This will include humans being in a position to know and describe the rules (especially through revelation and intuition), having the capacity to follow the rules, and being morally responsible agents who are able to choose to follow these rules. We can finally, and jointly, suppose that a broad (philosophical) conception of power exists that allows for power to be properly both 'power-over' and 'power to act.' So, the government rightly has the power over its people to use force to punish disobedience to the law, and it also has the power to educate its people in divine law, thereby enabling them to love and worship God. Put differently, political power can be legitimately both dominating and empowering. Both Christianity and Islam seem to demand these suppositions and recognise that society should ideally be built upon these divine rules. This will be important to remember when analysing Akhtar's comparison of their relative political models.

This general plausibility of Islamic nomocracy, however, doesn't mean that Akhtar's model is without any philosophical difficulties. Akhtar, himself, acknowledges that the forceful imposition of any divine law upon unbelievers or the unwilling is problematic. There is the real possibility that the imposition of divine law is incompatible with the demands of that very law. We could put the problem like this: divine law calls for proper worship, and proper worship, by its very nature, should not be enforced, but rather be willingly offered from the heart. This recognition leads Akhtar to put great effort into responding to just such a challenge by Cragg.[33] Cragg argues that the paradigmatic use of force by the prophet Muhammad compromises his moral authority to call people to heart worship. Akhtar's response is that this sort of challenge rests on a false separation of individual hearts from social structures. He believes that societal transformation requires both structural sanctification and personal/individual sanctification. So, he criticises Christianity for focusing exclusively on the transformation of individual hearts while ignoring the transformation of evil structures, and Marxism (as an example) for focusing exclusively on changing infrastructure. Instead, he suggests that both are (somehow) transformed together, and that the idea that we can "purify the institutions – and the heart will follow" is just as valid a principle as the other way around.[34] In short, he holds that enforced sanctification of social structures is a legitimate pathway towards achieving citizens being willing to seek personal sanctification. The legitimacy of this dynamic may be fairly interrogated, but, in any case, the problem raised by Cragg exists in any form of theistic divine command meta-ethic. Cragg's critique can therefore be fairly levelled at the first four of the Ten Commandments of Judaism (and Christianity). There, it appears that worship *is* enforceable by law in some sense, and so Akhtar's model remains in play.

The philosophical credentials of Islamic nomocracy, then, are generally acceptable. The critical question is therefore whether such a meta-ethic is true. My next two points lead us to strongly doubt it.

---

[33] Ibid., 129.
[34] Ibid., 127.

2. Akhtar's case is pragmatically questionable

Akhtar (and Islam) is optimistic that the application of divine law (the *shari'a*) to society by government can realistically create a just and prosperous society. My contention is that this optimism is unjustified. This is largely because the human moral capacity described by his Islamic nomocratic model appears overly optimistic in the face of real-world human experience. In short, the track record of political Islam simply does not support the claim.

Even allowing that I'm coming from an avowedly Christian point of view, history clearly seems to testify that the profound moral distortion evident in all human individuals and institutions appears too great to be overcome by mere religious education or governmental enforcement. I do not mean, of course, that the rule of law through government is *entirely* impotent: law *can* move hearts and shape society. It can do so (legitimately) through incentives and threat. For example, it can paint attractive pictures of utopian societies and terrifying pictures of judgment. It can describe laws that appeal to intuition and conscience, empower through education and enforce through punishment. I willingly concede that it is a necessary requirement of any truly just society that its government enacts and enforces laws that coincide with divine law. But while it might be necessary, it is far from sufficient. And it is far from sufficient because it does not have any clear mechanism to overcome sin if sin is an inherent and serious flaw in human will.

Akhtar (and Islam), of course, does not agree with me on this point. But even if he can convincingly show that law *can* somehow deal effectively with human sin, this does not overcome the problem of the empirical evidence showing that it *has not*: the Islamic model simply does not have a good track record of being able to fully deliver what it promises. The historical record shows that this model is not able to create a Muslim society that is ideally just, prosperous, and worshipful. The contemporary Muslim political philosopher Ovamir Anjum concedes that:

> Two observations about Islamic civilization have been commonplace, shared by Western as well as, often, Muslim observers. The first is the success and predominance of law in Islam; Islam is seen as "nomocratic and nomocentric." The second is the failure of Islamic politics or the Muslim political enterprise to enact coherent and stable political institutions and of Islamic normative political thought to

provide realistic guidance to governments or avert cycles of tyranny, violence, and rebellion.[35]

It is important to note that Anjum makes this point in order to support a revisionist case that Islamic nomocracy as traditionally conceived is inadequate. Nevertheless, he does not dispute the observed failure of Islamic nomocracy to deliver what it promises.

I am not claiming that Islam is *entirely* impotent to create a just and prosperous society. That would be a great surprise to many Muslims who have lived their lives happily within traditional Muslim communities! I simply want to dispute Akhtar's strong claim that "politically empowered Islam... historically, at least, gave us peace, scholarship, political security, and stability for millennia in several parts of the world" in a way that is markedly superior to any other political system.[36] I do not share Akhtar's optimism that coercive political power—of any kind—has the required power to save a world full of sin. Politicians, even those with divine law on their side, are left with the same dilemma as Mr Incredible:

> No matter how many times you save the world, it always manages to get back in jeopardy again. Sometimes I just want it to stay saved for a little bit. I feel like the maid: "I just cleaned up this mess, can we keep it clean for ten minutes?? Please."[37]

In summary, the idea that societal sanctification can originate politically, as much as personally, needs much more work. Certainly, Muslims recognize that Islamic nomocracy is yet to deliver it.

3. Akhtar's case is religio-politically unimaginative

To my mind, the most serious weakness of Akhtar's account concerns his lack of imagination concerning possible models of political engagement for any religion. He asserts, without detailed supporting argument, that only four possible models exist: submission, agitation, absorption, and 'imperial/missionary' absorption (with each incorporating the previous). Akhtar then assumes that only an absorption method is able to "sanctify politics" and allow it to create a just and prosperous society (along the lines mandated by divine law).

---

[35] Anjum, *Politics, Law, and Community in Islamic Thought*, 1.
[36] Akhtar, *Islam*, 2.
[37] Brad Bird, dir., *The Incredibles*, Walt Disney Pictures, 2004.

But why should we agree with him about this? I contend, instead, that myriad possibilities for societal transformation exist within the submission and agitation methods, but Akhtar fails to recognise them because he remains wedded to an Islamic legislative model. Not only has he failed to recognise them in general, but he has failed to recognise them in Christianity. He therefore dismisses the Christian account as a weak submission method that has either no interest in political power or a public agenda of submission masking an insidious power game. Here, Akhtar is at best dismissing crude Christian accounts, and at worst demolishing straw political theologians.

I contend instead that contemporary Christian political theology offers a range of sophisticated models that Akhtar has ignored altogether.[38] They include models that do not repudiate power, but instead adopt a radically different concept of the sort of power that is required for societal sanctification by divine law, and then pursue that power passionately. This article is not the place to spell out the details of such alternatives, but the mere fact of their existence shows that Islamic nomocracy bears potential unexamined defeaters.

Conclusion
This brief consideration of Shabbir Akhtar's political arguments should render it no surprise that Islamic nomocracy (in its various guises) has held appeal for generations of Muslims as a preferable religio-political model. Akhtar has persuasively shown it to be a philosophically plausible theistic model that has created liveable societies that many have found satisfying. What Akhtar has not done, however, is provide strong arguments that Islamic nomocracy is either the true religio-political account or a preferable model to Christian alternatives. The patchy track record of actual Islamic nomocracies, combined with the existence of sophisticated Christian political theologies ignored by Akhtar, render his account impotent.

---

[38] For one excellent example among many, see O. O'Donovan, *Resurrection and Moral Order: An Outline for Evangelical Ethics* (Grand Rapids, MI: Zondervan, 1994). Or, closer to my Australian home, J. Cole, *Christian Political Theology in an Age of Discontent* (Eugene, OR: Wipf and Stock, 2019).

Chapter 2

STRIVING FOR GOD
Extending Islam in Peninsular Arabia

Ruth Nicholls[1]

At the core of Semitic languages, typically there is a three consonantal letter root which is modified in a formalised manner to create nouns, verbs, adjectival, and adverbial type constructs. The foundational root of '*Islam*' is *slm*. This root includes the concepts of peace, wholeness, wellbeing, and safety, and is so used in the Arabic greeting, *(as)salam 'alaikum* – peace be upon you. Interestingly, in the index of the English edition of the Saudi Arabian published *The Noble Qur'an*, there is only one reference given for the word 'peace.'[2] The word '*Islam*,' the name given by God to the Prophet (Q5:3), is also from the root *slm* but comes from a derivative form (IV) to which another letter had been added (I)*Islm*). In this form it means 'submission, surrender, resignation.' In the context of the religion there is the added rider of submission or surrender to the 'will of Allah.' By adding '*m*' to the *slm* root and changing the vowels, it becomes '*muslim*' – one who has surrendered: in the case of the religion again 'to the will of Allah.' Not surprisingly, at the heart of Islam is the demand to 'surrender, be in submission to, act in obedience to the will of Allah' either willingly or as revealed to the Prophet and as subsequently developed, by force if required. That is, force has a divine sanction. While the word 'surrender' in English is

---

[1] Ruth Nicholls was until recently the Administrator of the Arthur Jeffery Centre for the Study of Islam, Melbourne School of Theology and is currently an honorary Research Fellow with the Centre. Ruth lived and worked for many years in a Muslim country where she became particularly interested in Sufism and folk Islam.

[2] Muhammad Taqi-ud-Din al-Hilali and Muhammad Muhsin Khan, *Translation of the Meanings of the Noble Qur'an in the English Language* (Madinah: King Fahd Complex for the Printing of the Holy Qur'an, 1999).

not always used in the context of war, its meaning and usage reflect that background.

From the Quranic record, Muhammad was called to be a Messenger of God whose original divine injunction appears to be to 'warn' of the 'wrath to come' (Q 74:1-7) and return people to the 'true worship of Abraham.' While it is considered that the first revelations were given around 610, it is believed that the Prophet went public with these messages from about 613.[3] The Prophet's initial audience was the people of his own tribe, the Quraish of Mecca, the place of his birth. Was the Prophet a captivating preacher? Was he able to win converts through his words and their presentation? Did those listening find his message compelling?

For whatever reason, the Prophet had little success among his own people. In fact, there was growing opposition to and rejection of both the Prophet, his message, and subsequently his small group of followers. Indeed, it was this opposition, ridicule and rejection that led to the migration to Medina. In reading between the lines it would appear that there were underlying, deeper significant issues propelling the move to Medina. Were the Messenger's attacks on idol worship threatening to the Quraish's trading acumen and their hold on the Ka'ba with its associated pilgrimages and fairs? Did the well-established, recognised merchant Quraish of Mecca feel menaced by the appearance of this Preacher, a relatively insignificant member of their tribe, calling them to change? Did his call to 'believe in him,' 'obey his teaching – albeit from Allah' include assumptions of authority and power? Interestingly, in Ibn Ishaq's record, one of the tribes (Thaqif) recognised that the Prophet's call to 'believe in him' also involved a question of authority which became their reason for refusing his message.

> If we actually give allegiance to you and God gives you victory over your opponents, shall we have authority over you? He (Muhammad) replied, "Authority is a matter which God places where He pleases." He replied: "I suppose you want us to protect you from the Arabs with our breasts and then if God

---

[3] These are assumed dates. It is generally thought that the Prophet first heard his call about 610 but did not start preaching until about 613. While 632 is given as the date of his death, Anthony McRoy raises questions concerning it in "The Deaths of Jesus and Muhammad: Implications for Historicity," *CSIOF Bulletin* 8/9 (Melbourne: MST Press, 2016), 48–56.

gives you the victory someone else will reap the benefit! Thank you, No!"[4]

Prior to the emigration to Medina, emanating from the rejection of the Meccan Quraish, Muhammad had been taking opportunities at various fairs to

> ...ask them to believe in him and protect him until God should make clear to them the message with which he had charged the prophet.[5]

While the Prophet believed he had a message from Allah, according to this record, the Prophet was not asking the people to believe in Allah as he was proclaiming him, but 'in himself.' In addition, he was also asking for 'their protection.' Obviously as an orphan who had lost his primary protector and supporter Abu Talib and given the opposition of the other members of the Quraish, his tribe, this need of 'protection' must have weighed heavily on him. Within a tribal society, 'protection' lay at the foundation of its organisation. This tribal protection was essential in case of attack: it was one's support and defence.

While the Meccans and the Thaqif rejected his message, it was at one of these fairs, a group of Khazraj from Yathrib, who were neighbours of the Jews whom they also raided, met with the Prophet. Apparently, in retaliation to these raids, the Jews had threatened the Khazrajites with the coming of a prophet who would support them (the Jews). On hearing Muhammad's message, these Khazrajites accepted the teaching, becoming Muslims, saying

> We have left our people, for no tribe is so divided by hatred and rancour as they. Perhaps God will unite them through you. So let us go to them and invite them to join this religion of yours; and if God unites them in it, then no man will be mightier than you.[6]

It is worth noting that embodied in this reply is the claim that religion plays both a political and social role: that Allah through religion might unite these warring tribes and restore their intertribal social harmony.

---

[4] A Guillaume, *The Life of Muhammad: A translation of Ibn Ishaq's Sirat Rasul Allah* (Oxford: Oxford University Press, 1955), 195.
[5] Ibid., 194.
[6] Ibid., 198.

It was in the following year, again at the fair, twelve Khazrajites, who became known as Helpers *Ansar*,

> "gave the apostle the pledge of women." This was before the
> duty of making war was laid on them.[7]

It is generally considered that this act constitutes the first Pledge at Al-'Aqaba. According to Ibn Ishaq, at the time of the second pledge of Al-'Aqaba during further negotiations with the Khazrajites, the main issue raised by the Prophet and Abu Bakr was to invite their allegiance on the basis of protection.[8]

> "I invite your allegiance on the basis that you protect me as
> you would your women and children."[9]

In their reply, however, this promise was spelt out definitively to include war:

> ...we will protect you as we protect our women. We give
> our allegiance and are men of war possessing arms...

Ibn Ishaq in commenting about this second pledge given by the Khazrajites makes it very clear that they understood that war was a possibility.

> ...they bound themselves to war against all and sundry
> for God and the apostle... one of the Leaders told me,
> "We pledged ourselves to war in complete obedience to
> the apostle in weal and woe, in ease and hardship and
> evil circumstances... and that in God's service we would
> fear the censure of none."

Obviously, from the moment the Prophet began to interact with the Khazrajites, they understood that in adopting this messenger and his message, war was part of the deal. That, according to Ibn Ishaq, was even before Allah's permission to fight! Asad in his *The Message of the Qur'an* comments,

---

[7] Ibid.
[8] Ibid., 203.
[9] Ibid., 205.

Since the exodus of the Muslims from Mecca to Medina state of open war had existed between them and the Meccan Quraysh.[10]

Given such a scenario, perhaps the Prophet was wanting or even waiting for a revelation from Allah to fight. After all, fighting was a normal part of Arabian tribal life, especially since it resulted in honour and booty for the winners. The psychological significance of such a revelation for the Prophet would have been morale boosting and for his followers—Muslims and Ansar—an authentication of his authority and a justification of his leadership.

According to a concordance of the Qur'an compiled by Muhammad Al A Raby Alazuzy, the Chief Official Interpreter of Islamic Law (Amin al Fatwa)[11] in Lebanon, the Prophet of Islam is recorded as being involved in eight war events, one of which includes the conquest of Mecca.[12] Interestingly he does not include these events in the *Jihad* category but under the section entitled *Muhammad.*[13] According to this analysis, during his 19 years (613-632) of being the Messenger of God, the Prophet averaged such an event about every two and a half years. However, basing an average on the total length of his prophethood distorts the record. More accurately these 'war events' occurred following the migration to Medina in 622. On that basis, the average is more striking – eight in ten years! That is almost a war every year! While it can be claimed that essentially these were only tribal wars where person to person combat was part of the practice, any war has devastating consequences. The effects are felt not only by those involved in the actual fighting but also by those who have been impacted by it, while

---

[10] Muhammad Asad, trans. *The Message of the Qur'an* (Gibraltar: Dar Al-Andalus, 1997), 236.

[11] Muhammad Al A Raby Alazuzy, *Topical Concordance to the Qur'an*, trans. Aubrey Whitehouse (Melbourne: MST Press, 2018), 5.

[12] According to the Alazuzy Concordance, the eight wars in which the Prophet was involved were 'the battle of Badr', Q3:123, 8:17,19, 25, 41,43, 44, 48. 50, 68; Uhud, 3:121,122; The Trench, 33:20, 22, 25, 27; Hudabiyya 9:1-2. 48:1, 22, 24: Hunayn 9:25,27; Qureiza 8:27, 56, 56, 9: 101, 48:2, 59:5,6; Kheibar 59: 11,15; Tabuk 9:40,65, 101; the Conquest of Mecca, Tait and Bishara 5:3, 6:92. 8:43.64; 9:40; 17:60; 28:85; 32:29,30; 48:2,27:110:3. According to the index in the Saudia Arabian *The Noble Qur'an* the verses for Badr are 3:13, 8:5-19; 42-48; Uhud 3: 121-128, 140-148; Ditch 85:4-10; Hunayn 9:25; Tabuk 9:40-59; 81:99, 117, 118, 120-122 with no seeming reference to Hudabiyya, Qureiza Khaybar, Mecca, Tait or Bishara. However, neither of these concordances would claim to be exhaustive. The battle of the Trench is sometimes called the battle of the Ditch or the War of the Confederates.

[13] Alazuzy, *Topical Concordance*, 81–82.

those conquered suffer more intensely. Whatever, the impacts on that emerging religious community these 'wars' had lasting significance.

More striking though is the war record in Ibn Ishaq's account of the Prophet's life.[14] According to that record, the Prophet personally took part in 26 fights, in which he includes Badr, Uhud, Hudaybiya, Khaybar, the occupation of Mecca, Hunayn, and Tabuk.[15] Then, he also notes that there were 38 expeditions and raiding parties in which the Prophet was either involved or sanctioned. Obviously to this reporter, these events constituted a badge of honour. Given that these were all after the emigration to Medina, those early years of the *ummah* of Islam were hardly peaceful. Tor Andrae comments that it "was a military state which was growing in power like an avalanche,"[16] while Cotterell's book captures the sentiment by entitling one of his chapters, "Fighting always fighting."[17] Moreover, the Prophet himself in addressing these events explains them as 'striving for God.'

The remainder of this paper, then, will examine more closely, though briefly, the eight 'wars' that Alazuzy has identified from the perspective of the expansion of Islam. While the word 'war' has modern connotations, it is possibly better to understand these events as aggressive confrontations which included what in those days were warlike activities, though after the death of the Prophet they assumed the format of war characteristic of the times. It will also consider what appears to be the primary reason for that event and where possible the ongoing effects of that incident in the life of the Muslim *ummah* and consequently on the continuing expression of Islam. The raids will only be mentioned where they are needed to complete the picture.

So, was the progress of Allah's religion the result of physical aggression or the peaceful acceptance of the Prophet's teaching? To answer that question, one needs to ask the degree to which warfare and raiding were accepted practices for desert-living Arabic tribes. Given the limited resources of such an environment, raiding (*razzia*)

---

[14] Guillaume, *The Life of Muhammad*.
[15] Ibid., 659.
[16] Tor Andrea, *Mohammed: The Man and His Faith* (New York: Harper Torchbooks, 1960), 23.
[17] Peter Cotterell, *Muhammad: The Man who Transformed Arabia* (Melbourne: Acorn Press, 2011), 109.

was an accepted way of life. Some would even suggest a 'sport.' A raid was generally conducted as a means of obtaining some form of economic advantage: tradeable merchandise, camels, horses, food. Consequently, camel caravan traders, while an essential part of Arabian trading society, though limited in number, required protection when travelling through the various tribal areas. Loss of life, apparently, was minimal but if there was a loss blood feuds usually resulted. The closest relative or tribal protector was bound to redress the death though it is said that 'blood money' was being paid in camels by the time of the Prophet. So inter-tribal fighting was not uncommon, though blood feuds were not the only reason. While the tribes did combine to war against each other, stronger tribes would support and be supported by weaker ones whether as aggressors or defenders. However, even fighting was regulated. Glubb commented that,

> Carefully balanced and universally recognised systems governed both the hostilities between the tribes and the relationship between the tribes and merchants.[18]

There were also sacred months during which each tribe had agreed to neither raid, nor fight. During those times, the tribes would go on pilgrimages to sacred sites, hold trading fairs and engage in poetry competitions. Interestingly, Muhammad's own birth in 570CE took place around the time of the *War of the Elephant* when Abráha, the Christian Abyssinian ruler of Yemen unsuccessfully marched on Mecca. When Muhammad was a young teenager, it is said that he accompanied his uncles in their involvement in the "Wicked Wars" or "Sacrilegious Wars," a tribal engagement which occurred annually for about a five-year period. He is supposed to have gathered any sent arrows so they could be returned![19]

The context of Allah's injunction to fight.

According to Ibn Ishaq, it was from Medina that the Prophet sanctioned these fights and raids for which he had received divine permission. Apparently that was given sometime after the second pledge at Al- 'Aqaba, generally thought to have been in 622CE. Ibn Abbas comments that it

---

[18] John Bagot Glubb, *The Life and Times of Muhammad* (London: Hodder and Stoughton, 1970), 200.
[19] Ibid., 72.

was revealed immediately after the Prophet left Mecca for Medina, i.e., at the beginning of year 1 H.[20]

Permission to fight? That, in itself, raises a question. Since warfare was so much a part of tribal life, why did the Prophet need a revelation from Allah to fight? Was it because he disliked fighting as some would claim or was it just a preference to avoid confrontation with casualties?[21] Had Allah previously advised him against it? The answer seems from Sura 4:77 and 5:32 (though both are regarded as Medinan suras) that there was a prohibition to fight. Given that Mecca was the home of the Prophet's tribe, certainly fighting against one's blood relatives and one's basis of protection would have created difficulty and as such would not have been given much consideration. Also, given that the numbers of the Prophet's followers, including those who could fight for the cause, were few in number would have been a deterring factor. Indeed, the ridicule, rejection and the 'persecution' experienced meant some followers left for Abyssinia. Psychologically the impact of such behaviour was significant and would have influenced subsequent thoughts, attitudes and plans.

In addition, since there was such a poor response from the Quraish to his proclamations, did the Prophet consider there may be other means of gaining converts? If people were not willing to respond, should they be forced to do so? Was coercion one way that tribal society, in those days, maintained group cohesion and gained position? While it is not possible to revisit the tribal context of the Prophet's day, indications from current tribal practices would suggest that coercion in various forms still plays an important role in such contexts. Did he consider that fighting, since it was one of the regular ways of solving problems, would result in the triumph of his religion? He was, no doubt, aware of the Byzantine and Sasanian efforts to extend their spheres of influence, and so their religious ideals by war. Did the Prophet (after all he was human) expect that a revelation from Allah would 'strengthen' his authority and provide validity to his cause? Alternatively, should the result of any such activity have been a failure, that would bring discredit to both Allah and the Prophet, unless of course, Allah provided a 'revelation' justifying the 'failure.' That was certainly the case following the 'battle of Uhud.'

[20] Asad, *The Message of the Qur'an*, 512.
[21] Glubb, *The Life and Times of Muhammad*, 226.

According to Ibn Ishaq and subsequent exegetes, Allah's permission to fight is recorded in Q22:39-41.[22]

> Permission is granted to those who **fight** because they have been wronged. And God is truly able to help them; those who were expelled from their homes without right, only because they said: 'Our Lord is God.'

In this sura the word used for 'fight' is from 'qaatil' which is related to the word to kill or murder (qatal), rather than the word 'jihad.' However, the tafsir of Jalalayn as translated by Feras Hamza ties this revelation both to 'struggling (striving) in the way of God' and 'jihad.'[23]

> (39) Permission is granted to those who fight namely to the believers to fight back – this was the first verse to be revealed regarding the struggle in the way of God jihād because they have been wronged as a result of the wrong done to them by the disbelievers. And God is truly able to help them.

Thus, this particular exegesis makes it very clear that even 'fighting as killing and murder' was to be understood as 'striving in the way of God.' Ibn Abbas in exegeting Q22:40 also links this revelation with jihad.[24]

> Verily Allah helpeth one... against his enemies (who helpeth Him) who helps His Prophet in jihad. (Lo! Allah is Strong) to help His Prophet and whoever helps His Prophet, (Almighty) He is Mighty in His vengeance against the enemies of His Prophet.

That is the progress of the preaching/warning was linked to aggressively advancing the cause. The outcome, according to Q22:40-41, would bring economic benefit on the proviso that the believers adhered to the Prophet's teaching, which had its origins, so he claimed, in Allah. Other suras (from Medina) repeating the permission to fight include Q2:190, 193; 9:12-14.

---

[22] Unless otherwise stated quotes from the Qur'an are from *The Holy Qur'an: A new English translation of its Meanings* © 2020 Royal Aal al-Bayt Institute for Islamic Thought, Amman, Jordan, (http://www.aalalbayt.org)

[23] Tafsir al-Jalalayn, trans. Feras Hamza © 2020 Royal Aal al-Bayt Institute for Islamic Thought, Amman, Jordan, (http://www.aalalbayt.org)

[24] Tafsir Ibn 'Abbas, trans. Mokrane Guezzou © 2020 Royal Aal al-Bayt Institute for Islamic Thought, Amman, Jordan (http://www.aalalbayt.org)

Indeed, not only was the Prophet ordered to fight but he also encouraged others to do the same:

> So fight in the way of God; you are charged only with yourself. And urge on the believers; maybe God will restrain the might of the disbelievers; God is mightier and more severe in castigation (Q4:84).

'Fighting in the way of God' (في سبيل الله) occurs some 55 times in the Qur'an where it means to be 'involved in jihad.'[25] Fighting for Allah becomes a sign of commitment not only to the Prophet but also to Allah and Islam (Q4: 76; 9:44; 45; 9:15). Indeed, one of Allah's tests for a believer was the willingness to fight (Q9:16; 47:4, 31), to the point where Allah 'loves' those who fight on his behalf (Q61:4). Fighting, striving in the cause of Allah, is not only a command that demands obedience but it constitutes a spiritual value which reflects the commitment of the believer. Some would even put 'jihad' as a sixth pillar of Islam.

Progress by raids

So, permission to fight was divinely sanctioned. Yet, it would appear that the Prophet did not immediately take up arms against the Quraish. Rather, the Prophet chose another tactic. The emigrees from Mecca had been living in Medina for some six months and it is said they were facing economic difficulties.[26] Obviously, the Prophet would have known the practices of the Meccan traders who passed some distance from Medina on their way to and from Syria. On learning of the passing of a Mecca bound Quraishi caravan, the Prophet sent out a raiding party (January 623).[27] The prospect of bounty from a caravan must have been attractive, but since the emigrees were from Mecca themselves and of the Quraishi tribe, raiding their own no doubt caused consternation. The raiding party met the traders, but a local tribe mediated between the two. The raiding party returned empty-handed. A further raid was sent out in February 623. Though arrows

---

[25] Bernie Power, "Not Quite the Religion of Peace," *Quadrant Magazine*, https://quadrant.org.au/opinion/qed/2019/02/not-quite-the-religion-of-peace, cited November 3, 2020.

[26] Initially Medina was known as Yathrib. It is said that it was after the Battle of the Trench that its name was changed. For ease of expression, I have chosen to use Medina as the name throughout the remainder of the article.

[27] The dates given for these raids are taken from Glubb, *The Life and Times of Muhammad*.

were shot, it was also unsuccessful. Another unsuccessful raid led by the Prophet took place in June 623, but it did result in a 'win' for Islam – a friendship treaty was established with the Bani Dhamra. In another raid in September (623), while unsuccessful economically it also added to the surrounding support: another treaty. Allegiances would be valuable should there be war, though it is uncertain the degree to which these resulted in converts! There are records that the Prophet sent teachers to various tribes to inform them of Islam.

According to Glubb's list, a number of unsuccessful raids were conducted between June and October of that year. The raid of November (623) which the Prophet sent to Nakhla was apparently to ambush a caravan travelling from Taif to Mecca. The raid successfully took bounty but at the same time killed a Meccan and took captives. More significantly though, the raid took place on the last day of a 'sacred' month when traditionally 'raiding' and 'fighting' were 'forbidden.' At one stage it would appear, that the Muslims were also forbidden to 'raid' and 'fight' in those months (sura 9:5, 36). Allah's response to the Nakhla incident is recorded in Q2:217 and as such it qualifies the previous revelation.

> They ask you about the sacred month, and fighting in it. Say, 'Fighting in it is a grave thing; but to bar from God's way, and disbelief in Him, and the Sacred Mosque, and to expel its people from it – that is graver in God's sight; and sedition is graver than slaying.' They will not cease to fight against you until they turn you from your religion if they are able; and whoever of you turns from his religion, and dies disbelieving – their works have failed in this world and the Hereafter. Those are the inhabitants of the Fire, abiding therein.

Jalalydn's tafsir as translated by Hamza is as follows:

> Thus the Prophet... sent forth the first of his raiding parties... The disbelievers reviled them for making fighting lawful in a sacred month and so God revealed the following: They ask you about the sacred the forbidden month and fighting in... 'the sacred month.' Say to them 'Fighting... is a grave thing... is heinous in terms of sin; but to bar... people from God's way, His religion, and disbelief in Him... and to bar from the Sacred Mosque that is Mecca and to expel its people the Prophet... and the believers from it – that is graver... more heinous in terms of sin than fighting in it in God's sight; and sedition your idolatry is graver than your slaying' in it. They

the disbelievers will not cease to fight against you O believers until so that they turn you from your religion to unbelief... whoever of you turns from his religion and dies disbelieving – their good works have failed that is they are invalid in this world and the Hereafter... Those are the inhabitants of the Fire abiding therein.

So basically, fighting against unbelievers takes precedence over traditionally sanctioned practices: moreover, idolatry is a greater sin than 'slaying' an unbeliever. Also, the revelation carries with it a demand to 'submit' to Allah's ways. To 'die disbelieving' had dire consequences.

A Meccan dead, a caravan captured, endless attempted raids against the Quraish would hardly have improved relations between the Meccans and the Muslims. Obviously, harassing the Meccans by raiding their caravans was part of the Prophet's strategy. Was it just economics that was driving this plan? Was this the Prophet's way of revenging the treatment he and his followers had received at the hand of the Quraish? Was he deliberately impoverishing the Quraish to make himself (Islam) great? Indeed, a Meccan sura (42:39-41) gave divine sanction to such actions. In Allah's revelation (quoted above) there was the reminder that the 'unbelievers' would not stop their attacks, presumably giving the Prophet permission to keep 'fighting.' The next raid was planned. A Quraishi caravan was due to leave Syria in January (624) bringing back considerable economic benefit to Mecca. The Quraish became aware of the planned attack, so chose a different route, but had called Mecca to arms. Asad in his commentary writes:

> The fact that the Prophet... had on this occasion made his plans known so long in advance suggests that the purported attack on the caravan was no more than a feint, and that from the very outset his real objective had been an encounter with the Quraysh army.[28]

Badr

The Prophet with his army (Q8:5-8) and the Meccans (though not the caravan) met a Badr (March 624 – AH2). A fight ensured. The Muslims, though Quraish themselves, now had a new allegiance: it was no longer tribal, it was to the *ummah,* the community of Islam.[29]

---

[28] Asad, *The Message of the Qur'an*, 236.
[29] Cotterell, *Muhammad: The Man who transformed Arabia*, 89.

Many significant Meccans who opposed the Prophet were killed, allowing the Muslims to triumph, apparently with the help of angels (Q3:124; 8:9-10) and divine support (Q8:17). Indeed, the Prophet received what he wanted, a further sanction for the advancement of Islam by war. Allah's command (Q8:39) was:

> And fight them until sedition is no more and religion is all for God; then if they desist, surely God sees what they do.

Commentators suggest that Badr was a decisive moment for Islam. Allah had shown He was on their side; the bounties of war and the ransom paid for captives had improved their economic lot. Their detractors were shown that these Muslims were a recognisable force. The believers would have felt vindicated. Asad adds this comment:

> ...the movement inaugurated by Muhammad was not an ephemeral dream but the beginning of a new political power and a new era different from anything that Arabian past had known.[30]

He continues:

> It may be safely assumed that until then only a very few of the Prophet's Companions had fully understood the *political* [sic]implications of the new order of Islam.... After the battle of Badr... they became aware that they were on their way towards a new social order... the idea of sacrifice through *action* [sic]. The doctrine of action... was consciously realised... and the intense activism which was to distinguish Muslim history in the coming decades and centuries was a direct, immediate consequence of the battle of Badr.[31]

As a consequence of the battle of Badr, Allah had strong words for those who became afraid and wanted to turn back (Q8:15 – 'no retreat permissible'), which became a permanent law.'[32] For those who died in the cause of Islam there was a promise: Paradise[33]

> Count not those who were slain in God's way, as dead, but rather, living with their Lord, provided for [by Him]. Q3:169 (cf. Q2:154, 3:158, 169).

---

[30] Asad, *The Message of the Qur'an*, 237.
[31] Ibid., 237.
[32] Ibid., 240.
[33] Ibid., 300 (cf. Cotterell, *Muhammad*, 91).

Also, though it would seem that initially all booty belonged to Allah and the Apostle (Q8:1) this was modified later with Allah and the Apostle receiving a fifth, with the rest being distributed to 'near of kin, and the orphans, and the needy and the wayfarer' (Q8:41).[34] A practice which was subsequently followed.

Uhud

In April 624 – AH2, the Meccans in retaliation mounted a raid on Medina. While there was some physical loss to the Medinans, the raid was largely unsuccessful but for the Muslims it meant food. Hence it is sometimes called the 'Porridge Raid.'[35] During 624 in May, June, and August, the Prophet continued with various raids, while widening the targets the degree of success varied. In the September the Muslims managed to capture another Quraishi caravan. Not surprisingly the Quraish were further incensed and planned a retributive attack on the Prophet in Medina. Gathering support from some surrounding tribes, the Meccans took up their places outside Medina at Uhud (March 625). There was consternation in Medina. Some were willing to take up arms and fight; others from the Medinans initially agreed and then reneged. The Prophet and his followers were basically outnumbered. Tribal style warfare occurred and initially the Muslims had the upper hand. However, the Muslim archers, it appears, being more interested in booty, left their post and the situation turned. The Prophet was injured, and many Muslims were killed. The outcome was essentially a draw. The Meccans left unable to take the advantage. The Muslims retired to their homes in Medina though the next morning the Prophet pursued the Meccans (Q3:172-174). The Meccans were unwilling to engage in further conquest and so the Muslims returned to Medina.

While Alazuzy only allocates two verses to this battle Ibn Ishaq claims that much of Sura Imran (3:121-199) stems from Allah's interaction with the Prophet in relation to this incident. The failure at Uhud, Allah declared, was to 'test the believers' (3:140) and to teach them 'patience in adversity' (3:142), while refusing to fight would result in hell-fire (3:156). By implication refusing to fight was both a failure to obey the Prophet, and thus Allah.

---

[34] Ibid., 245.
[35] Glubb, *The Life and Times of Muhammad*, 199.

Ending opposition

Throughout the story of the growth of Islam in those early days, there was another practice that was acceptable, though it could carry with it the demand for redress: eliminate the opposition which could take any form: Assassination! Extermination! Ethno-cleansing! Such models are still in use today. Even the Prophet's flight to Medina apparently was prompted by a Quraishi assassination attempt on his life and later it is said that the Jews also attempted to do the same. The Prophet himself was not averse to using this method alongside sanctioned 'traps' and 'deception.' The satirical poets of his day suffered at his hands, including Ka'ab of the Jewish Bani Nadr tribe.

While Badr might have meant triumph for the Prophet, the continuing rejection by the Jews and Christians in Medina caused angst. Both Jews and Christians were at odds with the Prophet over Allah's revelations and their understanding of their revealed Scriptures. The Prophet's response was to charge the Jews and Christians with 'changing' or 'corrupting' their texts (Q 5:12-140). Taking advantage of an incident in the market involving Jews and Muslims (April[?] 624) the Prophet lay siege to the 'fortress' of the Bani Qaynuqa. No Arabian allies came to their aid though Abdullah bin Ubayy interceded with the Prophet on their behalf. The tribe escaped with their lives and moveable possessions. Some travelled as far as Syria. The Prophet and the Muslims benefitted from their lands and anything they could not take with them. Allah's revelations which are said to date from this event are:

> O you who believe, do not take Jews and Christians as patrons; they are patrons of each other. Whoever amongst you affiliates with them, he is one of them. God does not guide the folk who do wrong (Q5:51).

> O you who believe, do not take as patrons those who take your religion in mockery, and as a game, from among those who were given the Scripture before you and [from among] the disbelievers and fear God if you are believers (Q5:57).

According to Ibn Ishaq, the Prophet is reported to have said "Kill any Jew that falls into your power."[36]

---

[36] Guillaume, *The Life of Muhammad*, 369.

As a consequence, the Jewish tribe, Bani Nadr, plotted against the Prophet aiming to kill him. He became aware of it. Then, citing that they had broken their treaty, demanded that they should leave in 10 days. They, too, were allowed to leave: most went to nearby Khaybar, destroying their homes but leaving their weapons of war (Q59:2). Further directions were also given regarding the distribution of booty (Q59:7).

'The Trench'

The Meccans, not satisfied with the outcome of Uhud and the constant harassment of raiding parties, decided to make another foray on Medina (March – April 627). Obtaining co-operation from some of their associated surrounding tribes, together with some Jewish support, they marched on Medina with a sizeable force. The Prophet had some warning and on the advice, it is said, of a Christian convert to Islam, dug a ditch around at least parts of Medina. The battle has subsequently been named the battle of 'the trench' or 'ditch' (Q33:20, 22, 25, 27), though sometimes called the 'War of the Confederates.' The 'confederates' were confused by this new war tactic and found it difficult to mount an attack. Meanwhile the Muslims (and Medinans) were very fearful (Q33:10-11); some refusing to fight, others reneging. While the Quraish had used bribes to boost their numbers, the Prophet also attempted to use bribes to dissuade some of the tribes from continuing. It is said that dissension, due to underlying distrust, weakened the alliance. Along with the lack of food for the animals and inclement weather and angel intervention the Meccans withdrew (Q33:9, 25).

The power and influence of Mecca and so too the Quraish had been shown to be no match to the power and might of the Muslims and their Prophet. Not surprisingly, as a consequence a number of tribes sought to align themselves with the Prophet. What was their motive? Was it in response to the Prophet's teaching? Was it a fear that if they were attacked, they would suffer the fate of the defeated? Was it that they wanted to be associated with the stronger party?

Qurayza

Frustrated by continued opposition of another Jewish tribe, Bani Qurayza, including their support of the Meccans at Uhud in violation, it is said, of the treaty agreements, the Prophet surrounded their 'fortress.' The Qurayza surrended, possibly anticipating to be treated like the Bani Qaynuqa and Nadr. Basically, one of their clan leaders turned against them, though it was the Prophet who endorsed the decision. Following Arabian custom, the men were killed, the women and children made slaves and their property and goods given to the Muslims. The Prophet received a fifth (Q 33:26-27) as well as was customary added to his harem.

Hudaybiya

It was about a year later (March 628 – 6AH) that the Prophet decided to make a *bona fida,* lesser pilgrimage (*'umrah*) to Mecca. Some of the Bedouin tribes who had associated themselves with the Prophet declined to join him. Setting up camp at Hudaybiya, just outside the sacred area, the Prophet sent Uthman, his own son-in-law as an envoy into Mecca, requesting permission to enter to complete the pilgrimage and sacrifice the animals. It was rumoured that Uthman had been killed, prompting the Prophet to institute the 'oath of allegiance' to ensure support among his followers. The Meccans did attack but the Muslims took captives, though later freeing them. The Meccans under the leadership of Abu Sufyan refused the Muslims entry. A stalemate resulted. The Prophet and the Muslims ultimately agreed on a 'peace treaty.' The Muslims would not enter Mecca that year but the following year the Meccans would leave for three days to allow the Muslims access to the Ka'ba. It also made provision for the Muslims and the Meccans to interact on a more regular basis. Although seemingly defeated, the Prophet and his party sacrificed their animals. While this foray didn't advance the Muslim hold on Mecca, a number of individuals from Mecca as well as some surrounding tribal groups did align themselves with the Prophet, though not necessarily for religious reasons. The Prophet's influence on Arabia was growing. While the Muslims initially were not happy with a number of the conditions, ultimately it was considered a victory (Q48:1). According to Rizvi:

> It is recorded that during the two years following this treaty, more people accepted Islam than during the whole nineteen years since the inception of the mission.[37]

Khaybar

[37] *The Life of Muhammad The Prophet: Battles* (www.al-Islam.org), accessed November 3, 2020.

Still the Jews of Khaybar and scattered Christians were resistant to both the Prophet and his message. In addition, they were apparently planning an assault of the Prophet, inviting others to join them. In March 629 – 7AH the Prophet attacked their fortresses, killing the men and taking the women and children as captives while gaining an extensive booty. The Prophet also added another Jewess to his harem. According to Ibn Ishaq,

> God struck terror to the hearts of the men of Fadak when they heard what the Apostle had done to the men of Khaybar. They sent... an offer of peace on condition that they should keep half of their produce."[38]

Here was the beginning of the *dhimmi* status that was to determine the conditions for both Jews and Christians living under Islam. Ultimately, they became people without rights. This policy would be more formally developed as it was subsequently implemented. Basically, the Jewish opposition had been dealt with but the Prophet's anger and frustration at both Jews and Christians has influenced Muslim relations with those two groups to this day.

Mecca 'falls'

On the basis of an intertribal conflict which involved a tribe allied to the Muslims, the Prophet took the opportunity to renege on the Treaty of Hudaybiya and attack Mecca (January 630AD – 8 AH). Abu Sufyan was sent to Medina to negotiate but his advances were refused. As the Muslims progressed towards Mecca they were joined by other tribes. Abu Sufyan with several others, while assessing the Muslim contingent, was taken to the Prophet where Abu Sufyan and those with him accepted Islam. The Prophet send them back to Mecca with the promise that everyone who stayed in their house would be safe in the attack. There was no fighting and limited resistance. The leaders of the Quraish were now in submission to the Prophet who at that time entered the Ka'ba, destroying its idols but retaining its black stone. The Prophet's proclamation of 'the One God,' Allah was now a physical reality among many of the tribes surrounding the Mecca- Medina area. The pilgrimages, *umra* and *haj* became part of accepted Muslim practice. To the Prophet the religion of Abraham had been restored at its rightful place (Q2:125-127). According to Rizvi, other tribes were now invited to join Islam, though some tribes were still resistant.

---

[38] Guillaume, *The Life of Muhammad*, 523.

Hunayn

A significant percentage, it would appear, of at least the western Arabian tribes, had allied themselves to the Prophet. However, the extent to which they were truly Muslim might be questioned in view of developments following the Prophet's death. Some central Arabian tribes, especially those not too far from Medina, were still idol worshippers. Two of these, the Hawazin and Thaqif attacked the Muslims at Hunayn, not far from Mecca. The Muslims almost lost the battle, some fleeing, but they finally succeeded. Some of the attackers escaped to Ta'if, a walled city, which was besieged for a day. The Hawazin and their families were taken by the Muslims, though they were later released. Many of the Hawazin turned to Islam, it is said, because of the release of the captives.

Tabuk

In AH 9, (September-October 630) the Prophet set out for North West Arabia (Syria), in response to a perceived threat of an invasion of (north) Arabia by Heraclius. It was a campaign for which the Prophet raised money. Given the heat of the summer, its progress was limited and was terminated at Tabuk – the threat of invasion unfounded. With a significant number of Arabian tribes having aligned themselves to the Prophet, Andrae following Wakidi suggests that the Prophet was already seeking to move beyond Arabia.[39] Allah had announced that the Prophet should take 'the truth' and 'manifest it over every other religion'. While this expedition didn't reach Syria, a number of Christian princes did surrender and began paying taxes to the Prophet, in accordance with the will of Allah (Q9:29): a practice that still continues.

Conclusion

Was the expansion of Islam, in those early days the result of the Prophet's preaching or political manoeuvring including raids and warfare? Certainly, after the migration to Medina, it would appear that wars and raids contributed significantly to the expansion of the religion. Yet, one must ask the question, was it the message, political expediency and/or fear—a weapon that the Prophet strongly advocated—that saw the Arab tribes adopt Islam? Glubb writes:

---

[39] Andrae, *Mohammed*, 168.

...we know that the Apostle was steadily but cautiously widening his field of operations. He began by suppressing the opposition... and making agreements with tribes... With considerable skill, he used the threat of armed forces to win political victories, but he always preferred diplomacy to arms.

According to Tor Andrae,

During his last years in Medina Mohammed's sovereignty embraced practically the whole of Arabia. A large number of tribes sent emissaries to him, and voluntarily accepted Islam, while others submitted only after military pressure.

On the other hand, Gabriel writes,

At the time of Muhammad's death no more than perhaps one-third of Arabia had been exposed to Islam in any way, and far less than a third of the population, perhaps no more than 20% or so had actually professed it.[40]

Certainly, in his treatment of the Meccans in the encounter at Hudaybiya and the 'Conquest of Mecca' he used diplomacy, and when approaching some of the tribes, diplomacy was his *operandus modi*. However, can it really be said that the Prophet preferred diplomacy? He does not seem to hesitate to assassinate opposition and took whatever opportunities arose to take up arms against the Jews and others, for which he claimed he had valid reasons.

There are records of the Prophet sending 'teachers' to various tribes to warn them of Hell and to call them from idolatory, to observe the prayer ritual and live in obedience to the Will of Allah. Some accepted, some at least initially rejected.

From Ibn Ishaq's account, the Medina years of the Prophet were filled with an aggressive extension of Islam. Significant sections of the Qur'an (such as Q3, *The House of Imran*, Q8 *The Spoils of War*, Q9 *Repentance*, Q33 *The Confederates*, Q48 *The Victory*, Q59 *The Gathering*) deal with these battles. According to Nöldeke's chronology, only 24 out of 114 suras, that is about a quarter, are from the Medinan period with many of the revelations appearing to deal with 'behaviour' rather than the message. [41] In Ibn Ishaq's *sira*, the

---

[40] Richard A, Gabriel, *Muhammad: Islam's First Great General* (Norman, OK: University of Oklahoma Press, 2007), 205.
[41] Alazuzy, *Topical Concordance*, 97.

longest section is the third part: *Muhammad's migration to Medina, His Wars, His Triumph and Death* which occupies 471 pages of Guillaume's translation, or almost some 60% of the work. Obviously to Ibn Ishaq it was this latter period of 'wars and raids' that was the more important story to tell.

As a consequence of these battles much of the conduct and practice of aggressively advancing Islam was established. 'Striving for God' became the battle cry of the Prophet and 'jihad' became both a moral and religious obligation. Under Allah, martyrdom was elevated while retreating was condemned and refusal to fight criticised and threatened with hell-fire (Q3:156. 9:24). Sura 9:29—

> Fight those who do not believe in God, nor in the Last Day, and who do not forbid what God and His Messenger have forbidden, nor do they practise the religion of truth, from among of those who have been given the Scripture, until they pay the jizya tribute, readily being subdued.

—has its origin from this period, with the added injunction in 9:73 (cf. 9:123) to:

> ...struggle against the disbelievers and the hypocrites, and be harsh with them; for their abode will be Hell, an evil journey's end!

Glubb's claim is that the 'ultimate triumph' of the Prophet 'was not due to his military success but to his personality.'[42] He continues,

> ...whatever we think of his spiritual mission, we can readily admit that the Messenger of God had an instinctive touch in politics and diplomacy.[43]

On the other hand, Gabriel—in *Muhammad: Islam's first great General*—writes,

> ...had Muhammad not succeeded as a military commander Islam might have remained... an interesting religious sect relegated to a geographical backwater.[44]

A preacher? A prophet? A politician? A military leader? Obviously, it was not just one of these but the combination of them all. Did the

---

[42] Glubb, *The Life and Times of Muhammad*, 312.
[43] Ibid., 313.
[44] Gabriel, *Muhammad*, pxviii.

spread of Islam result from his preaching? That was at least the launching place but much of the early progress, especially after the migration to Medina was obviously a result either directly or indirectly of wars and raids. Interestingly, it wasn't too long after the Prophet's death, that the Muslim armies set out to claim the world for Islam. In so doing, they were just following a model that was already accepted practice, had received divine sanction, with not only Allah's approval but was his command.

Bibliography

Andrae, Tor. *Mohammed: The Man and His Faith*. New York: Harper Torchbooks, 1960.

Al A Raby Alazuzy, Muhammad. *Topical Concordance to the Qur'an*. Translated by Aubrey Whitehouse, edited by Ruth Nicholls. Melbourne: MST Press, 2018.

Asad, Muhammad. *The Message of the Qur'an: Translated and explained*. Gibraltar: Dar al-Andalusa, 1980.

Gabriel, Richard A. *Muhammad: Islam's First Great General*. Norman, OK: University of Oklahoma Press, 2007.

Glubb, John Bagot. *The Life and Times of Muhammad*. London: Hodder and Stoughton, 1970.

Ibn Ishaq. *The Life of Muhammad: A Translation of Ibn ishaq's Sirat Rasul Allah*. Translated by A. Guillaume. Oxford: Oxford University Press, 2007.

McRoy, Anthony. "The Deaths of Jesus and Muhammad; Implications for Historicity." *CSIOF Bulletin* 8/9 (2016): 48–56. Melbourne: MST Press.

Chronological List of Significant Battles and Raids[45]

First raid under Humza	January 623
Raid near Rabigh (arrow shot)	February 623
Bani Dhamra raid (treaty)	June 623
Number of unsuccessful raids	June – October 623

---

[45] Based on various lists provided in Glubb, *The Life and Times of Muhammad*. Spelling follows Glubb's.

Dhi as Ushaira raid (treaty)	September 623
Nakhla raid (a death)	November 623
Badr	March 624
Response raid to Meccan raid.	April 624
Raid of Dhu Amr	June 624
Bahran raid	August 624
Capture of Quraish caravan	September 624
Battle of Uhud	March 625
Al Raji incident.	May 625
Bir Moona	June 625
Return to Badr	March 626
Dhat al Riqa raid	June 626
Dumat al Jandal raid	August 626
Seige of Medina (trench)	March – April 627
Encounter with Bani Quraidha	April 627
Bani Lihyan raid	October 627
Bani Mustaliq raid	December 627\January 628
Truce of Hudaibiya	March 628
Conquest of Kheibar	September 628
Muslim pilgrimage to Mecca	February 629
Battle of Mota	September 629
Occupation of Mecca	January 630
Battle of Hunain	February 630
Siege of Ta'if	February-March 630
Muhammad to Medina	March 630
Expedition to Tabuk	September-October 630
Death	June 632

Chapter 3

CALIPHATE: QURANIC CONCEPT?

Bernie Power[1]

The name could not be more ironic. Some years ago, I visited the large 'Gallipoli Mosque' in Auburn, Sydney. The Gallipoli peninsula is, of course, in western Turkey where Turkish troops inflicted a humiliating defeat on Australian soldiers in 1915 during the First World War. Australians cherish the name Gallipoli as a reminder of the courage of the ANZAC troops under fire: Turks celebrate it as a great historical victory over the infidel invaders. In November 1914, the Muslim Caliph, the Ottoman Sultan Mehmed V had called for a holy war against the Triple Entente forces. He wrote:

> Of those who go to the *Jihad* for the sake of happiness and salvation of the believers in God's victory, the lot of those who remain alive is felicity, while the rank of those who depart to the next world is martyrdom. In accordance with God's beautiful promise, those who sacrifice their lives to give life to the truth will have honor in this world, and their latter end is paradise.[2]

The Turkish Muslims won this important campaign. After reading thousands of pages of Turkish archives, including soldiers' diaries, historian Professor Harvey Broadbent concluded that the Turks were "fighting for their religion as much as for their homeland."[3]

---

[1] Dr Bernie Power is a lecturer with the Arthur Jeffery Centre for the Study of Islam at Melbourne School of Theology, and a Mission Partner with Interserve, Australia. He is the author of several books on the Christian-Muslim interface.

[2] https://www.history.com/this-day-in-history/ottoman-empire-declares-a-holy-war, accessed September 8, 2020.

[3] Eleanor Hall and Alice Matthews, "Gallipoli 2015 through Enemy Eyes: Historian Harvey Broadbent Tells the Turkish Side of the Story," *ABC News*, published March 4, 2015, https://www.abc.net.au/news/2015-03-04/harvey-broadbent-tells-turkish-side-of-gallipoli-story/6279772.

For a group of settlers (the Gallipoli Mosque was built by Turkish immigrants in 1979) to name a prominent institution after an important military and religious triumph in the country they defeated seemed somewhat insensitive. I was pondering the equivalents: a British-owned pub named 'The Battle of Waterloo' in Paris? Or an American franchise restaurant called 'The FatMan' in Nagasaki?[4]

But it was a later meeting that was even more ironic. On the footpath a few streets away, a group of heavily-bearded young men had set up a table selling *Hizb u-Tahrir* literature. Much of it related to the re-establishing of the Caliphate, which they called the Khilafah. After some discussion, I pointed out that it was Mustafa Kemal Attaturk, Turkey's triumphant general at Gallipoli and later their first president, who had abolished the Caliphate in 1924. "If an important Muslim leader put an end to it, why do you want to re-institute it?" I asked. One of the men replied through clenched teeth:

> Attaturk was a traitor. He was a *kaafir* like you! But we will re-establish the Khilafah, and follow it even here in Australia, whether you like it or not.

For fourteen hundred years, the Caliphate had been a fixture in the Islamic political landscape. After Muhammad's death in 632 AD (CE), according to Muslim sources, his best friend Abu Bakr took over the reins of the Muslim community as the *caliph* or representative of Muhammad in every respect except prophethood. The caliph was to be the political and military ruler, 'the commander of the faithful', and the administrator of the *shari'a*. Following his death in 634, Abu Bakr was replaced as caliph by 'Umar bin al-Khattab (634-644 AD), who was followed by Uthman bin Affan (644-656 AD), and then by Ali bin Abu Talib, Muhammad's son-in-law (656-661 AD). These four were called the 'rightly-guided' or *rashiduun* caliphs.

Interestingly, they all came into the role by different methods. Abu Bakr was never officially designated as leader by Muhammad but gained the position after some very deft political manoeuvring which led to his public proclamation as the *caliph*. Eager to avoid the same uncertainty, Abu Bakr appointed Umar as his replacement. On

---

[4] 'Fat Man' was the code name for the nuclear bomb dropped on Nagasaki.

his deathbed Umar established a committee of six people to select the next caliph from amongst themselves, and they chose Uthman. Following Uthman's assassination, Ali was asked to take the role by a group of Muhammad's companions. Clearly there was no one accepted way of accession to leadership in early Islam.

On Ali's death, at the hands of another Muslim, the situation deteriorated. Ali's eldest son, Hassan, took the role initially, but after seven months he abdicated in favour of Mu'awiya, on condition that Mu'awiya did not designate a successor but would allow an electoral council to appoint one. On his deathbed, Mu'awiya reneged on this treaty and anointed his son Yazid as caliph. Yazid called on Hussein, Ali's second son, to pledge fealty to him. Hussein refused and opted to fight instead. He was beheaded by Yazid at the battle of Karbala in 680 AD. Yazid then established the dynastic Umayyad caliphate based in Damascus. It continued until 750 AD. However 'the party of Ali', *Shi'at Ali,* believed that the *imamate* belonged to Muhammad's physical descendants. They followed the *Shi'a* imams, an alternative leadership also based on the dynastic principle. Later, they also divided amongst themselves as the followers of the fifth imam, (the Zaidis), or the seventh imam (the Ismailis) or the twelfth imam, Imam al-Mahdi. His adherents believe that he has been in occultation from 874 AD until an expected return at the end times.

The Abbasids overthrew the Umayyad rulers in 750 AD, and established a new dynasty of caliphs, ruling from Baghdad until 1258 AD. However, one of the Umayyads escaped to Spain and set up a rival caliphate in Cordoba in 756 AD which continued until 1031 AD. As a result, from 756 to 910, there were two rival caliphs.

The Fatimid Caliphs, who were Ismaili Shias, ruled mostly from Cairo from 910 to 1171AD, and set up their own caliph. Consequently, for over 100 years from 929 to 1031, three men claimed to be the caliph at the same time, in Cordoba, Baghdad and Cairo.

The Almohad dynasty, also caliph-led, ruled North Africa from 1147 to 1256 AD, resulting in three caliphs, ruling from Baghdad, Cairo, and Marrakesh. The Fatimid dynasty ended in 1171 when it was overtaken by Saladin of the Ayyubid dynasty. From 1171 to 1258, there were two caliphs operating from Baghdad and Marrakesh.

The Ottoman Caliphs ruled from Turkey from 1451 to 1924. The Madhi Caliph ruled in Sudan from 1885 to 1899. The Ahmadiyya sect, considered to be heretical by most Muslims, has proclaimed its leader in Qadiani, India, as Caliph from 1908 and that dynasty continues until the present day.

Based on these varying claims, there has always been a caliph of one type or other, and sometimes two or three competing caliphs, often at war with each other. Mostly they have followed a dynastic system, where an incumbent was replaced by his son or a close male relative. For 424 of the 1388 years since 632 AD up to today, that is for over 30% of Islamic history, there have been two or more claimants to the role of caliph.

Those listed above are not all of the Islamic dynasties that have existed. As the Islamic *umma* splintered, many other kingdoms, emirates and sultanates rose and fell in different locations throughout the Middle East, North Africa and Asia. Examples include the Mughal emperors ruling in India and the Safavids in Iran. These kingdoms often fought against each other, or allied together to fight other Muslim rulers. The Qarmatians were an Ismai'ili sect which established their rule from Bahrain. They considered pilgrimage to Mecca to be a superstition, and in 906 attacked the returning caravan, killing 20,000 pilgrims. In 930 they sacked Mecca and Medina, filling the Zamzam well with corpses and taking the Black Stone. They sold it back to the Abbasids in 952 for a huge ransom.

The abolition of the Caliphate by Mustapha Kemal Attaturk in 1924 was a blow to Islam. They no longer had a universally-accepted leader who could call the whole *umma* to jihad. In recent years, radical groups, such as the Muslim Brotherhood and *Hizb-u-Tahrir*, have called for the re-establishment of the Khilafah. Taqiuddin an-Nabhani, the founder of *Hizb ut-Tahrir*, wrote:

> This vital issue, i.e. the changing of every Islamic land to Dar-ul-Islam and unifying it with the other Islamic lands, is a goal that we must strive to achieve. The method used to achieve this goal is the establishment of the Khilafah as a ruling system through which the country is changed to Dar-ul-Islam and then unified with the other Islamic lands.[5]

---

[5] Taqiuddin an-Nabhani, *Political Thoughts* (London: Al- Khilafah, 1999), 122.

As ISIS began winning important victories in Syria and Iraq in 2014, a crowning moment came when <u>Abu Bakr al-Baghdadi</u> was declared the new Caliph at the mosque in Mosul. Tens of thousands of Muslims from all around the world flocked to join his army. However he killed himself and three of his own young children, by detonating a suicide vest while being pursued by American troops and army dogs in October 2019. Most Muslims did not accept him as a legitimate caliph.

So it is obvious that the concept of the caliph as an international leader is firmly established in Islamic thinking. However, is it as tightly rooted in Islamic law? And more specifically, what does the Qur'an teach about the caliphate?

The noun *khalifa*

The relevant noun based on the *kh-l-f* root is *khalifa*, which appears only twice in the Qur'an in its singular form, and its plural forms *khulafa'* or *khala'if* are found in seven verses.[6]

The first occurrence of *khalifa* is in Q.2:30, in the story of the creation of Adam. Adam is mentioned 26 times in the Qur'an, and details about him are found in 84 verses in eleven chapters.[7] This would appear to be a significant use of the term, since it defines the word *khalifa* in the context of the first human being.

In Q.2:30 Allah announces to the angels: "I am making on the earth a *khalifa*."

The English translators take quite different directions in rendering this term *khalifa*. Muhammad Asad renders it as 'one who

---

[6] The other words that are not verbs (see later) that come from this root have meanings unrelated to succession, so they have been ignored for this study. They are *khilaafin* ('opposite' - 6 occurrences), *khalf* ('behind/after' - 22 occurrences), *khilfat* ('alternating' - 1 occurrence), *khawaalifi* ('those who remain behind' - 2 occurrences), *khalifina* ('those who stay behind' - 1 occurrence), *mukhalafuuna* ('those who remained behind' – 4 occurrences), *mukhlifa* ('will fail' – 1 occurrence), *ilhtilaafi* ('alternation' – 7 occurrences), *mukhtalifan* ('varying' – 10 occurrences) and *mustakhlafiina* ('trustees' - 1 occurrence)

[7] Q2:30-39; 3:33,59; 5:27; 7:11-28, 172; 15:26-43; 17:61-65; 18:50,51; 19:58; 20:115-124; 36:60; 38:71-85

shall inherit it' i.e. the earth. In a footnote, he adds 'a successor' or 'a vicegerent.'[8] Maududi and Yusuf Ali use "vicegerent", Pickthall "viceroy," Abdul Haleem and Ghali opt for "a successor,"[9] The Saheeh International versions calls it "a successive authority."[10] Al-Hilali and Khan see it as a communal, not individual, reference and translate the term as '(mankind) generations after generations.' Clearly a translation of the term involves a theological interpretation.

The term 'vicegerent' and its implications

'Vicegerent' is a transliteration of the Latin terms *vice* 'in the place of' and *gerere* 'to carry.' Collins Dictionary defines it as "a person <u>appointed</u> to <u>exercise</u> all or some of the authority of another, esp [sic] the administrative powers of a <u>ruler</u>; <u>deputy</u>."[11] The term has a long and distinguished Christian history. The Byzantine emperors were titled God's vicegerents on earth,[12] King John I became vicegerent under the Pope,[13] and Thomas Cromwell was appointed 'Vice-Gerent in Spirituals' by King Henry VIII.[14] In Milton's *Paradise Lost* (Chapter 10), God the Father addresses Jesus Christ:

> But whom send I to judge them? whom but thee,
> Vicegerent Son? To thee I have transferred
> All judgement, whether in Heaven, or Earth, or Hell.[15]

Clearly this term denotes some-one of great honour, power and authority.

So it appears that there is a 'high' view of the word *khalifa* which translates it as 'vicegerent' or 'viceroy,' a ruling individual who enjoys esteem and capability. A 'middle' view would be 'successor,'

---

[8] http://www.muhammad-asad.com/Message-of-Quran.pdf, accessed September 10, 2020.
[9] https://quran.com/2/30, accessed September 9, 2020.
[10] https://www.searchtruth.com/chapter_display.php?chapter=2&translator=29 &show_arabic=1, accessed September 9, 2020.
[11] https://www.collinsdictionary.com/dictionary/english/vicegerent.
[12] Anthony R. Littlewood, *Byzantine Court Culture from 829 to 1204* (Cambridge, MA: Harvard University Press, 1988), 21.
[13] Charles Henry Browning, (1898). *The Magna Charta Barons and their American Descendants with the Pedigrees of the Founders of the Order of Runnemede Deduced from the Sureties for the Enforcement of the Statutes of the Magna Charta of King John* (Philadelphia: Janaway Publishing, 2016), 14.
[14] Gilbert Burnet, *The History of the Reformation of the Church of England* (Charleston, SC: Nabu Press, 2011), 1:135.
[15] http://gutenberg.org/cache/epub/26/pg26-images.html, accessed September 10, 2020.

which describes a person who is a chronological progression or replacement of another or others with no necessary ethical or functional implications. A 'low' view would be to translate it as undifferentiated humanity, a corporate identity.

Jalalayn's commentary on Q.2:30

Like the translators, the commentators are divided, or at least appear to be divided, on the meaning of the term.

TABLE 1

Arabic text of Jalalayn's *tafsir*	Literal meaning of the Arabic text	Feras Hamza's translation
(*'idh qaala rabbak lilmalaa'ka*)	(When your Lord said to the angels)	(when your Lord said to the angels)
(*'ani jaa'il fil arD khalifa*)	(I am making on the earth a *khalifa*)	(I am appointing on earth a vicegerent)
yakhlufuni	he is succeeding/replacing me	who shall act as My deputy
ayy yanuub 'anii (see below)	i.e. he is deputising for me	
fi tanfeedh ahkami fiha	in implementing my rulings in it	by implementing My rulings therein
wa huwa 'adam	and he is Adam	and this vicegerent was Adam

Tafsir Jalalayn[16] seems to take a 'high' view when it exegetes this verse as:

...your Lord said to the angels, "I am appointing on earth a vicegerent who shall act as My deputy by implementing My rulings therein — and this vicegerent was Adam."[17]

That is what the English translation by Feras Hamza on the Aal Albayt website of Altafsir.com presents Jalalayn's commentary as

---

[16] This commentary was begun by Jalal ad-Din al-Maḥalli in 1459 and then completed after his death by his student Jalal ad-Din as-Suyuti in 1505.

[17] https://www.altafsir.com/Tafasir.asp?tMadhNo=1&tTafsirNo=74&tSoraNo=2&tAyahNo=30&tDisplay=yes&UserProfile=0&LanguageId=2, accessed September 9, 2020.

TABLE 2

saying. However an examination of Jalalayn's original Arabic text[18] (TABLE 1 above) reveals that the translator has added a key word, as is shown in the table. Note: the words in brackets are siply repeating what is in the Qur'an. Words that are not in brackets are Jalalayn's commentary on the verse.

In the first instance, Hamza translates the word *khalifa* as 'vicegerent.' But note the key insertion in the last phrase of Jalalayn's commentary: *wa huwa 'adam*, "and he is Adam," is translated by Hamza as "and *this vicegerent* was Adam" (emphasis mine).

Arabic text does not have the word 'vicegerent' or any equivalent – this is an unwarranted addition in the English translation. By including it, Hamza upgrades the text to a 'high' view of the term *khalifa*.

Incidentally, there appears to have been some other interference with Jalalayn's Arabic commentary. The original

---

[18]https://ia801209.us.archive.org/12/items/TafseerAlJalalainMaaAnwar
AlHaraminJild1ArabicPDFBook/Tafseer%20Al%20Jalalain%20Maa%20Anwar%20Al
%20Haramin%20Jild%201%20Arabic%20PDF%20Book.pdf.

Arabic text has glosses or additions written in small print above and below the main text. (As per the example – TABLE 2 above.) They are connected to the main text by small arrows. They are highlighted here in boxes. These appear to be explanatory notes by a later editor. The phrase *ayy yanuub 'anii* 'i.e. he is deputising for me' is one of these notes and it is shown in the dashed box. Rather than just 'succeeding' the antecedent, the new incumbent is now 'deputising' for him.

The impression given is of an organised attempt to change the evidence to fit a certain theological perspective. This has been done firstly by adding phrases into the earlier Arabic text (see TABLE 3) which were apparently not there in the original, and secondly by then adding words in the English translation which were not in the Arabic text.

TABLE 3

Arabic text of Ibn Abbas' *tafsir*	Literal meaning of the Arabic text	Mokrane Guezzou's translation
(wa 'idh qaala)	(and when He said)	(And when your Lord said unto the angels)
wa qad qaala	and he had said	
(rabbak lilmalaa'ika)	(your Lord to the angels)	
alladhin kana fil 'arD	who were on the earth	who were already on the earth
(ani jaa'il)	(I am making)	(Lo! I am about to place a vicegerent in the earth),
khaaliq 'akhluq	creating, I create	
(fil 'arD)	(on the earth)	
min al'arD	from the earth	I am creating a vicegerent from the earth
(khalifa)	(a *khalifa*)	
badalan minkum	replacing you (pl.)	

Ibn Abbas' commentary on Q.2:30

The popular commentary named after Ibn Abbas,[19] *Tanwir al-Miqbas min Tafsir Ibn Abbas* [The Enlightenment Acquisition from the

---

[19] The attribution of this commentary to Ibn Abbas (619-687) is widely challenged. See Bilal Philips, *Usool at-Tafseer* (Riyadh: International Islamic Publishing House, 2005),

Commentary of Ibn Abbas], is translated by Mokrane Guezzou, on the Aal Albayt website of Altafsir.com. He places in his English translation some key words not found in the original Arabic text, and he omits other words. His translation of the commentary on this section of the verse is as follows:

> (And when your Lord said unto the angels) who were already on the earth: (Lo! I am about to place a vicegerent in the earth), I am creating a vicegerent from the earth.[20]

Ibn Abbas' Arabic text, its literal meaning and Guezzou's translation are shown in the table (3) above.

Guezzou chooses to translate the word *khalifa* as 'vicegerent' but he then repeats this word as though it was a part of Ibn Abbas' commentary, which it was not. Ibn Abbas gives no synonym for the noun. At the same time, Guezzou omits translating the important phrase 'replacing you (pl.)', which Ibn Abbas gives to explain the noun. This is obviously a reference to the angels that Allah was addressing (because it is plural), with the implication that they were ruling on the earth before the first man was created. The significance of this idea becomes clear in later verses. But for now it is enough to note there are unwarranted additions and omissions in the English translation, leaving the reader with impressions that are not justified by the original Arabic text. Both these translators are attempting to promote the term *khalifa* from a 'middle' view to a 'high' view.

Ibn Kathir's commentary on Q.2:30
A third key commentary, by Ibn Kathir (1300-1373), takes a different direction. He makes the following observations on Q2:30.[21]

> Adam and His Children inhabited the Earth, Generation after Generation.
> Allah reiterated His favor on the Children of Adam when He stated that He mentioned them in the highest of heights before He created them. Allah said,

---

64. It is most likely a collection by Abu Tahir Muhammad ibn Yaqub al-Fayruz Abadi (1329–1414) based on earlier works.
[20] https://www.altafsir.com/Tafasir.asp?tMadhNo=2&tTafsirNo=73&tSoraNo=2&tAyahNo=30&tDisplay=yes&UserProfile=0&LanguageId=2, accessed September 10, 2020.
[21] http://m.qtafsir.com/Surah-Al-Baqara/Adam-and-His-Children-inhabite, accessed September 10, 2020.

(And (remember) when your Lord said to the angels.)
This Ayah means, "O Muhammad! Mention to your people what Allah said to the angels, 'Verily, I am going to place a Khalifah on earth'.
Meaning people reproducing generation after generation, century after century, just as Allah said, 'And it is He Who has made you (Khala'if) generations coming after generations, replacing each other on the earth' (6:165),
'And makes you (Khulafa') inheritors of the earth' (27:62),
'And if it were Our will, We would have (destroyed you (mankind all, and) made angels to replace you (Yakhlufun) on the earth.' (43:60) and,
'Then after them succeeded an (evil) generation (Khalf))' (7:169).

He is clearly taking a 'low' view of the term *khalifa* by presenting it as 'people reproducing generation after generation, century after century'. Ibn Kathir's methodology is to look at the verse in context to discover the meaning of the word *khalifa*. The verse has two contexts: the immediate context of the passage in which it is found, and its wider context throughout the Qur'an.

He deals with the second one first. He notes that the noun in its other forms, *khalf, khulafa', khala'if* and the verb *yakhlufun,* denote the succession of generations. There is nothing here about power, authority or honour. It simply means historical replacement by one generation after another. This seems to be a reference to humanity in general, not to a specific individual.

Ibn Kathir then turns to the immediate context. He observes:

It appears that Allah was not referring to Adam specifically as Khalifah, otherwise he would not have allowed the angels' statement, "Will You place therein those who will make mischief therein and shed blood?" (Q2:30).

For the angels, these yet-to-be created humans were not seen in a positive light. They take a lower-than-low view of the term. They understand *khalifa* to refer to disobedient and blood-thirsty humans, not to a powerful and righteous leader who will rule according to Allah's law, a vicegerent.

Ibn Kathir continues with his commentary, proposing three theories as to how the angels came upon this knowledge.

The angels meant that this type of creature usually commits the atrocities they mentioned. The angels knew of this fact, according to their understanding of human nature, for Allah stated that He would create man from clay. Or, the angels understood this fact from the word Khalifah, which also means the person who judges disputes that occur between people, forbidding them from injustice and sin, as Al-Qurtubi said.

The first relates to humanity's low origin of being made from clay,[22] whereas they as angels were made from light.[23] The second relates to the meaning of the word *khalifa* as a judge, a role needed only where law-breaking occurs.

This is interesting in that Ibn Kathir has not provided any evidence for the latter definition which he cited from Al-Qurtubi. He then adds a third theory, angelic prescience, by claiming that "they had knowledge that this creation would commit mischief on it, as Qatadah mentioned."

Ibn Kathir continues with the angels' ongoing objections:

This is only a question for the sake of learning about the wisdom of that, as if they said, Our Lord! What is the wisdom of creating such creatures since they will cause trouble in the earth and spill blood "If the wisdom behind this action is that You be worshipped, we praise and glorify You (meaning we pray to You) we never indulge in mischief, so why create other creatures?"

The logic of this is compelling. Why would Allah create a race of beings (humans) who will bring trouble while the current beings (angels) bring only obedient worship?

Ibn Kathir's commentary then takes a different direction.

Allah said to the angels in answer to their inquiry, "I know that which you do not know," meaning, "I know that the benefit of creating this type of creature outweighs the harm that you mentioned, that which you have no knowledge of. I will create among them Prophets and send Messengers. I will also create

---

[22] 3:59; 6:2; 20:55; 23:12; 15:26,28,33; 30:20; 37:11; 55:14.
[23] This concept is not found in the Qur'an. It comes from the Hadith: Sahih Muslim bk 42 no 7134. See http://sunnah.com/muslim/55/78.

among them truthful martyrs, righteous believers, worshippers, the modest, the pious, the scholars who implement their knowledge, humble people and those who love Allah and follow His Messengers."

He has moved very quickly towards a 'high' view of the word *khalifa*, but it is of a corporate entity, of people who are obediently ethical. It is not one individual who exhibits these qualities to a high degree and then attempts to lead others to the same path. However, Ibn Kathir's deduction is an unsubstantiated surmise. Allah's enigmatic and unexplained answer does not convey this meaning at all – it is simply a statement that 'Allah knows best.' There is no content in it about what He means. Ibn Kathir is simply guessing in the dark. But he continues:

> It was said that the meaning of Allah's statement, "I know that which you do not know" is, "I have a specific wisdom in creating them, which you do not have knowledge of." It was also said that it is in answer to, "While we glorify You with praises and thanks and sanctify You" after which Allah said, "I know that which you do not know." Meaning, "I know that Iblis is not as you are, although he is among you." Others said, "Will You place therein those who will make mischief therein and shed blood – while we glorify you with praises and thanks and sanctify You" is their request that they should be allowed to inhabit the earth, instead of the Children of Adam. So Allah said to them, "I know that which you do not know) if your inhabiting the heavens is better, or worse for you." Ar-Razi as well as others said this. Allah knows best."

This passage contains some interesting insights. It implies that, just as the angels could not guess what Iblis (Satan) would do and become in the future, likewise they could not guess what humanity might become. Secondly it suggests that the angels wanted to inhabit the earth themselves instead of humans. Allah points to this scenario later when He threatens to replace humanity on the earth with angels (Q43:60). Ibn Abbas' commentary above has also raised this, with the phrase 'replacing you (pl.).' It implies that angels were ruling the earth before humans were sent down to inhabit it.

Reading the rest of the Adam story in the Qur'an gives the impression that the angels were right about humanity. Despite the covenant with Allah (Q20:115), both Adam and his wife ate of the tree, (Q7:22) and thus disobeyed *'asa* Allah and went astray *gawa*.

(Q20:121) Then their private parts became obvious to them and they covered themselves with leaves (Q7:22; 20:121). Satan had made them slip from the place where they were. (Q2:36) Allah called out to them: "Did I not forbid you that tree and tell you that indeed Satan is an open enemy to you?" (Q7:22). So Allah ordered them all out of paradise (Q2:36).

Adam and his wife begged for forgiveness (Q7:23), and Allah forgave them (Q2:37; 20:122). Allah then repeated the command to leave, and Adam and his wife along with Satan were cast out of paradise and down to the earth (Q7:24–25; 2:38; 20:123).

The term stating that Adam 'disobeyed' is a strong one. The verb 'aṣa is also used of the people of Israel who rebelled in the desert (Q2:61) and killed the prophets (Q3:112). Likewise Pharaoh 'disobeyed' (Q73:16; 79:21), as did the people who rejected the message of the prophets Noah (Q71:21), Hud (Q11:59), David and Jesus (Q5:78), and Muhammad (Q4:42). Adam and his wife's signature move, eating the forbidden fruit, is not a promising start for humanity. Clearly the angels were correct.

Ibn Kathir finished this section with the phrase "Allah knows best." It was a common literary device used by Muslim historians and theologians when they recognised that they had wandered outside of their limits of knowledge or expertise. It is ultimately an admission of ignorance.

The khalifa reference in Q38:26
There is a second occurrence of the noun khalifa which, at first glance, seems more promising. One individual was appointed who could legitimately carry out judging or ruling. Allah says to the Israelite king:

> O David, I have made you a vice-gerent (khalifa) on the earth,
> so judge between people with justice and do not follow your
> desire (Q38:26).

This is the sole instance in the Qur'an where the term khalifa is used in a judicial sense.

Again the context is important. This verse is at the conclusion of a story (Q38:21-26) in which two 'brothers' climb over the wall into David's praying place, frightening him. They tell him that they have a matter for him to judge and they request a just verdict. One claimed that the other owned ninety-nine ewes and had forcefully persuaded him to hand over his only ewe. David said that the man was wrong to do this, and that such oppression was common and those who believe and do righteous deeds are few. The Qur'an then states:

> And David guessed/thought that We [i.e. Allah] had tried/tested him and he sought forgiveness of his Lord and fell down prostrate and repented (Q38:24).

Allah declares that David was forgiven and has a place near Allah and a good abode (Q38:25). Then the verse follows about David being make a *khalifa* on earth, called to judge with justice, not following his desire (Q38:26).

The translators into English again present a range of terms for *khalifa*. Yusuf Ali, Maududi and Usmani opt for 'vicegerent,' Pickthall 'a viceroy,' Abdul Haleem 'mastery,' Ghali chooses 'a succeeding (literally: Caliph) (Messenger),' Khattab has 'an authority,' and Sahih International and Hilali/Khan 'a successor.'[24] This prompts a whole range of questions: who would David be 'vicegerent' for? He was already the king (see Q38:17-20). He could not be the Caliph of Muhammad who did not yet exist. Could he be the Caliph of Allah? And why were previous kings or prophets not given this title? Why wasn't Muhammad called a Caliph of Allah?

The story raises another important query: why did David feel the need to seek forgiveness and repent?

The commentators al-Baidawi and Jalalayn connect it with the biblical story of David and the parable from the prophet Nathan.[25] David's repentance was due to his adultery with Bathsheba and the killing of her husband Uriah.[26] Jalalayn add some extra-biblical details about the two visitors and David's sexual partners.

> These two were angels who had come in the form of two disputants between whom there was supposed to have occurred

[24] https://quran.com/38/23-33, accessed September 10, 2020.
[25] According to Yusuf Ali, *The Holy Qur-an: English Translation of the Meanings and Commentary* (Madinah: The Custodian of The Two Holy Mosques King Fahd Complex for the Printing of the Holy Qur-an, 1413 AH [1992]), 1375 n4171.
[26] 2 Sam. 11:1–12:25.

the situation mentioned—but only hypothetically —in order to alert David (peace be upon him) to what he had done. He had ninety nine women but desired the woman of a man who had only her and no other. He David had married her and consummated the marriage.[27]

Ibn Abbas' commentary actually names Uriah.[28] This would fit in with the remainder of Q38:26 where David is warned by Allah, as Yusuf Ali translates it,

> ...nor follow thou the lust (of thy heart), for it will mislead thee from the Path of Allah; for those who wander from the Path of Allah is a Chastisement Grievous, for that they forget the Day of Account.[29]

The inference is that David is not qualified to judge others when he is guilty himself.

Al-Hilali and Khan take a different view. They imply that David's remorse and repentance arose because he had judged the case too quickly, after hearing only one side. They translate Q38:23 as: "[Dawud] (David) said (immediately without listening to the opponent): 'He has wronged you...'"[30] Their brackets include words which are not a part of the Arabic text. Some other commentators agree: "David's fault here is his hastiness in judging before hearing the case of the other party."[31] Again no evidence is provided for this view and the text or context do not imply or support this idea.

Whichever is the correct interpretation, the clear teaching is about David's regret and contrition and Allah's warning in the context of some failure or disobedience.

---

[27] https://www.altafsir.com/Tafasir.asp?tMadhNo=1&tTafsirNo=74&tSoraNo =38&tAyahNo=22&tDisplay=yes&UserProfile=0&LanguageId=2, accessed September 10, 2020.
[28] https://www.altafsir.com/Tafasir.asp?tMadhNo=2&tTafsirNo=73&tSoraNo =38&tAyahNo=23&tDisplay=yes&UserProfile=0&LanguageId=2, accessed September 10, 2020.
[29] Ali, *The Holy Qur-an*, 1377–1378.
[30] Muhammad Taqi-ud-Din al-Hilali and Muhammad Muhsin Khan, *The Noble Qur'an: English Translation of the Meanings and Commentary* (Madinah: The Custodian of The Two Holy Mosques King Fahd Complex for the Printing of the Holy Qur-an, 1427 AH [2006]), 614.
[31] Ali, *The Holy Qur-an*, 1377 n4176.

The other seven uses of this noun are all plural of which there are two forms, *khulafaa'* (Q7:69; 7:74; 27:62) and *khalaa'if* (Q6:165; 10:14; 10:73; 35:39).

The plural noun: *khulafaa'*

This form is found in three verses.

Q7:69 is a warning from the Arab prophet Hud to the people of 'Ad after their disbelieving leaders declare to him: "Indeed we see in you foolishness, and truly we think you are one of the liars." (Q7:66) He tells them:

> Remember that Allah made you *khulafaa'* (successors) after Noah [whose generation was drowned in the Flood], and increased you in stature substantially. Ultimately the people of 'Ad did not respond to Hud. They were destroyed when Allah "afflicted them with different kinds of punishment" (Q.89:13).

Q7:74 records the words of the Arab prophet Salih to the people of Thamud:

> And remember when He [Allah] made you *khulafaa'* (successors) after 'Ad [who had been destroyed] and settled you in the land... Like their predecessors, the people of Thamud were soon destroyed, this time by an earthquake (Q7:78)

The Messenger (seen as Muhammad by most commentators) asked his own generation: who is better, Allah or those gods that the idolators propose as His partners? He answers his own question, saying:

> Is it not the one who answers the distressed when he calls, and removes the evil, and makes you *khulafaa* (successors) on the earth? (Q27:62).

Besides this verse's mention of Allah removing evil, it is sandwiched between the stories of Allah destroying Sodom and Gomorrah during Lot's time (Q27:54-58) and the threat of distress upon the unbelievers and wrong-doers (Q27:66-70).

The plural noun *khalaa'if*

This plural form of the word *khalifa* is found in four verses.

Q6:165 is a statement of the successive generations of the earth, all of whom are being tried by Allah.

> And it is He who made you *khalaa'if* (successors) of the earth. And He raised some of you over others in ranks so that He might test you in what He has given you. Surely your Lord is swift in punishment and certainly forgiving and merciful.

The previous verse reminds the readers that every person earns [al Hilali and Khan add '(sin)'[32]] against himself, and no-one with a burden can bear the burdens of others. The scene is set for a grand assize with no outside help, where each person is responsible for their own actions, evil or otherwise.

Q10:13,14 outline Allah's purpose in creating each new generation: '

> And indeed We [Allah] destroyed the generations before you when they did wrong. And their messengers came to them with clear signs, but they were not believing. In this way We requite the criminal people. Then We made you *khalaa'if* (successors) in the earth after them so that We might see how you work.

Every new cohort is placed on earth as test for them. Allah scrutinises their performance, in the hope they will be better than their ancestors who sinned.

Q10:73 is preceded by the story of Noah sent to preach to his generation.

> They denied him, but We saved him and those with him in the ship. And We made them into *khalaa'if* (successors), and We drowned those who denied Our signs. So see what was the end of those who were warned.

This is the now-familiar cycle: warning → judgement →destruction → replacement by a *khalaa'if* succeeding generation → warning for the *khalaa'if* 'succeeding generation.'

The last verse containing this word is found in Q35:38,39:

---

[32] al-Hilali and Khan, *The Noble Qur'an*, 199.

Indeed Allah is the knower of the unseen of the heavens and the earth. Indeed He is the knower of what is in the breasts. It is He who made you *khalaa'if* (successors) in the earth. So whoever disbelieves, then upon him is his disbelief. And the disbelief of the unbelievers adds nothing but hatred with their Lord. And the disbelief of the unbelievers adds nothing but loss.

The succession of each new generation seems to take place always in an ocean of disbelief, resulting in hatred from Allah and loss.

The verbs connected to *khalifa*

The word *caliph* is based on the root *KH-L-F*. The basic Form I verb *khalafa* occurs only five times in the Qur'an. It means 'to replace,' as when Moses told his brother Aaron to temporarily replace *'akhlufni* him as the Israelite leader while the latter went up the mountain (Q7:142, 150). Or it can mean 'to succeed,' as when later generations followed earlier ones.

The context or result of these five verses is always negative. In the story of Moses, while Aaron replaced Moses as leader he oversaw the construction and idolatrous worship of the golden calf, earning his brother's and Allah's ire (Q7:148-150; 20:85-94). The other occurrences of the verb also occur within a framework of judgement. In Q43:60, after describing Pharaoh's obduracy, Allah says: "If it were Our Will, then We would have made angels to replace *yakhlufuun* you on the earth." Al Tabari's *tafsir* notes that Allah could theoretically 'exchange' *badala* the people of Israel with angels because of the former's intransigence.[33] This verb does not, however, mean that every new generation replaced by Allah will necessarily be more righteous. In Q7:169, the rebellious Jews were replaced by another generation *khalf* which inherited the Book but chose the goods of this low life and then claimed they would be forgiven. In Q19:59, those who wept when they heard the verses of Allah recited were succeeded by a generation *khalf* which gave up their prayers, followed their lusts and would soon meet evil. A change does not always bring an improvement.

---

[33] https://muflihun.com/43?tafid=8167#60, accessed September 9, 2020.

The other verb that comes from this root is the Form X[34] *istaFMaLa'* meaning 'to grant succession.' It occurs in four verses: two are negative, one is neutral, and one has positive connotations. Q6:133 is revealed in the context of judgement where the people were doing wrong. It warns the listeners:

> If [Allah] wills, He can destroy you, and grant succession *yastakhlif* after you to who He wills, just as He raised you from the seed of another people. (Q.11:57)

This was a threat from the prophet Hud to the people of 'Ad:

> If you turn away [from my message]... my Lord will grant succession to another nation besides you and you will not harm Him in a single thing.

When the people complained to Moses in Q7:129, that his conflict with the Pharoah was bringing them trouble, Moses replied:

> It may be that your Lord will destroy your enemies and grant you succession on the earth.

There was not a clear promise, but the Jewish acquisition of Egyptian lands was presented as a possibility (see Q7:110; 20:57; 26:35).

The fourth verse, however, does make a specific and positive promise. This seems to be a statement of the Messenger to the hearers. It is one of the **349** passages which begin with the command 'Say' *qul* where the Messenger is being coached on how to respond to questions. In this passage, he tells his hearers:

> Allah promised those among you who believe and do good works that He will certainly grant you succession in the land (or 'on the earth') as he granted succession to those before you (Q24:55).

Of the nine occurrences of a verb drawn from the *KH-L-F* root, and relating to succession or replacement,[35] only one promises a positive

---

[34] Arabic verbs, like Hebrew, are based on three letter roots. There can be ten forms of each verb, designated by the Latin numbers I to X, with extra letters added to the three root letters. The basic Form I has the structure *FaMaLa* for First, Middle and Last root letters. Form X verbs have the structure *istaFMaLa*.

[35] The other verbs from this root – Form II ('to leave behind' - 1 occurrence), III ('to oppose, differ' - 2 occurrences), IV ('to break, fall' - 14 occurrences), V ('to remain

outcome, one is uncertain and the remaining seven have negative connotations.

A remarkable addition to a commentary

This paper has so far been a comprehensive listing and analysis of every word in the Qur'an, whether verb or noun, relevant to the root *kh-l-f* which pertains to the concept of a *khalifa* or successor. It is remarkable that the well-respected commentator Ibn Kathir follows his insightful exegesis of Q2:30 relating to the *khalifa* with the following paragraphs:

> **"The Obligation of appointing a Khalifah and some related Issues."**
>
> Al-Qurtubi, as well as other scholars, said that this Ayah (2:30) proves the obligation of appointing a Khalifah to pass judgements on matters of dispute between people, to aid the oppressed against the oppressor, to implement the Islamic penal code and to forbid evil. There are many other tasks that can only be fulfilled by appointing the Imam, and what is necessary in performing an obligation, is an obligation itself. We should state here that Imamah occurs by either naming a successor, as a group among Ahl As-Sunnah scholars said occurred – by the Prophet – in the case of Abu Bakr, or hinting to a successor. Or, the current Khalifah names a certain person as Khalifah after him, as Abu Bakr did with 'Umar. Or, the Khalifah might leave the matter in the hands of the Muslim consultative council, or a group of righteous men, just as 'Umar did. Or, the people of authority could gather around a certain person to whom they give the pledge of allegiance, or they could select one among them to choose the candidate, according to the majority of the scholars.
>
> The Khalifah must be a responsible adult Muslim male, able to perform Ijtihad (independent legal judgements), bodily able, righteous, with knowledge of warfare and politics. He also must be from the tribe of Quraysh, according to the correct view, but it is not necessary that he be from the tribe of Bani Hashim, or that he be immune from error, as the Rafidah (Shiites) falsely claim.
>
> When the Khalifah becomes an immoral person (Fasiq), should he be impeached There is disagreement over this

---

behind' - 1 occurrence) and VIII ('to differ' - 35 occurrences) have meanings unrelated to succession, so they have been ignored for this study.

matter, but the correct view is that he is not to be removed, because the Messenger of Allah said, "Unless you witness a clear Kufr regarding which you have clear proof from Allah."

Does the Khalifah have the right to resign from his post? There is a difference on this issue. It is a fact that Al-Hasan bin `Ali removed himself from the position of Khalifah and surrendered it to Mu`awiyah. However, this occurred because of a necessity, and Al-Hasan was praised for this action.

It is not permissible to appoint two Imams for the world or more at the same time. This is not allowed because the Messenger of Allah said, "Whoever came to you while you are united and tried to divide you, then execute him, no matter who he is." This is the view of the majority of scholars. Imam Al-Haramayn stated that Abu Ishaq allowed the appointment of two or more Imams when the various provinces are far away from each other. However, Imam Al-Haramayn himself was indecisive about this view.

The inclusion of this passage at this place in the commentary is as disappointing as it is remarkable. The impression given is that these views about the Caliph, the problems which arise from it and the answers to these problems can be logically derived or deduced from the Qur'anic text, because it is placed in a Qur'anic exegetical work. In fact, the Qur'an says nothing about the need for, the appointment of and the qualities of a universal leader for the Muslims as this text implies. No such office is even hinted at, let alone provided with the precise detail found in the above description. This is simply a *post factum* endorsement of the political status quo.

Summary and conclusion:
So what does the Qur'an say about the *khalifa*?

There are only two occurrences of this word (in the singular) in the whole Qur'an.

The first is in Q.2:30 concerning the creation of Adam. Translators of the Qur'an take one of three approaches
(i)   a 'high' view, by rendering it as 'vicegerent' or 'viceroy,' an individual representing a powerful and esteemed entity

80

(ii)   a 'middle' view, by presenting it as 'successor', a chronological replacement of previous incumbents, or

(iii)   a 'low' view, to refer it to the first human or humans, since the verse continues in the plural.

The earliest commentators wrote in Arabic. However some translators into English have tried to 'upgrade' the definition of *khalifa* by adding or removing words or phrases not found in the Arabic text. They promote the 'vicegerent' label, even if the Arabic text does not warrant this. There are also question-marks about some of the commentaries: Ibn Abbas' *Tanwir alMiqbas* was almost certainly not written by him, and Jalalayn's *Tafsir* shows signs of later editing.

If the term *khalifa* referred to Adam, as some commentators say, rather than to humanity in general, then the picture of the *khalifa* is not a positive one. Adam and his wife disobeyed Allah and were cast out of paradise along with Satan, causing humanity to be born and live on earth rather than in paradise. This was not a good inheritance for a vicegerent to pass on to one's progeny.

The second occurrence of the singular noun *khalifa* is in Q38:26, where David is told that he has been made a *khalifa* on earth and should judge people with truth and not follow his desire or lust. The context is some sin of David which resulted in remorse, repentance and forgiveness.

The seven occurrences of the plural form, either *khulafaa'* or *khalaa'if,* all refer to generations which succeed those who have been destroyed by Allah because of their disobedience and sin.

The nine occurrences of a verb drawn from the *KH-L-F* root, also relate to succession or replacement. One pledges from Allah a positive outcome, one is uncertain and the remaining seven have negative implications.

As we worked through these eighteen references in the Qur'an, we saw that they raise more questions than they answer. But it is clear that it is impossible from them to construct a political system in which a single *khalifa* rules on earth as the representative of Allah or of Muhammad. Yet this is exactly what the commentator Ibn Kathir does in his auxilliary paragraph, as do many translators and scholars who propose the 'high' view of this term in the Qur'an. It would be more honest to admit that the administrative office of Caliph began due to political expediency, because Muhammad did not nominate a successor. The role evolved gradually and was developed by competing groups and historical events. The problems that arose, such as how to choose a Caliph, were solved in different ways by various generations, and some of the answers to those problems are as disputed today as they ever were. The Qur'an apparently provides no solutions to any of them or they would have been settled long ago.

Which brings us back to our earlier reference to the Gallipoli Mosque. According to the mosque's official website, "The name of the mosque—Auburn Gallipoli Mosque—reflects the shared legacy of the Australian society and the main community behind the construction of the mosque, the Australian Turkish Muslim Community."[36] However Australians and Turks understand the significance of the Gallipoli event, this 'shared legacy', in quite different ways. Like the beaches on the Gallipoli peninsula in 1915, history, and theology, are always contested ground, a matter of perspective.

Likewise the role of the Caliph, as an idea and in reality, has been contested from the very beginning. It remains to be seen what will become of it in the future. Will another Caliph rise to power? If so, where will he come from and what will he do? To answer these questions, we can only take recourse to the oft-quoted refrain of Muslim theologians and commentators throughout the ages: Allah knows best.

Further Reading:
Arnold, Thomas W.
> *The Caliphate*. London: Routledge, 1965.

Azmeh, Wayel.
> "Misconceptions About the Caliphate in Islam" (May, 2016), https://onlinelibrary.wiley.com/doi/abs/10.1111/dome.12083.

---

[36] https://web.archive.org/web/20110216053649/http://www.gallipolimosque.org.au/mosque_history.aspx?iPageID=5, accessed September 13, 2020.

Kennedy, Hugh.
   The Prophet and the Age of the Caliphates. 2nd ed. Harlow, UK:
   Pearson Education, 2004.

Chapter 4

THE DHIMMITUDE OF THE WEST:
A New Trajectory?

Mark Durie[1]

Dhimmitude is an Islamic phenomenon. It describes the condition of submission to Islamic dominance, yet without conversion to the Islamic faith.

Under classical theological formulations, developed in the first centuries of Islam, the region where Islam rules is known as Dar al-Islam 'the House of Islam.' From the very beginning the Dar al-Islam included many non-Muslims, indeed they were normally in the majority after initial conquest. Based on the example of Muhammad's dealings with the conquered Jewish farmers of Khaybar, Fadak, Tayma and Wadi-l Qura, the institution of the *dhimma* pact was developed in Islamic law to define the legal status of those who refused to convert to Islam. The dhimma was granted by Muslim conquerors as a concession to the vanquished: an institutional legal framework which promised a measure of religious freedom, and determined the social and economic place of non-Muslims in the Islamic state. In return the people of the pact, known as *dhimmis*, were required to pay tribute in perpetuity to the Muslim Community (the Umma), and to adopt a position of humble servitude to it.

The Quranic verse which dictates the fundamental character of dhimmitude is Sura 9:29:

> Fight against those who do not believe in Allah nor in the Last
> Day, and do not make forbidden what Allah and His Messenger

---

[1] Dr Mark Durie is a Senior Research Fellow at the Arthur Jeffery Centre for the Study of Islam at Melbourne School of Theology, Director of the Institute for Spiritual Awareness and a Writing Fellow with the Middle East Forum.

have made forbidden, and do not practice the religion of truth, of those who have been given the Book [i.e. Jews and Christians], until they pay the jizya [tribute paid as compensation] readily and are humbled.

Within Islamic polity, all non-Muslims who are not objects of war or slaves are considered by the shari'a to be dhimmis – communities who are allowed to exist within the Dar al-Islam by virtue of surrender under the conditions set by a dhimma pact. These are the permanently conquered peoples of Islam.

The term dhimma is often translated as 'pact of protection,' and the conquered non-Muslims are described as 'protected.' This is misleading. The Arabic verb *dhamma* means 'blame, find fault, censure for evil conduct,' so in its original use, the word *dhimma* implied blame or fault: it referred to a covenant, the non-observance of which would incur a liability. It is therefore better translated as 'pact of liability.'[2]

The historian Bat Ye'or has documented the social, political, economic and religious conditions of dhimmi communities—Jews and Christians—in the Middle East.[3] This is a sad history of dispossession and decline. Legal provisions applying to dhimmis ensured their humiliation and inferiority, and to this was added the often crippling taxes which were allocated to support the Muslim community. Under conditions of dhimmitude there was also a constant risk of jihad conditions being reinvoked—of lawful massacre, enslavement and looting—if the dhimmi community was considered to have failed to live up to the conditions of their pact.[4] According to some jurists, a single non-Muslim's failure to keep the dhimma conditions could result in the whole community losing their protection, and the jihad restarting.

History records many examples where dhimmis were attacked by their fellow Muslim citizens on such grounds, for

---

[2] Mark Durie, *The Third Choice: Islam, Dhimmitude and Freedom* (Melbourne: Deror Books, 2010), 123.
[3] Bat Ye'or, *The Dhimmi: Jews and Christians Under Islam* (Rutherford, NJ: Fairleigh Dickinson University Press, 1985); *The Decline of Eastern Christianity Under Islam: From Jihad to Dhimmitude, Seventh–Twentieth Century* (Rutherford, NJ: Fairleigh Dickinson University Press, 1996); *Islam and Dhimmitude: Where Civilizations Collide* (Cranbury, NJ: Fairleigh Dickinson University Press, 2002).
[4] Durie, *The Third Choice*, 155ff.

example the massacres of the Jews of Granada in 1066, and of the Christians of Damascus in 1860.

Like sexism and racism, dhimmitude is not only manifested in legal and social structures, but in a psychology of inferiority, a will to serve, which the dominated community adopts in self-preservation. This was described by Bat Ye'or:

> The law required from dhimmis a humble demeanor, eyes lowered, a hurried pace. They had to give way to Muslims in the street, remain standing in their presence and keep silent, only speaking to them when given permission. They were forbidden to defend themselves if attacked, or to raise a hand against a Muslim on pain of having it amputated. Any criticism of the Koran or Islamic law annuled the protection pact. In addition the dhimmi was duty-bound to be grateful, since it was Islamic law that spared his life.

> The whole corpus of these practices... formed an unchanging behaviour pattern which was perpetuated from generation to generation for centuries. It was so deeply internalised that it escaped critical evaluation and invaded the realm of self-image, which was henceforth dominated by a conditioning in self-devaluation... This situation, determined by a corpus of precise legislation and social behaviour patterns based on prejudice and religious traditions, induced the same type of mentality in all dhimmi groups. It has four major characteristics: vulnerability, humiliation, gratitude and alienation.[5]

As one Iranian convert to Christianity put it, "Christianity is still viewed as the religion of an inferior class of people. Islam is the religion of masters and rulers, Christianity is the religion of slaves." Often dhimmi Christians can be seen to collude to conceal their own condition, finding themselves psychologically unable to critique or oppose it.

Today Islam is exerting an increasing influence on the destiny of Western cultures. Through immigration, oil economics, cultural exchange and terrorism, the remnants of what was once Christendom has been compelled to attend to Islam and its distinctive understanding of inter-religious relations. It is no coincidence that there was a dramatic increase in the use of the word 'Abrahamic' after 9/11, to refer to a supposed family connection between

---

[5] Ye'or, *Islam and Dhimmitude*, 103–104.

Judaism, Christianity and Islam, as the basis of European culture was discovered to be 'Abrahamic.' This reflects an Islamic understanding that Abraham was a Muslim, and the common core of Judaism and Christianity was in fact Islam all along.

Although many of the laws of dhimmitude were dismantled during European expansion and colonisation, they have been making a comeback in many Islamic societies, and ISIS even attempted to fully restore the dhimma system.

Within a religiously conservative Islamic worldview, there are limited options for the roles that non-Muslims communities can play. The only real alternative to 'enemies of Allah' is the submission and submissiveness of dhimmitude.

The requirement that non-Muslims affirm and serve Islam, or else find themselves at war with it, greatly limits the repertoire of responses that dhimmified Christians can have towards it. Where there are grounds for confrontation, the only way of struggling permitted to the dhimmi is by saying soft things and employing praise. Such political correctness is itself an injustice that needs to be exposed and challenged. This dynamic, when combined with the meanings of 'struggle' (jihad) that Islam claims as its divine right without apology of any kind, can intimidate and debilitate Christians who are free and do not live under Islam. The cumulative effect can be that the gross injustices come to seem as somehow excusable or unexceptional.

A glaring example is the weak international response today to the persecution of non-Muslims (not just Christians) under Islam. This is epitomised in the slavish attitude adopted by Mary Robinson, UN High Commissioner for Human Rights, in a statement she read to an *Organisation of Islamic Conference Symposium on Human Rights in Islam* held at the Palais des Nations in Geneva in 2002. After offering praise, Robinson praised the inherent righteousness of Islam:

> It is important to recognize the greatness of Islam, its civilizations and its immense contribution to the richness of the human experience, not only through profound belief and theology but also through the sciences, literature and art.

> No one can deny that at its core Islam is entirely consonant with the principle of fundamental human rights, including

human dignity, tolerance, solidarity, and equality. Numerous passages from the Qur'an and sayings of the Prophet Muhammad will testify to this. No one can deny, from a historical perspective, the revolutionary force that is Islam, which bestowed rights upon women and children long before similar recognition was afforded in other civilizations.

...And no one can deny the acceptance of the universality of human rights by Islamic States.[6]

Observe here the dhimmi themes of gratitude, affirmation of moral superiority of Islam (with the implication of inferiority of the infidel), and the denial of any possible voice of protest against human rights abuses in Islamic states. It is a classical dhimmi strategy to avoid confrontation by affirming what is best in Islam. Change for the better is only allowed to arise from values which Muslims can see as springing from their faith itself. This strategy conceals and disempowers the moral worth of non-Muslim value systems. It is the strategy of those whose existence is marginal and threatened.

For those living in liberal democracies this cannot be a healthy way to engage with the 'other' that is Islam. It establishes a framework in which Islam takes on the role of a dominator that expects to be praised, admired, and stroked. From the Islamic side, the reaction to deserved criticism of Islam can be shock, denial and outrage.

In 2007, a letter entitled "A Common Word between Us and You" was addressed by 138 Muslim scholars to the Christians of the world. It received an appreciative response from a group of Yale theologians in a full-page advertisement taken out in the New York Times, which was endorsed by 300 Christian leaders, including such well-known figures as David Yonggi Cho, Robert Schuller, Bill Hybels, Rick Warren and John Stott. Consistent with the worldview of dhimmitude, the Yale theologians adopted a tone of grateful self-humiliation and self-inculpation, using expressions such as:

- "It is with humility and hope that we receive your generous letter";
- the Muslims' letter was "extraordinary" and written in "generosity";

---

[6] Mary Robinson, March 15, 2002.

- "we ask forgiveness of the All-Merciful One and of the Muslim community around the world."

No comparable expressions of humble gratitude or confession of guilt had been offered from the Muslim side. No doubt the Christians believed they were relating from a position of strength, by invoking Christian virtues of humility and self-examination. However, they appear not to have taken account of the dynamics of dhimmitude and the possibility that these statements could be understood by Muslims as a display of self-acknowledged inferiority.[7]

For Christians there is a challenge here. In adapting to this requirement of grateful service, Christians can interpret their own submissiveness in gospel categories of forgiveness and service. Yet from the Islamic side this just looks like 'submission,' i.e. the programme of 'Islam' itself is working. Islam interprets such submissiveness as its rightful due, not an expression of grace, and affords itself the right to the feeling of generosity. Likewise international aid is seen as tribute, a rightful due.

Another cost of this dynamic is a widespread Islamic pattern of claiming the role of victim, whilst inculpating others for problems not of their making. Since Islam is not confronted with its own difficulties, whilst having its virtues affirmed, Muslim communities have permission to feel themselves aggrieved. This is enormously costly for the ongoing social and economic development of Islamic nations, and it is costly for Western societies.

9/11 was a horrific wake-up for the West. Just as, in the worldview of the shari'a, the violence of jihad is intended to produce conditions leading to surrender to the dhimma, so 9/11 and other violent assaults triggered off waves of submissive gestures towards Islam from Western leaders, beginning with George Bush's declaration immediately after 9/11 that Islam is 'non-violent': "The face of terror is not the true faith of Islam. That's not what Islam is all about. Islam is peace."

---

[7] Ironically, while this dialogue was being conducted in the pages of the *New York Times*, the Royal Aal al-Bayt Institute for Islamic thought, which had initiated and hosted the Common Word process on the Muslim side, was broadcasting fatwas on its website by its Chief Scholar which condemned converts from Islam to Christianity as apostates, characterising them as deserving of death or else they should be stripped of all legal rights and treated legally as non-persons (because they ought to be dead).

President Obama, in his turn, expressed gratitude for America's supposed debt to Islam in a speech to the Turkish Parliament: "We will convey our deep appreciation for the Islamic faith, which has done so much over the centuries to shape the world – including in my own country."

President Sarkozy of France declared that Islam is "one of the greatest and most beautiful civilisations the world has known," and Tony Blair, announcing a grant for the study of Islam, rejected the possibility that Islam could be anything but peaceable: "The voices of extremism are no more representative of Islam than the use in times gone by of torture to force conversion to Christianity represented the teachings of Christ." The great irony in Blair's remarks is that Muhammad, the founder of Islam, unlike Christ, did use torture and violence to further his religious goals.

On the ground, agencies of government have been impacted by the climate of appeasement. One of the more notorious examples has been the poor response of British police services and other agencies to a pandemic of grooming and sex-trafficking gangs, in which the large majority of traffickers have been Muslims, and the victims non-Muslim young teenage girls. The number of victims is estimated to be in the tens of thousands, or even more. Repeatedly, when the perpetrators have finally been brought to justice, the authorities have been shown to have been reluctant to pursue investigation and prosecution. A number of harrowing testimonies have been presented of victims who attempted to get help from the police, without success. One Dr Ella Hill (a pseudonym adopted for reasons of safety) reported that when she approached the police five times after being trapped by a trafficking gang, with X-rays of broken bones in hand as evidence, they told her "there was nothing they could do about it." Hill, who managed to escape the trafficking gang and went on to qualify as a doctor, has come to attribute police inaction to the training the police receive in the UK concerning race and religion. Her sexual abuse was expressed, in the words of her abusers, in terms of her race and religion: she was abused by her tormentors as a white Christian, but, as she explained,

> How the police have been trained for a long time is to preserve inter-racial relations, to not raise any racial hatred, to not accuse people of doing something in the name of religion which could cause anti-Muslim prejudice, or anti-Islamic prejudice. So this is

91

the way that the police have been trained for a long, long time – years and years and years – so they are looking at it from completely the wrong way around. They are looking at it from the perpetrators' perspective, rather than from the victims' perspective, where a victim has been a victim of identity-based violence, where they have been attacked because of their race, and they've been attacked because of their religious status, which is a non-Muslim... whatever it is that the perpetrators feel is the religious justification for that person deserving punishment... The way that the system has been set up, it has been set up to have protected groups, and white people and non-Muslim people are not a protected group.[8]

In the unfolding of this scandal, there has been an intersection of a broader social agenda of appeasement towards Islam in the UK with the grid of identity politics, in which white people are considered to be the oppressors of coloured people. By this understanding, Muslims are by definition victims, not perpetrators.

In the wake of a series of media reports about these gangs in 2017, Trevor Phillips, the former head of the UK's Equality and Human Rights Commission had said, "What the perpetrators have in common is their proclaimed faith. They are Muslims, and many of them would claim to be practising. It is not Islamophobic to point this out, any more than it would be racist to point out, that the most active persecutors of LGBT people come from countries where most people are, like me, black."[9] In March 2020, Trevor Phillips was expelled from the Labor party for expressing such views, which were alleged to be Islamophobic.

These developments must be seen against the background of rising concern in the UK about the formation of Muslim communities which pursue separation, a concern which has focused on the rise of shari'a courts as an alternative legal system. In 2016 Prime Minister Theresa May committed an independent review of shari'a law in the UK, to inquire whether their activities are compatible with British law, specifically in their treatment of women

---

[8] Interview of Dr Ella Hill on Triggernometry, "I Am a Grooming Gang Survivor," YouTube, July 20, 2020, https://youtu.be/etpAtC2S0uQ.

[9] Rebecca Perring, "Trevor Phillips Attacks Political Correctness for Failing to Tackle Muslim Child Sex Gang," *Express*, published August 11, 2017, https://www.express.co.uk/news/uk/839905.

in relation to arrangements for divorce, domestic violence and custody of children.

In recent decades communities, across Western nations have been subjected to a series of terrifying violent attacks linked, according to the testimony of the perpetrators, to Islam. At first the response of many Western leaders has been to publicly praise Islam, and express gratitude for it, in the face of this violence.

In the 1930s, psychologist Walter Cannon proposed that an animal, when stressed, can adopt one of two visceral reactions: 'fight' or 'flight.'[10] There are other alternatives. One is the 'freeze' response. Another is what Shelley Taylor, psychology professor at UCLA in 2000 called the 'tend and befriend' response, whereby, an animal responds to stress by caring for offspring— 'tending'—and by affiliating with others – 'befriending.'[11] The impetus to 'tend and befriend' can also be directed towards the source of the threat, as when a dog which is being chastised by his master lies down and begins to lick the master's feet. Among humans, captive-captor bonding, the "Stockholm Syndrome," is a manifestation of this visceral response.

Over the longer term, 'befriend' responses towards Islam, marked by expressions of affection and respect towards both Muslims and Islam, have proved unsatisfactory. Displays of submissive respect have not led to the cessation of jihadi violence, and growing numbers of citizens have settled into a deep and informed discontent with what they regard as a dangerous and unsuccessful policy of appeasement.

After finishing up as Prime Minister, Tony Blair came to a more critical view of Islam's potential to drive violence. The rise of ISIS and the extraordinary devastation it unleashed focused his mind, as it did for many. In response to ISIS, Tony Blair commented that "many millions" of Muslims hold views which are "fundamentally incompatible with the modern world."[12] Rejecting

---

[10] Walter Cannon. *Wisdom of the Body* (New York: Norton, 1932).
[11] Shelley E. Taylor, "Tend and Befriend: Biobehavioral Bases of Affiliation under Stress," *Current Directions in Psychology Science* 15, no. 6 (2006): 273–277.
[12] Matt Broomfield, "Many Millions of Muslims Fundamentally Incompatible with the Modern World, Says Tony Blair," *Independent*, published March 27, 2016,

claims that western policies have caused the rise of Islamic terrorism, Blair acknowledged that ISIS seeks, not dialogue, but dominance, which must be forcibly resisted.

Other Western leaders have shifted in their position on Islam (or Islamism) from praise to resistance. President Macron of France responded to the ritual killing of schoolteacher Samuel Paty by calling the battle with 'Islamism' an 'existential' struggle. He also said that France would not renounce the caricatures of Muhammad which Samuel Paty had shown to his students to teach them about freedom of speech. Already before Paty's assassination, Macron had announced a suite of proposals to contain the influence of radical Islam in France, including greater regulation of mosques and imams. He said, "We don't believe in political Islam that is not compatible with stability and peace in the world."[13]

Undoubtedly Macron's policy of resistance to Islamic dominance and rejection of Islamic separatism reflects a changing mood in the general French population, many of whom have lost whatever appetite for appeasement they once had. Macron's statements has predictably been met with howls of outrage from the Muslim world.

Across the West, dhimmitude was the flavour of the decade following 9/11. However, the continued manifestations of jihadi violence, the fallout from ISIS, and growing concern about what Trevor Phillips has called "sleepwalking our way to segregation": these are gradually awakening the West to the existential challenge conservative Islamic polity presents to Europe and the West.[14] Europe is currently going through a period of realignment of popular attitudes to Islam and to the expectations of how Muslim minorities should function. There are signs that the trajectory towards dhimmitude, of willing submission to Islamic dominance, is being increasingly resisted, even if it has not yet been fully overturned. Yet,

https://www.independent.co.uk/news/world/ middle-east/many-millions-muslims-fundamentally-incompatible-west-says-tony-blair-a6954796.html.

[13] Patrick Wintour, "Macron's Clash with Islam Sends Jolt through France's Long Debate about Secularism," *The Guardian*, published October 26, 2020, https://www.theguardian.com/world/2020/oct/26/ macrons-clash-with-islam-sends-jolt-through-frances-long-debate-about-secularism.

[14] "Britain Sleepwalking to Segregation," *The Guardian*, published September 19, 2005, https://www.theguardian.com/world/2005/sep/19/ race.socialexclusion.

it is late in the day for this change to be happening, and the eventual outcome for Europe is far from clear.

Bibliography

Bat Ye'or. *The Dhimmi: Jews and Christians Under Islam*. Rutherford, NJ: Fairleigh Dickinson University Press, 1985.

—. *The Decline of Eastern Christianity Under Islam: From Jihad to Dhimmitude, Seventh–Twentieth Century*. Rutherford, NJ: Fairleigh Dickinson University Press, 1996.

—. *Islam and Dhimmitude: Where Civilizations Collide*. Cranbury, NJ: Fairleigh Dickinson University Press, 2002.

Cannon, Walter. *Wisdom of the Body*. New York: Norton, 1932.

Durie, Mark. *The Third Choice: Islam, Dhimmitude and Freedom*. Melbourne: Deror Books, 2010.

Taylor, Shelley E. "Tend and Befriend: Biobehavioral Bases of Affiliation under Stress," *Current Directions in Psychology Science* 15, no. 6 (2006): 273–277.

Chapter 5

ISLAM and GEOPOLITICS

Elizabeth Kendal[1]

How, asked Erasmus in 1530, have the Ottomans "reduced our religion from a broad empire to a narrow strip?"

The answer is rudimentary. Since the dawn of Arab imperialist expansion (AD 633), the armies of Islam had been the strongest on the planet.

While they did suffer some set-backs—defeated by "Greek fire"[2] at Constantinople (678), defeated by Charles Martel in the Battle of Tours (732)—generally speaking, the armies of Islam were dominant; they came, they saw, they conquered.

But even as Erasmus was voicing his lament, Renaissance energy was rising in Europe; the tide was turning. In 1492, after 700 years of struggle, Crusaders liberated Portugal and Spain. In 1571, Europe's Holy League won a pivotal battle on the water, defeating the Ottomans in the Battle of Lepanto. Ultimately, in 1683, Austrian and Polish forces defeated Ottoman forces and turned back the battle at the Gates of Vienna.

---

[1] Elizabeth Kendal is an international religious liberty analyst and advocate. She serves as Director of Advocacy at Canberra-based Christian Faith and Freedom (CFF) and is an Adjunct Research Fellow at the Arthur Jeffery Centre for the Study of Islam at Melbourne School of Theology.

[2] In AD 672, having conquered Syria and Egypt, the armies of Islam set out to conquer Constantinople. This culminated, in AD 674, in a naval clash in the Sea of Marmara between Caliph Mu'awiya's Arab Muslim fleet and Byzantine forces. Though outnumbered, the Byzantine fleet possessed superior naval skill and a secret weapon: "Greek fire," the world's first flame thrower. Armed with this devastatingly powerful weapon, the Byzantines set the enemy fleet and the waters surrounding it ablaze in unquenchable fire. See Thomas F. Madden, *Istanbul* (New York: Viking, 2016), 125–127.

It was not that Islam had grown weak; rather that Christian Europe had grown strong.[3] Through advances in science, technology, economics and military strategy, the armies of free and innovative Europe were now superior to the armies of repressive and stagnant imperial Islam.[4]

By 1945, Islam had been on the losing side of two world wars,[5] the Ottoman Empire had been dismembered and the Caliphate had been abolished. Disillusioned and humiliated, Muslims were increasingly inclined to reject political Islam as backward and embrace political secularism as the gateway to modernity. It was a totally different world.[6]

So what happened?

How has Islam come to be such an influential political player in world affairs and such a profound threat to freedom and peace just half a century after it was presumed dead, a relic of the past confined to irrelevance in the "dustbin of history"?

I have written elsewhere on how global population and religious trends converged in the later part of the 20th century to produce the Islamic uprisings of 1979.[7]

---

[3] Thomas F. Madden, "The Crusades: Then and Now," Augustine Institute, 2011–2012 Archbishop's Lecture Series (https://vimeo.com/33043624).

[4] Rodney Stark. *How the West Won: The Neglected Story of the Triumph of Modernity* (Wilmington, DE: ISI Books, 2014).

[5] During World War One (1914–1918) Germany brokered an alliance with the Ottoman Empire. Enacting the dream of Islamophile German Emperor (Kaiser) Wilhelm II, the Sultan agreed to call for jihad in the British, French, and Russian colonies. This, they believed, would pave the way for a German-Ottoman victory. They gambled and lost. For the Sultan this included loss of Empire. In World War Two (1939–1945), the Mufti of Jerusalem, Mohammed Amin al-Husseini aligned Arab, Bosnian and Albanian Muslims with Adolf Hitler's anti-Semitic Nazis. This too was a gamble which resulted in loss, particularly loss of Islamic prestige. See Barry Rubin and Wolfgang G. Schwanitz, *Nazis, Islamists and the Making of the Modern Middle East* (New Haven, CT: Yale University Press, 2014).

[6] In December 1948, when the 58-member United Nations General Assembly voted to adopt the Universal Declaration of Human Rights (UDHR, https://www.un.org/en/universal-declaration-human-rights). Saudi Arabia was the *only* Muslim-majority state to protest the UDHR's un-Islamic provisions; specifically Article 16 on marriage, and Article 18 on Religious Freedom.

[7] Elizabeth Kendal, "Trends in Global Persecution," the home page of her website (http://www.elizabethkendal.com).

Consequently, this paper will focus solely on how international geopolitics has served to advance the agenda of the post-1979, revived and energised *Dar-al-Islam* (house of Islam) as it continues to pursue *success* over the *Dar-al-Harb* (house of war).[8]

"HASTEN TO SUCCESS": HOW THE WAR IS WAGED

Well might we say, "Islam is back!"[9] However, the armies of the *Dar-al-Islam* remain weaker than the armies of the *Dar-al-Harb*. As such, Islam's battle for supremacy remains an asymmetric conflict. Consequently, it is imperative that we understand how asymmetric conflict is prosecuted.

Understanding Asymmetric Conflict

An asymmetric conflict is one fought between unequal forces: one weak, one strong.

Traditionally, a weak force would not pick a fight with a strong force unless the status quo was intolerable. This was because the only alternative to winning was losing, and generally that meant dying in a pool of blood on a remote battlefield.

Today, however, there is an alternative to winning or losing and dying in battle. Today, in our sophisticated, technological and interconnected world, political mileage is up for grabs. Today, a militarily weak force like Hamas can advance a political agenda precisely by picking a fight it knows it cannot win and then making political mileage out of being weak and getting clobbered![10]

Lacking military might, the weaker force relies on psychological tactics designed to foment terror, sow confusion, and lessen the enemy's resolve.

---

[8] Essentially a statement of faith and call to prayer, the *Adhan* does contain one promise: the promise of *success*, *"Hasten to success."*

[9] Elizabeth Kendal, *After Saturday Comes Sunday: Understanding the Christian Crisis in the Middle East* (Eugene, OR: Wipf and Stock, 2016), 59–60.

[10] The political aims of Hamas include securing victim status for Palestinian Arabs and international condemnation and demonisation of Israel. In this Hamas has been hugely successful, at the cost of many thousands of Palestinian lives.

Terrorism is a psychological tactic, as is the use of "human shields"[11] and the "false flag."[12]

Islamic jihadists exploit human shields when they establish bases in, and fire rockets or launch provocations from, hospitals (e.g., Gorazde, Bosnia),[13] schools and kindergartens (e.g. Gaza),[14] UN posts (e.g. Lebanon),[15] UN and safe havens (e.g. Srebrenica, Bosnia),[16] and even from behind pro-democracy rallies (e.g. Andijan, Uzbekistan).[17]

False flag operations have been executed repeatedly in the Syrian conflict by besieged rebel/jihadist forces desperate for a US intervention on their behalf. Indeed, the most famous atrocities of the Syrian conflict—the Houla Massacre (2012) and the gas attacks in

---

[11] When a weak force provokes the enemy from behind a line of unarmed civilians, they can be said to be using humans as shields. The strong force must then decide whether it will withhold fire (to protect the civilians) or return fire, in which case civilian casualties are all but guaranteed. If it opts to return fire, the "massacre" will be reported, along with sensational (often staged) images, by eager, gullible journalists who accept the victimhood narrative unquestioningly in their rush for the exclusive scoop.

[12] A "false flag" operation is one in which the weaker force perpetrates an appalling attack that is then attributed to the enemy. Generally, this means acquiring enemy uniforms and then brutally slaughtering disposable civilians while making sure there are eyewitnesses, including reporters who are desperate to be first with exclusive reports and sensational images.

[13] Vaughn S. Forrest and Yossef Bodansky, "The Truth About Gorazde," A Report for the Task Force on Terrorism and Unconventional Warfare, House Republican Research Committee, U.S. House of Representatives, Washington, DC, 20515, May 4,1994 (http://www.srpska-mreza.com/library/facts/Gorazde.html).

[14] Terrence McCoy, "Why Hamas Stores Its Weapons Inside Hospitals, Mosques and Schools," *Washington Post*, published July 31, 2014, https://www. washingtonpost.com/news/morning-mix/wp/2014/07/31/why-hamas-stores-its-weapons-inside-hospitals-mosques-and-schools/

[15] Human Rights Watch, "Why They Died, Civilian Casualties in Lebanon during the 2006 War," September 2007 – specifically section VI, "Hezbollah Conduct During the War" (https://www.hrw.org/reports/2007/lebanon0907).

[16] Elizabeth Kendal, "Bosnia and Herzegovina: Religious Tensions Rising," (under subheading "Creating Context: History's Wedges"), World Evangelical Alliance Religious Liberty Commission, September 29, 2006, http://elizabethkend al.blogspot.com/2011/04/bosnia-and-herzegovina-religious.html.

[17] Elizabeth Kendal, "Why Andijan Changed Everything," Religious Liberty Monitoring, March 23, 2007, http://elizabethkendal.blogspot.com/2007/03/ uzbekistan-why-andijan-changed.html.

Ghouta (2013),[18] and Khan Sheikhoun (2017)[19]—were all false flags.[20]

Historian Richard Landes explains: "All asymmetrical wars take place primarily in the cognitive arena, with the major theatre of war the enemy's public sphere.

> The mainstream news media – their journalists, editors, producers – constitute a central front of this cognitive war: the 'weak' but aggressive side cannot have success without the witting or unwitting cooperation of the enemy's journalists.[21]

The goal is "Information Dominance" (ID).

Strategic analyst Gregory Copley contends that by the second decade of the 21st century, Information Dominance had become "the primary warfighting strategic weapon of aspirant powers." This, he explains, is

> largely due to the fact that the rise of the electronic age, in its later stages encompassing the computer age, meant that most minds were within reach, and most strategic outcomes could be determined by the reach of components of ID... [including] linguistic messaging... [and] imagery or computer code to affect the abilities or will of the target audience. [22]

"Agitprop (agitation propaganda)," he explains, "is the 'performance art' of psychological strategy," for like all warfare, psychological

---

[18] Concerning the Ghouta gas attack, see the 5,000 word analysis by Seymour M. Hersh, "Whose Sarin?" which was published in London Review of Books, January 7, 2016, after all mainstream media refused to publish analysis so contrary to the official narrative (https://www.lrb.co.uk/the-paper/v35/n24/seymour-m.-hersh/whose-sarin).

[19] Elizabeth Kendal, "Syria and Chemical Weapons: Listen to the Experts," Religious Liberty Monitoring, June 29, 2017, http://elizabethkendal.blogspot.com/2017/06/syria-and-chemical-weapons-listen-to.html.

[20] Elizabeth Kendal, *After Saturday Comes Sunday*. Chapters 7 and 8 examine some of the most critical psyops of the Syrian conflict, including the Houla Massacre (chapter 7) and the Ghouta gas attack (chapter 8).

[21] Richard Landes, "Islamism is winning the cognitive war – thanks to manipulative and gullible journalists," *Daily Telegraph*, published April 4, 2013 (no longer accessible), http://www.theaugeanstables.com/2013/04/04/islamism-is-winning-the-cognitive-war-thanks-to-manipulative-and-gullible-journalists (only partial), quoted in Elizabeth Kendal, *After Saturday Comes Sunday*, 130.

[22] Gregory R. Copley, *Sovereignty* (Alexandria, VA: International Strategic Studies Association, 2018), 256–257.

warfare "requires its own version of 'boots on the ground' or ships in the straits: physical action against targets."[23]

Terrorism is but one component of Agitprop. Another is destabilizing-chaos which, as counterinsurgency expert David Kilcullen explains, can be achieved by way of "anonymous funding, amplification of online messaging, offers of training or equipment through 'cut-outs' such as tactical training companies or non-government organisations, or 'false flag' operations."[24]

One man's peril is another man's opportunity

Traditionally, if a weak king was threatened—either by domestic opposition or an aggressive neighbour—he would seek protection from an even stronger king. If the stronger king saw value in the weak king, then he would broker an agreement to guarantee protection in exchange for economic and/or geostrategic gains. The weak and subordinate king (the vassal) would pay tribute, pledge loyalty, and grant the stronger controlling king (the suzerain) essentially whatever he wanted, e.g. access to ports, the right to station troops in the territory, the right to exploit resources, etc. So long as the vassal abided by the covenant, he and his state would be secure. Similarly, a strong king might reach out pre-emptively to a weak king, essentially exploiting his vulnerability.

As such, small, vulnerable, weak states and weak rulers were rarely independent.

Not much has changed!

However, unlike sovereign kings, democratically elected governments rule by consent of the governed. No democratically elected government will intervene in a foreign conflict, propup a foreign regime or send aid to non-state actors if they fear it might cost them their political life.

Consequently, before any strong democracy commits itself to action, an acceptable narrative must be established and a massive campaign undertaken to saturate the electorate with propaganda. It

---

[23] Gregory R. Copley, "Agitprop Meets the Social-Media Age," Defense and Foreign Affairs Strategic Policy 7 (2020).
[24] David Kilcullen, "Home of the Hateful, Fearful and Heavily Armed," *The Australian*, May 30, 2020, https://www.theaustralian.com.au/inquirer/land-of-the-fearful-home-of-the-heavily-armed-and-hateful/news-story/6ec95cf2dd7ea519d084ed99dc3fd450.

is imperative that the voting public view the weak, imperiled force as a victim worthy of support. Meanwhile, the opposing stronger force must be so thoroughly demonised that anyone *not* voicing support for a "humanitarian intervention" is sure to be widely mocked and vilified.

It is often the case that politicians wanting to justify and legitimise a "humanitarian intervention" will send out a signal on what "red line" would need to be crossed before military aid could be justified. Once the red line is crossed – or at least, is *believed* to have been crossed (they are *not* the same) – then the intervention simply must proceed to avoid a national loss of face.

In truth, these "humanitarian interventions" are just military interventions determined by *realpolitik*. They are only presented as "humanitarian" for domestic consumption. While unpalatable, this does explain why "humanitarian interventions" are so selective and why Christians facing violent religious persecution, ethnic cleansing and even genocide in strategically located or resource-rich **allied** states never see one.[25]

The problem with backing weak regimes is that it inevitably necessitates turning a blind eye to the organised crime that keeps illegitimate client-states and puppet rulers financially viable and therefore stable.[26]

COLD WAR GEO-POLITICS
Afghanistan
In December 1979 – ten months after Iran's Islamic Revolution and one month after the Siege of Mecca – Soviet troops entered Afghanistan to help the People's Democratic Party of Afghanistan (PDPA; communist) put down an escalating Islamic insurgency.

Soviet-Afghan cooperation was nothing new; they were next-door neighbours after all. Since the 1950s the Soviets had assisted the Afghan monarch and subsequent governments with numerous

---

[25] Elizabeth Kendal, "The Humanitarian/Moral Intervention: An Exercise in Duplicity," Religious Liberty Monitoring, September 15, 2013, http://elizabethkendal.blogspot.com/2013/09/the-humanitarianmoral-intervention.html.
[26] Christopher Deliso, *The Coming Balkan Caliphate* (Praeger Security International, 2007), specifically chapter 7.

programmes to advance modernisation – modernisation which Afghanistan's revived and energised Islamists were now resisting.

Hoping to minimise Afghan resistance, the Soviets deployed Muslim troops from the USSR's Central Asian republics. However, Muslim solidarity proved a greater problem, and only four months after they were deployed the Muslim troops were recalled. It was a pivotal moment in Soviet-Muslim relations.[27]

During the 1980s, the US armed, funded and backed the Afghan mujahideen as they resisted the "Soviet occupation". While the opportunity to wage a proxy war against the Soviets in Afghanistan might have seemed irresistible, putting high-powered weapons (including anti-aircraft weapons) into the hands of revived and energised Islamic jihadists was anything but smart – as anyone with a basic understanding of Islam, and a basic awareness of the prevailing trends in the Muslim world, would have known.

POST-COLD WAR
...not much changes
Through the 1980s, war raged on in Afghanistan as anti-Communist uprisings rocked the Soviet bloc. In February 1989, the Soviet Army pulled out of Afghanistan. In November 1989, the Berlin Wall came down. By year's end, Soviet-backed Communist regimes had fallen in Czechoslovakia, Romania, Bulgaria and Albania.

In 1991, Soviet Communist Party chief and champion of *glastnost* (openness) and *perestroika* (restructuring), Mikhail Gorbachev, survived an attempted coup before ceding power to Boris Yeltsin, who dismantled the Communist Party and oversaw the dissolution of the Union of Soviet Socialist Republics (USSR).

Despite the fact that the Cold War was over, the US allowed its obsession with Russia, and its Cold War myopia, to perpetuate on through the 1990s, blinding it to the real and present danger of revived and energised revolutionary and Wahhabi fundamentalist Islam.

---

[27] Marlène Laruelle, *Beyond the Afghan Trauma: Russia's Return to Afghanistan* (Washington, DC: The Jamestown Foundation, 2009).

EUROPE: A Green Corridor Through the Balkans

In the 1990s the US-led West supported Catholic Croat, and Bosnian and Albanian Muslim separatists as they systematically dismantled Yugoslavia to the detriment of the majority Orthodox Serbs who, unlike the Croats and Muslims, had been allied to the West through two World Wars.

Bosnia

In March 1992, Bosnian Islamist Alija Izetbegović instigated war when he unilaterally and illegally declared the republic of Bosnia and Herzegovina independent of Yugoslavia.[28]

In his October 2003 obituary to Alija Izetbegović, scholar and diplomat Damjan de Krnjevic-Miskovic wrote:

> "As Yugoslavia was falling apart, Izetbegović helped to found the Party of Democratic Action (SDA) – a party composed overwhelmingly of Bosnian Muslims – whose slogan was 'In Our Land, With Our Faith." This was in 1990, the same year [his book entitled] the *Islamic Declaration* was reprinted in Sarajevo. Famously, the book proclaimed that "there can be no peace or coexistence between the 'Islamic faith' and non-Islamic societies and political institutions." It argued that in countries where Muslims do not represent a majority of the population, the "Islamic order" could not be "implemented," and that the "Islamic authority [...] may turn to violence."[29]

Christopher Deliso – a journalist with expertise in economics, Byzantine history, and the Balkans – comments in his book *The Coming Balkan Caliphate*:

> During the Nazi occupation of Yugoslavia in WWII, Izetbegović had been a recruiter for the Bosnian Muslim Handzar ('Dagger') Division, which swore loyalty to Hitler and his 'New Europe', and was committed to killing Christian Serbs and Yugoslav Jews.[30]

---

[28] Article 5 of the Constitution of Yugoslavia (1974) granted the republics the constitutional right to self-determination, including a right to secede, but only on the condition that all Yugoslavia's republics and provinces consented to the borders being changed.

[29] Damjan de Krnjevic-Miskovic, "Obituary: Alija Izetbegovic, 1925–2003," *The National Interest*, October 22, 2003, http://nationalinterest.org/article/obituary-alija-izetbegovic-1925-2003-2458.

[30] Deliso, *The Coming Balkan Caliphate*, 5.

Is it any wonder that Bosnia's Orthodox Serb minority (comprising 31 percent) resisted this brazen and illegal act? After World War II and the horrors of the Holocaust in Yugoslavia,[31] no Serb would want to be an ethnic minority in a Muslim-Croat dominated state! Neither would any Serb with an ounce of historical memory desire a return to dhimmitude![32]

Undeterred, Izetbegović insisted that Bosnia's Serbs should not be permitted to break away from break-away Bosnia. In 1995 he convinced US President William (Bill) Clinton (1993–2001) to enter the war on the side of the Bosnian Muslims.

And so it was, that the US administration of President Bill Clinton aligned with the Islamist ambitions of Alija Izetbegović who, despite already having support from Iran—which was funnelling arms and fighters into Bosnia, via Croatia[33]—needed more firepower, specifically airpower from a legitimising source.

All that was needed was an acceptable narrative that would legitimise a "humanitarian intervention." "Red lines" would have to be crossed – or at least, be *believed* to have been crossed. It was a job for the masters of agitprop; a joy for Western elites positively infatuated with Izetbegović and riven with Russophobia which routinely spilled over into contempt for all things Orthodox.

Not only did the "Iranian Pipeline" have Washington's support, but Washington provided a further "14,000 tons of weapons, valued at over $200 million." It also gave Izetbegović the green light to use Iranian weapons however he saw fit.[34]

---

[31] See "The Jasenovac Extermination Camp: Terror in Croatia," http://www. holocaustresearchproject.org/othercamps/jasenovac.html.
[32] Elizabeth Kendal, "Bosnia and Herzegovina: Religious tensions rising," under subheading "Creating Context: History's Wedges," World Evangelical Alliance Religious Liberty News and Analysis, September 19, 2006, http://elizabethkendal.blogspot.com/2011/04/bosnia-and-herzegovina-religious.html.
[33] Yossef Bodansky and Vaughn S. Forrest, "Iran's European Springboard?" September 1, 1992.
Report for US Task force on terrorism & unconventional warfare, House Republican Research Committee, http://www.srpska-mreza.com/library/facts/bodansky1.html.
Also: Robert Block, "US turns blind eye to Iran arms for Bosnia," *Independent*, June 3, 1994, https://www.independent.co.uk/news/world/europe/us-turns-blind-eye-to-iran-arms-for-bosnia-1420068.html.
[34] Deliso, *The Coming Balkan Caliphate*, 9.

The war only ended—or more correctly, froze—after the Dayton Accords partitioned the state between a Muslim-Croat Federation and a Serb "entity"—the Republika Srpska (Serb Republic)—in which the Serbs would retain a high degree of autonomy. It is a partition no fundamentalist Muslim accepts – even to this day.

Kosovo

Between March 1998 and June 1999, US President Bill Clinton aligned the US with the Kosovo Liberation Army (KLA)—a proscribed terrorist organisation comprised mostly of Albanian Islamists and irredentists—in its war to dismember Orthodox Serbia and claim Serbia's ancient historic and religious heartland of Kosovo and Metohija for Serbia's predominantly Muslim ethnic Albanian minority.[35]

Serb resistance ended on 11 June 1999 after NATO illegally— i.e. without the approval of the UN Security Council—bombed Belgrade, the capital of Serbia, a nation that had never threatened the US or any NATO state.

For a detailed exposé of the consequences of that "humanitarian intervention," visit Kosovo Crucified.[36] The report documents the post-war cultural destruction of Kosovo and Metohija which took place between June 1999 and May 2001. It provides the name and location of each church and monastery attacked, the KFOR (Kosovo Force/UN "peace-keepers") zone of responsibility, the level of destruction, and the church or monastery foundation date.

For example:
(1): The Monastery of the Holy Trinity [targeted by Albanian Muslims in July 1999[37]].
Location: Musutiste near Suva Reka.
KFOR zone of responsibility: Germany.

---

[35] Metohiija comes from the Greek μετόχια / metóchia, meaning "monastic estates." This southwestern region of Kosovo had been the seat of the Serbian Orthodox Church since the 14th century; countless Orthodox churches and monasteries were planted throughout its hills.
[36] "Kosovo Crucified," special edition by the Serbian Orthodox Diocese of Raska-Prizren (http://www.kosovo.net/ckos/page_01.htm).
[37] "Holy Trinity Monastery" (http://www.kosovo.net/estrojica.html).

Level of destruction: level VII (attacked with explosives; building materials removed).
Foundation date: the monastery was founded in 14th century.

After listing the 107 churches and monasteries destroyed in that two-year period, the report proceeds with pictorial evidence of what can only be described as cultural genocide under NATO's watch.

For Russia—at the time too weak to assist her Orthodox sister—being forced to watch this cultural genocide was especially painful.

According to analyst Gregory Copley, President Bill Clinton engaged in "punitive actions against Serbia, starting at the beginning of his Administration in 1993, to satisfy his personal political alliance with long-standing Albanian (and later Bosnian Muslim) associates. Those links had begun when he was Governor of the State of Arkansas (1979–1981 and 1983–1992).

> What is significant is that this use by the Clinton Administration of information dominance to win support for its desired courses of action, empowered increasingly by the evolution of the internet and social media, ultimately worked against the US and NATO interests while causing lasting damage to Serbia and the Balkans as a whole.[38]

Christopher Deliso writes concerning the break-up of Yugoslavia:

> Ironically, every Balkan 'independence' drive has simply led to a new dependency – nowadays on foreign creditors, political overseers, and international institutions. The West's divide-and-conquer approach to the Balkans has yielded numerous attractive results for foreign investors, in everything from prime seaside real estate in Croatia, Montenegro and Bulgaria to dirt-cheap investments in major Serbian industry, as well as telecommunications and media markets everywhere.[39]

He continues:

> The bastard twin of the global economic order represented by multinational corporations, financial markets, and institutions,

---

[38] Gregory R. Copley, "Pivot: Did NATO's Serbian War Set the Stage for the Decline of Western Power?" Defense and Foreign Affairs Strategic Policy 3 (2020).
[39] Deliso, *The Coming Balkan Caliphate*, 141.

Islamism preys on the intrinsic weakness and inefficiencies of the new Balkan order to achieve its objectives.[40]

He concludes:

So long as preserving corrupt foreign relations takes precedence over national and international security, the war on terror will never be won. And when it is the case that terrorism cannot be investigated because blocking its criminal funding channels would cause fatal tremors in the global economic system – this is when we know that terrorism is here to stay.[41]

The US-NATO war against Serbia discredited the US and NATO and devastated the Balkans. Even more critically, it advanced the Islamist dream of a "Green Traverse" or "Green Corridor"—an Islamic land-bridge—stretching from Turkey through Thrace-Macedonia-Kosovo-Sanjak-Bosnia, projecting into Europe.[42]

AFRICA: Islam Advanced: Terror Takes Root
Ivory Coast
Since 2002, West African Islamists have preyed on the economic interests of former colonial power **France**, to achieve their objectives in **Ivory Coast (Côte d'Ivoire)**.

By aligning themselves with French interests, against the anti-neo-colonial/anti-*FrançAfrique* policies of President Laurent Gbagbo (a Christian and ardent nationalist), the Islamists were able to secure French support for regime change in Abidjan.[43] That support included French collusion in the plot to steal the November 2010 election, despite objections from Ivory Coast's constitutional court. France then provided military aid—including attack helicopters and boots on the ground—which enabled the Islamists to achieve a regime change by force while claiming the moral high-ground.[44]

---

[40] Ibid., 144.
[41] Ibid., 152.
[42] Srdja Trifkovic, "U.S. Policy and Geopolitics of Jihad: The Green Corridor in the Balkans," May, 2009. This must-read article is based on the author's presentation and an accompanying discussion at a meeting in Copenhagen on 17 May 2009. It is one of a series of essays collected in the book *Kosovo: The Score 1999-2009*, published by the American Council for Kosovo and the Lord Byron Foundation for Balkan Studies, 2009, http://gatesofvienna.blogspot.com/2009/05/ green-corridor-in-balkans.html.
[43] *Françafrique* refers to exploitative French neo-colonialism in Francophone Africa.
[44] Elizabeth Kendal, "Ivory Coast: where Islamic and Western interests converge," Religious Liberty Monitoring, April 7, 2011, http://elizabethkendal.

To advance its own economic and geo-strategic interests, France advanced and powered Islamists at the expense of Ivory Coast's mostly Christian and animist southern peoples.[45] The result was a puppet regime beholden to France and to Islamic militants, many of whom have been incorporated into the security services. Such a regime is anything but secure. Peace remains tenuous.[46]

Libya

Muammar Gaddafi was indeed a cruel, eccentric, megalomanic dictator. He was, however, ardently anti-Islamist, fully cognisant of the existential threat posed by revived and energised fundamentalist Islam.

In 1989, at a meeting in Baghdad of Arab monarchs, heads of state and senior officials, Gaddafi urged Arab leaders to unite against the threat posed by "radical-extremist Islamic groups that are seeking to take over the Middle East."[47] The Arab leaders rejected Gaddafi's urgings, believing they could exploit the jihadists as proxies.

In December 2003—just two years after the 9/11 terror attacks in USA—Gaddafi surrendered his Weapons of Mass Destruction and allied with the West in its War on Terror, keeping al-Qaeda in the Islamic Maghreb contained and hamstrung for years.

In August 2011, under the cover of the "Arab Spring," Islamic jihadists stormed the Libyan capital, Tripoli, courtesy NATO air-support. Two months later, Gaddafi was dragged from a drainpipe and savagely lynched to shouts of "Allahu Akbar." Rejoicing at the news, the jihadists' Western backers effused that democracy could

blogspot.com/2011/04/ivory-coast-where-islamic-and-western.html. Also: Thabo Mbeki, "What the World Got Wrong in Côte D'Ivoire," Foreign Policy, April 29, 2011, https://foreignpolicy.com/2011/04/29/what-the-world-got-wrong-in-cote-divoire.
[45] Ivory Coast, Religious Liberty Monitoring, April 2011, https://elizabethkendal.blogspot.com/2011/04.
[46] Elizabeth Kendal, "Ivory Coast: Troubles Far From Over," Religious Liberty Monitoring, March 9, 2017, http://elizabethkendal.blogspot.com/2017/03/ivory-coast-troubles-far-from-over.html. At the time of writing (August, 2020), with elections looming, Ivory Coast seems perched on the brink of civil war. See "Cote D'Ivoire: Police allow machete-wielding men to attack protesters," Amnesty International, August 18, 2020, https://www.amnesty.org/en/latest/news/2020/08/ cote-d-ivoire-police-allow-machete-wielding-men-to-attack-protesters.
[47] Yossef Bodansky, *High Cost of Peace* (Roseville, CA: Prima Publishing, 2002), 31 (quoted in Kendal, *After Saturday Comes Sunday*, 78–79).

now take root in Libya.[48] However, as is normally the case, terrorism gave rise to terrorism.

Exploiting the chaos, a multitude of jihadists and Sahelian mercenaries and separatists raided Libya's armouries. Mali,[49] Burkina Faso and Niger have not been the same since.[50] What's more, transnational terrorist organisations have established bases in the Sahel and are training jihadists from across the continent.

Meanwhile, conflict continues to rage in Libya between the anti-Islamist forces of the Tobruk-based Libyan National Army (backed by Russia and anti-Muslim Brotherhood Egypt and United Arab Emirates) *and* the mostly Islamic jihadist forces of the illegitimate, UN-manufactured and recognised "unity government" (backed by pro-Muslim Brotherhood forces, neo-Ottoman Turkey and Qatar).[51]

In March 2011, as the battle for Tripoli raged, Gaddafi explained why an unstable Libya was not in the West's interests. "Should the situation be unstable," he warned, "Al-Qaeda will establish its rule and Libya will get transformed into another Afghanistan. Millions of refugees will flood Europe, which will make the whole Mediterranean region suffer." Gaddafi was quite sure the West would not want that![52]

MESOPOTAMIA: Shi'ite Crescent Invades Fertile Crescent
Because I have covered the geopolitics of the Battle for Mesopotamia at length in my book, *After Saturday Comes Sunday: Understanding the Christian Crisis in the Middle East*, I do not intend to spend much time on it here.[53]

---

[48] Kendal, *After Saturday Comes Sunday*, chapter 6.
[49] Religious Liberty Monitoring, Mali, http://elizabethkendal.blogspot.com/search/label/Mali.
[50] "The Complex and Growing Threat of Militant Islamist Groups in the Sahel" (Infographic), Africa Center for Strategic Studies, February 15, 2019 (see https://africacenter.org/?s=sahel).
[51] For some background on the political situation in Libya, see Elizabeth Kendal, "Libya: Storm Clouds Gather," *Religious Liberty Prayer Bulletin* 353 (2016): http://rlprayerbulletin.blogspot.com/2016/04/rlpb-353-libya-storm-clouds-gather.html.
[52] "Muammar Gaddafi: 'We Do Not Believe the West Any Longer,'" YouTube, video, 9:42, published April 1, 2011, https://youtu.be/gVcefsgO4zM.
[53] See http://www.elizabethkendal.com/books/after-saturday-comes-sunday.

It is enough to say that the West's interventions in Iraq and Syria have advanced and empowered Islamic forces at the expense of regional security and the Fertile Crescent's vulnerable minorities.

These interventions proceeded in defiance of Russia whose centuries-long engagement with Islam and decades-long ties to the region meant it not only had valuable insights but well-established networks on the ground.

Iraq

Counter-terrorism expert Yossef Bodansky explains how in late 2002, as Washington mounted its case for regime change in Baghdad, President Putin advised the US administration of President G.W. Bush that instead of going after Saddam Hussein it should concentrate instead on the real sponsors of Islamic terror, specifically Pakistan and Saudi Arabia, and put an end to the Saudi funding of Wahhabi extremism.[54]

Russia insisted that the greater problem was that of the prevailing radical and militant trends. It warned the US that if it was to proceed with regime change in Baghdad it had better be prepared to deal with radicalised populations, Sunni Islamist militancy, a radical Shi'ite population under Iranian influence, the flow of al-Qaeda operatives, as well as Kurdish-Turkish and Turkmen-Arab hatreds.

In November 2002, Moscow offered to engineer a "pre-emptive coup" that would remove Saddam while keeping the stabilising structures in place.

Not only did Washington reject Moscow's offer, but the CIA deliberately leaked the information, betraying the Russians who then refrained from sharing any more intelligence with the CIA. Actually, the US had already chosen its course: a US-led alliance would invade a largely defenceless Iraq, overthrow the dictator, and establish a democracy more amenable to US interests.[55]

---

[54] Yossef Bodansky, *The Secret History of the Iraq War* (New York: Regan Books, 2004).

[55] Once the largest in the region, Iraq's air-force was virtually eliminated in 1991 during Gulf War One.

In 2004, as he watched it all unfold, Jordan's King Abdullah lamented the spectre of "Shi'ite Crescent" of Iranian influence rising over the Middle East, stretching from Tehran through Baghdad to Damascus.[56]

Western policy in Iraq facilitated: (1) the creation of Al-Qaeda in Iraq (AQI) which subsequently evolved into Islamic State in Iraq (ISI), then – after splitting – into ISIS and ultimately IS; (2) the rise of the "Shi'ite Crescent" (better known as the Iran-led, Shi'ite-dominated, Axis of Resistance); and (3) the genocide of the West's war time ally,[57] the indigenous Christian nation of Assyria.

Syria

Just as it had done with regards to Iraq, Russia urged the US against pursuing regime change in Damascus, warning that Syria is not Tunisia, nor is it Egypt – to the contrary, it is far more complex and diverse; the minority-led government had majority support and would not quickly fall.[58]

But alas, it was all in vain. Not only was Russia ignored, but all Christian voices were ignored and silenced – buried under a mountain of propaganda and derision.

And so it was that the US aligned with Wahhabi Saudi-Arabia and pro-Muslim Brotherhood forces Qatar and neo-Ottoman Turkey (all Islamists and appalling human rights-abusers) in their plot to effect regime change in Damascus under the cover of the "Arab Spring." The Turkey-Arab goal was to re-orient Syria, incorporating Damascus into the north-south Sunni axis so it might better serve Sunni interests. Of particular interest was the construction of a "Sunni" pipeline, which would transport Persian Gulf oil and gas

---

[56] Ian Black, "Fear of a Shia Full Moon," *The Guardian*, January 26, 2007, https://www.theguardian.com/world/2007/jan/26/worlddispatch.ianblack.

[57] W. A. Wigram, *Our Smallest Ally: A Brief Account of the Assyrian Nation during the Great War* (New York: Macmillan, 1920).

[58] A December 2011 poll commissioned by Qatar revealed that while a majority of regional Arabs (i.e. Saudis, Qataris, Jordanians etc) supported regime change in Damascus, a majority of Syrians (55%) *did not*. As an integral player in the regime change alliance, Qatar was embarrassed by the results, which did not remain on-line for long. The results were only restored to the internet after they were re-packaged, and Syria's result was dissolved within the combined results for "The Levant." See Kendal, *After Saturday Comes Sunday*, chapter 7.

113

from Qatar through Saudi Arabia and Syria to Turkey, for sale to Europe.[59]

Having facilitated the ascent of revolutionary Iran, the US was now desperate to frustrate its ambitions: including its goal of establishing an Axis of Resistance land-bridge stretching from Tehran to the borders of Israel; and its plan to construct an east-west "Shia" pipeline[60] that would transport Persian Gulf oil and gas from Iran through Iraq to Syria for sale to Europe at a far cheaper price than the UK-US could manage through their hugely expensive BTC pipeline.[61]

While frustrating Iranian ambitions and protecting US energy interest are still major reasons why the US continues to pursue regime change in Damascus—albeit now by way of economic siege—another motivation has recently come to the fore.[62]

On 12 May 2020, America's Special Representative for Syria, James Jeffrey confirmed that the US presence in Syria will continue for the purpose of maintaining pressure on America's "enemies." "My job," Jeffrey explained, "is to make [Syria] a quagmire for the Russians."[63]

It is worth noting that when Russia entered the Syrian war in September 2015, Damascus was on the brink of collapse. Only six months earlier (March 2015) the al-Qaeda-dominated jihadi alliance, *Jaysh al-Fateh* (Army of Conquest) had seized control of Idlib. A few

---

[59] See http://www.elizabethkendal.com/wp-content/uploads/ME-Map.pdf.
[60] Ibid.
[61] Operated by British Petroleum (BP), the BTC pipeline traverses mountains and war zones, skirting non-aligned Armenia, to carry crude oil from Baku, Azerbaijan, through Tbilisi, Georgia, to Ceyhan on Turkey's Mediterranean coast (close to America's Incirlik Air Base on the eastern edge of Adana).
[62] Elizabeth Kendal, "Syria: Damascus Under Siege," *Religious Liberty Prayer Bulletin* 554 (2020): http://rlprayerbulletin.blogspot.com/2020/06/rlpb-554-syria-damascus-under-siege.html. See also "Syria: Caesar's inhumanity," *Religious Liberty Prayer Bulletin* 556 (2020): http://rlprayerbulletin.blogspot.com/2020/ 07/rlpb-556-syria-and-lebanon-church-in.html.
[63] David Brennan, "U.S. Syria Representative Says His Job Is to Make the War a 'Quagmire' for Russia," *Newsweek*, May 13, 2020. https://newsweek.com/us-syria-representative-james-jeffrey-job-make-war-quagmire-russia-1503702. That an American official could display such complete disregard for human life – including hundreds of thousands of Syrian Christians (1.2 million before the war) – is both astonishing and deeply distressing.

months later (May 2015) Palmyra fell to Islamic State. By August 2015, *Jaysh al-Fateh* was shelling Latakia (the Alawite heartland and a sanctuary for many thousands of displaced Armenian and Assyrian Christians) and Islamic State was on the edge of Damascus poised to sever the M5 Highway. That would have cut the nation in two, severing Aleppo (the commercial capital) and Latakia (the Alawite heartland) from Damascus, the nation's capital and nerve centre.

Had that occurred, then the genocide of Syria's Alawites and Christians would have followed, and Syria would have descended into a Libya-style hell.

On Monday 28 September 2015, Russian President Vladimir Putin addressed the United Nations General Assembly in New York. Like analyst David Goldman, I would describe Putin's speech as "the most lucid account of the state of the world I have heard from any national leader in decades."[64]

The extraordinary speech is certainly worth watching and/or reading.[65] President Putin's speech is reminiscent of his 2013 open letter to the American people. Entitled: "A Plea for Caution from Russia," by Vladimir Putin, the open letter was published as an op-ed in the New York Times on September 11 (9/11), 2013, just as the US was contemplating launching missile strikes on Syria in response to a rebel false flag operation. It too is worth a read.[66]

Another document worth reading is Russia's draft proposal for a new Syrian constitution.[67]

---

[64] David Goldman, "Take Putin at his word: Social disintegration in the Middle East is the issue," *Asia Times*, September 30, 2015, https://asiatimes.com/ 2015/09/take-putin-at-his-word-social-disintegration-in-the-middle-east-is-the-issue.

[65] Russian President Vladimir Putin Address to the U.N. General Assembly, September 28, 2015, C-Span video (with translation), https://c-span.org/video/ ?328385-4/russian-president-vladimir-putin-address-un-general-assembly, quoted at length in Kendal, *After Saturday Comes Sunday*, 221–223. See also "The Full Transcript of Russian President Vladimir Putin's Speech at the United Nations General Assembly," *Newsweek*, September 29, 2015, https://newsweek.com/ transcript-putin-speech-united-nations-377586.

[66] Vladimir Putin, "A Plea for Caution from Russia," Op-Ed, *New York Times*, September 11, 2013, https://www.nytimes.com/2013/09/12/opinion/putin-plea-for-caution-from-russia-on-syria.html.

[67] "Russia's draft proposal for a new Syrian constitution," Middle East Media Research Institute, February 9, 2017, https://www.memri.org/reports/russian-draft-proposal-new-syrian-constitution.

Unlike the US-backed constitutions of Afghanistan and Iraq, which enshrine Islamic Shari'a as the ultimate authority, Russia's draft proposal for a new Syrian constitution envisages a free, sovereign and democratic, multi-ethnic, multi-faith nation where all citizen are equal before the law. The draft proposes that the Syrian Arab Republic be henceforth known as the Syrian Republic (Article 1). Democracy is guaranteed (Article 2). Religious freedom is guaranteed (Article 3). Cultural and ideological diversity are guaranteed (Articles 1,4, 6) as is political pluralism (Article 5). Equality, and freedom of expression are guaranteed (Articles 13 and 20) and women are empowered (Article 19).

One cannot read President Putin's open letter (2013), or his speech to the UNGA (2015), or Russia's draft proposal for a new Syrian constitution (2017) without wondering, "Why does the US insist Russia is the enemy?"

GEOPOLITICS: Open to Exploitation

For too long now, the *Dar al-Harb* has allowed itself to be divided: West versus East with Islam projecting through the middle.[68] In March 2014, strategic analyst Gregory R. Copley commented that the West, particularly the US, has "sustained the Cold War against Russia as the successor state to the USSR."

"The continuation of the Cold War by the West," writes Copley, "would have been of profound concern to US Pres. Ronald Reagan, who, with British Prime Minister Margaret Thatcher, saw the need to win the Cold War as a change to end *de facto* hostilities against the Russian people, and bring a post-Soviet Russia into the West. But this was not understood by the successor leaders to Mr Reagan and Baroness Thatcher: all those who followed seemed to wish to perpetuate the Cold War and its primary instrument, the North Atlantic Treaty Organization (NATO):

> The result is that Russia, despite its desire to be part of the West, is once again forced into the position of geo-strategic adversary to the US, and at a time when the US hardly can afford to create new adversaries.

---

[68] Kendal, *After Saturday Comes Sunday*, chapter 11.

More recently, in February 2020, Copley wrote an editorial in which he lamented the "four major clouds of self-deception which currently constrain the players in the present global strategic architecture."[69]

> "The third cloud of self-deception," writes Copley, "is the Western belief that the Russian Federation is still the Union of Soviet Socialist Republics (USSR) under the Communist Party of the Soviet Union. Russia today is led by nationalists; the Soviets were communists and globalists... By conflating Russia with the USSR, and insisting that it remain the enemy, the West has created a self-fulfilling prophecy."

Copley laments Western intransigence. "It is difficult to know," he writes (Nov 2019),

> whether the US Defence or State departments, each locked into ancient policies of support for Turkey (ever forgiving its sins against Cyprus, Egypt, the Kurds, the Greeks, Armenians, and others), have considered the long-term strategic interest of the US, or whether they are merely reiterating policy mantra of the past. They echoed the UK's support for Turkey since the Crimean War of 1853-56, with few pauses, merely because Turkey was seen as a bulwark against Russia... Erdogan no longer wishes to be a pawn for East or West, but cannot yet achieve that. He survives by playing one against the other.[70]

Not much has changed!

For that is exactly how Sultan Abdulmecid I won the Crimean War (1853–1856).

In 1853, Russia crossed into the Danubian Principalities on the Ottoman Empire's frontier, in defence of persecuted Orthodox Christians as was its right according to the Treaty of Küçük Kaynarca, brokered between the Russian Empire under Catherine the Great and the Ottoman Empire at the conclusion of the Russo-Turkish War of 1768–1774.[71]

[69] Gregory R. Copley, "Early Warning: The Strategic Importance of Self-Deception," *Defense and Foreign Affairs Strategic Policy* (2020).
[70] Gregory R. Copley, "Early Warning: When Ethics Collide with Strategic Logic," *Defense and Foreign Affairs Strategic Policy* (2019).
[71] See https://military.wikia.org/wiki/Treaty_of_Kucuk_Kaynarca

With the Ottoman Empire on the brink of collapse, the Sultan reached out to imperial Britain and imperial France which then entered the war on the side of the Turks. Britain and France were motivated in part by a determination to prevent any Russian imperial expansion, and in part by their desire to preserve their lucrative free trade agreements with the Ottoman Empire.

Rescued by the West, the Ottoman Empire was able to limp on for another 59 years at the cost of some three million Christian lives.

The idea that Christian Britain would aid the Muslim Turks against Orthodox Russia was not immediately popular in Britain. Queen Victoria was staunchly opposed, opining that it "would be in the interests of peace, and a great advantage generally, were the Turks to be well beaten."[72]

In order to justify Britain's entry into the war on the side of the Turks, Britain's elites fashioned a narrative around a Turkish psychological operation through which the Turks sacrificed thousands of unwitting human shields.[73]

British propaganda disparaged Orthodoxy as barely semi-Christian and demonised Russia as a monster and a threat, while romanticising Islam and proffering the Ottoman Empire as a worthy ally and victim of Russian imperialist aggression.

Historian Orlando Figes writes:

This was a war—the first war in history—to be brought about by the pressure of the press and by public opinion. With the development of the railways enabling the emergence of a national press in the 1840s and 1850s, public opinion became a potent force in British politics, arguably overshadowing the influence of Parliament and the cabinet itself.[74]

---

[72] Orlando Figes, *The Crimean War: A History* (New York: Picador, 2010), 145.

[73] Fully cognisant that Russia's Black Sea fleet had vowed to destroy any Turkish ships transporting arms and fighters to the Caucasus, Turkey sent out a flotilla. While the ships were indeed carrying arms and fighters to the Caucuses, they were also (unbeknown the Russians) carrying civilians, including numerous women and children. Some 2,700 Turkish fighters and some 1,500 unarmed civilians were killed in the Russian attack. Ibid., 141–147.

[74] Ibid., 147.

An expert in Russian history, Figes wrote *The Crimean War: A History*, precisely because he was concerned that the war's religious origins and motivations had for too long been ignored, obscured and misunderstood.[75]

Feeling betrayed, abandoned and absolutely mortified that Christian states had sided with the Turks, Tsar Nicholas lamented:

> Waging war neither for worldly advantage nor for conquests, but for a Christian purpose, must I be left alone to fight under the banner of the Holy Cross and to see the others, who call themselves Christians, all unite around the Crescent to combat Christendom? . . Nothing is left for me but to fight, to win, or to perish with honour, a martyr of our holy faith, and when I say this I declare it in the name of all Russia.[76]

Figes maintains, "These were not the words of a reckless gambler; they were the calculations of a believer."

The fact that Britain insisted that Russia was merely exploiting the Muslim persecution of Orthodox Christians as a pretext to advance its imperial ambitions, simply demonstrates the degree to which the West simply did not understand Russia.[77]

Not much has changed.

In 1683, Austrian and Polish forces turned back the battle at the Gates of Vienna sparing the West the suffering and trauma well known in the East.

Having endured centuries of Islamic imperialistic jihad, conquest, occupation, colonisation, discrimination, subjugation, dhimmitude and violent persecution—including massacres and

---

[75] Ibid.

[76] Ibid., 157.

[77] Historically, has Russia held deep spiritual-emotional ties to Constantinople, which she regards as her mother church. After Constantinople fell to the Turks in 1453, Russia took on the role of defender of Orthodox Christianity. Indeed, defence of persecuted Orthodox Christians was (and remains) integral to Russian foreign policy. Only during the 70-year-long communist captivity was this not the case. Indeed, the Soviets persecuted the Church mercilessly.

slavery—Eastern Christians do not have the luxury of blissful ignorance.[78]

Today, having suffered both Islam and Marxism, the East wants neither. The West however, having been spared both, is now embracing both.

And so the *dar-al-harb* remains divided and at war with itself, to the benefit of Islam, and to the detriment of global liberty and security.

ON THE HORIZON

Every nation – West and East – has its own interests and ambitions; some reasonable, some not. To think otherwise is naïve. But when it comes to containing and defeating revived and energised fundamentalist Islam, the interests of West and East converge. While we cannot change the past, it is imperative moving forward, that the Western mind be both reformed and informed, for many more crises loom large on the horizon.

HYPOTHETICAL: Consider this Scenario
(which actually is not very hypothetical at all)

War erupts between Azerbaijan and Armenia. Neo-Ottoman Turkey enters the fray on the side of its Turkic Islamist ally Azerbaijan. Both have long fantasized about wiping Armenia off the map. Boasting the latest Israeli-made armed drones; hosting the

---

[78] M. A. Khan, *Islamic Jihad: The Legacy of Forced Conversion, Imperialism and Slavery* (Bloomington, IN: iUniverse, 2009). Excerpt from page 322: "The Ottoman penetration into Europe in the 1350s and their capture of Constantinople later in 1453 opened new floodgates for slave-trade from the European front. In their last attempt to overrun Europe in 1683, the Ottoman army, although defeated, returned from the Gates of Vienna with 80,000 captives. An immense number of slaves flowed from the Crimea, the Balkans and the steeps of West Asia to Islamic markets. BD Davis laments that the 'Tatars and other Black Sea people had sold millions of Ukrainians, Georgians, Circassians, Armenians, Bulgarians, Slavs and Turks, which received little notice'. Crimean Tatars enslaved and sold some 1,750,000 Ukrainians, Poles and Russians between 1468 and 1694. According to another estimate, between 1450 and 1700, the Crimean Tatars exported some 10,000 slaves, including some Circassians, annually – that is, some 2,500,000 slaves in all, to the Ottoman Empire." Islamic slave raids in Russian-controlled territory continued to be launched from the Crimean Peninsula until Catherine the Great annexed the region in 1774.

valuable BTC pipeline; backed by Turkey and its jihadist proxies, Azerbaijan is brimming with confidence.[79]

As anticipated, Russia comes to the aid of its long-time ally and vassal, Orthodox Armenia.

In 1878, the Treaty of San Stefano placed the great majority of Armenians under the protection of Russia on the grounds that the Turks had not yet enacted sufficient reform. However, in the subsequent Treaty of Berlin (1878) that protection was removed at the behest of the British. In his 1939 memoir, wartime British Prime Minister Lloyd George lamented that due to

> our sinister intervention... Armenia was sacrificed on the triumphal altar we had erected. The Russians were forced to withdraw. The wretched Armenians were once more placed under the heel of their old masters.[80]

And we all know how that turned out; the result was genocide!

Russia is not about to let history repeat; there will be no Armenian genocide today. What's more, the last thing Russia wants is a neo-Ottoman Caliphate in its back yard!

What will the West do? Will the West enter the war on the side of NATO-member neo-Ottoman Islamist Turkey and US-UK-Israel-allied Azerbaijan? What sort of narrative could possibly justify a Western intervention on the side of Turks against Armenians? How much Russophobia would have to be whipped up for *that* intervention to be approved by the masses? (Hint: probably not much!) How would Western Christians respond? As was demonstrated during the Crimean War, Western churches have a long history of questioning whether the Eastern Orthodox are even Christian at all, despite their having persevered through centuries of religious discrimination, subjugation and violent persecution!

The prospect of an Islamic Caliphate expanding ever-eastwards – from Turkey through the Caucuses, its sights on Central Asia and Xinjiang, western China (a.k.a. East Turkistan);

---

[79] See https://www.bp.com/en_az/azerbaijan/home/who-we-are/operationsprojects/pipelines/btc.html.
[80] Taner Akçam, *A Shameful Act: The Armenian Genocide and the Question of Turkish Responsibility* (London: Consta, 2007), 258–259.

121

incorporating Afghanistan as well as nuclear-armed Pakistan – would excite transnational jihadists no end!

Consider a hypothetical in which Ethiopia dissolves into chaos. An unstable Ethiopia is in no-one's interest; save for the Islamists who are poised to pounce.[81] Islamic State has been recruiting in Amharic [language] for jihad in Ethiopia since at least July 2019. Islamists have long fantasised about Islamising the "Christian island" that is Ethiopia.[82]

Consider a hypothetical in which Indonesia's Papuan Provinces descend into genocidal hell. In 1962, to curry favour with Indonesia during its Cold War with the Soviets, the US brokered the New York Agreement which granted mostly Javanese Muslim Indonesia the right to administer resource-rich, mostly Melanesian Christian Dutch/West New Guinea. In 1969, a rorted referendum known as the Act of Free Choice (subsequently lampooned as the Act of No Choice) paved the way for Dutch/West New Guinea (Irian Jaya) to be officially incorporated into Indonesia. The West turned a blind eye then and has continued to turn a blind eye ever since. By 2020, racial-religious tensions are at boiling point. If conflict erupts, what will the West do? Will the West abandon the Christian Papuans—the legacy of Western missionaries—into the hands of the Indonesian military and its nationalist and jihadist proxies just to curry favour with Jakarta during its new Cold War with China? The mountainous jungles of resource-rich Papua would make an ideal base for transnational Islamic jihadists pursuing *success* in Southeast Asia and the Pacific.

RETURNING TO ERASMUS

Erasmus wrote his treatise, *De bello turcico* ("On the War Against the Turks"), to coincide with the Diet of Augsburg, an imperial assembly of the Holy Roman Empire convened in the Bavarian city of Augsburg in February 1530 at the behest of Charles

[81] Elizabeth Kendal, "Ethiopia: Church Protests; Watershed Days," *Religious Liberty Prayer Bulletin* 520 (2019): http://rlprayerbulletin.blogspot.com/2019/09/ rlpb-520-ethiopia-church-protests.html. See also Elizabeth Kendal, "Slaughter in Oromia: The Battle for Ethiopia Heats Up," *Religious Liberty Prayer Bulletin* 560 (2020): http://rlprayerbulletin.blogspot.com/2020/07/rlpb-560-july-update-incl-syria-iran.html.
[82] "Ethiopia has been for fourteen centuries a Christian island in a sea of pagans" – Ethiopia's Emperor Menelik, in a letter to European powers. See https://en.wikipedia.org/wiki/Menelik_II.

V, to discuss what he maintained were the two greatest threats facing Christendom: Lutheranism and Islam. For Erasmus it was imperative that Christendom—divided on account of the Reformation—be united in the face of the threat posed by the ascendant Ottoman Turks.[83]

Historian Jerry Brotton comments, that in the face of this existential threat,

> It had proved almost impossible to unite Christendom against the Ottomans: Venice remained on amicable commercial terms with them, while the French pursued repeated diplomatic and military alliances with [Ottoman Sultan] Süleyman as a bulwark against the Habsburgs [who ruled over the imperialist Royal House of Austria].[84]

Erasmus knew that "Christendom" needed reformation, insisting:

> If we want to heave the Turks from our necks, we must first expel from our hearts a more loathsome race of Turks, avarice, ambition, the craving for power, self-satisfaction, impiety, extravagance, the love of pleasure, deceitfulness, anger, hatred, envy.

He also knew that in the absence of unity and "a truly Christian spirit," evil would triumph.[85]

Not much has changed! For *that* is as true today as it was in 1530.

---

[83] Jerry Brotton, *This Orient Isle: Elizabethan England and the Islamic World* (London: Allen Lane, 2016), 30–31.
[84] Ibid., 31.
[85] Ibid., 31–32.

SECTION II

ISLAM AND POLITICS

REGIONAL EXPRESSIONS

Chapter 6

ISLAM in the NORTH CAUCASUS
and
RUSSIAN FEDERAL LAW

Denis Savelyev[1]

INTRODUCTION

Islam in the North Caucasus

Russian Federation is a home for approximately twenty-five million Muslims. There are around two hundred different ethnic groups in Russia, and fifty-eight of them historically follow Islam. Majority of the Muslims in Russian Federation are Sunni, with a small Shi'a population in the Southern Dagestan. There are four main Sunni schools of law (or *madhhabs*). The majority of the Sunni Muslims living in Russia belong to the Hanafi *madhab*, and a few republics in the North Caucasus follow Shafi'i *madhhab*.[2]

There are numerous differences between Muslims from different *madhhabs* and further dissimilarities depending on the ethnic group. In this article we will focus on the three republics in the North Caucasus which follow Shafi'i school of law, namely Dagestan, Ingushetia and Chechnya.

North Caucasus have a long history going back for at least a couple of centuries of rebellions against the Russian government.

---

[1] Denis Savelyev is originally from Russia where he worked as a lecturer and alternate director at Eurasian Missionary College in Kazan. Denis was also involved in church-planting before coming to Australia. He completed his MA and PhD at Melbourne School of Theology and then did his Post Doctural Studies on internal history of the Qur'an. Currently he is both the Administrator of the Arthur Jeffery Centre of Islam, Melbourne School of Theology and also a lecturer on Islam there.

[2] Елена Теслова, «Численность Российской Уммы достигла 25 миллионов человек,» (Russian Ummah has reached 25 million people), Anadolu Agency (07 March 2018), https://www.aa.com.tr/ru/заголовки-дня/численность-российской-уммы-достигла-25-млн-человек/1081820

There was a Russo-Caucasian war in the middle of the 19th century, an Islamic rebellion in Chechnya and Dagestan was crushed by the early Soviet state in the beginning of the 20th century. In the middle of the last century a lot of Chechens and Ingushs were deported to Kazakhstan by the Soviet government. There were two Chechen-Russian wars in the ninety nineties. Chechens even have an oft-repeated statement that Chechens suffer persecution every fifty years.[3] In 1998 two Dagestani villages – Karamakhi and Chabanmakhi – whose citizens decided to follow Wahhabi branch of Islam rebelled against the Federal Government, rejected the Russian Constitution, expelled the police and declared independence. In August 1999 Chechen militants headed by Shamil Basaev invaded Dagestan. They were hoping that Dagestani Muslims would join them in order to overthrow Russian government, but this never happened. Chechen militants' invasion was defeated and rebellion in Karamakhi and Chabanmakhi was quashed.

Internal Muslim conflicts during Chechen-Russian wars

During the Chechen-Russian conflicts Muslims from the different parts of the world came to fight alongside Chechens. Many of those Muslims were from a Wahhabi branch of Islam which followed the Hanbali school of law. There are four main sources for the Islamic law: The Qur'an, the *sunna* of Muhammad, *Qiyas* (Analogy), and *Ijma'* (Consensus).[4] Hanbali *maddhab* focuses mainly on the first two sources. Furthermore, Wahhabi Muslims reject the traditions that appeared after the period of the first four Muslim Caliphs. In addition, Chechens are very proud of their ethnicity and they have their own set of traditions (*adats*). Akhmad Kadyrov once said: "First of all – we are Chechens, and only then – Muslims."[5] Chechens are also adherents of Sufism (Islamic mysticism), which is

---

[3] Alla Dudayeva in her book about her late husband Dzhokhar Dudayev mentions him talking about deportations and annihilations of Chechens that they face every fifty years. Алла Дудаева, *Миллион Первый*, Ультра Культура, Екатеринбург, 2005, стр.60. A similar statement was recently made by Magomed Daudov, the Chairman of the Parliament of the Chechen republic. See «В Грозном состоялось собрание, посвященное Дню памяти и скорби народов ЧР,» (A meeting dedicated to the Day of remembrance and sorrow of the Chechen people was held in Grozny) Грозный Информ (10 Мая 2018), https://www.grozny-inform.ru/news/politic/95935/
[4] Andrew Rippin, Muslims, Their Religious Beliefs and Practices, (Routledge, London: 2012), p.93
[5] Вахит Акаев, «Специфика современного чеченского Ислама,» (Specificity of the Modern Chechen Islam), *Россия и Мусульманский Мир*, 2008, №11, стр.42

considered by many Hanbali Muslims to be a heresy.[6] The influence of the Wahhabi teachings in Chechnya grew and some of Chechen leaders started to actively oppose it.[7] In 1998 Akhmad Kadyrov openly opposed the spread of Wahhabism in Chechnya and proposed to officially prohibit Wahhabism in the Chechen Republic and to deport Wahhabi fighters and preachers. The main reasons for this was the attack of Wahhabism on traditional Chechen Islam and terrorist acts perpetrated by the Wahhabi fighters.[8] In 1999 Akhmad Kadyrov declared insubordination to Aslan Mashadov (then the president of Chechnya) and announced support for the anti-terrorist operation of the troops of the Russian Federation.[9] In a way it was a choice of a lesser evil. Chechens would not have territorial independency, but the threat of Wahhabi teachings to traditional Sufi Islam in Chechnya would be eliminated and another campaign of Russian Federal troops against Chechens would be avoided. In exchange for a relative Chechen autonomy Russia kept territorial integrity and terrorist acts have stopped.

Islam in the North Caucasus and Politics

Since the majority of Muslims in the North Caucasus rejected Wahhabi teachings and actively opposed it, there is a reason to think that traditional Islam in the North Caucasus is compatible with Russian federal laws. However, Russian Federal Government often turns a blind eye to the situation in Caucasian republics in return for relative peace. In this article we will look at several different spheres where this is the case.

Persecution of Christians
Apostacy in Islam

Despite the different views on the role of *qiyas* and *ijma'* on the Islamic law, all Muslim schools of law agree on the issues that are described in the Qur'an and the *sunna* of Muhammad. The *sunna*, or example of Muhammad, is mainly derived from the *hadith* literature.

---

[6] See for example a Hanbali scholar stating that Sufis are out of the fold of Islam: https://www.youtube.com/watch?v=_z6Wvyrm1GU

[7] Ахмат Кадыров, «Война среди нас самих!» (War Is Among Us!), https://web.archive.org/web/20110903225543/http://www.kadirov.ru/node/8

[8] Ахмат Кадыров, «Через референдум Чечня прозреет!» (Chechnya will see the light through referendum!), https://web.archive.org/web/20110724061104/http://kadirov.ru/node/88

[9] «Кадыров Ахмад (Ахмат-хаджи),» (Kadyrov Ahmad (Ahmat-hajji), Кавказский Узел, https://www.kavkaz-uzel.eu/articles/13679/

There are six major *hadith* collections accepted by all Sunni Muslims. According to Sahih al-Bukhari (the most authoritative hadith collection) a Muslim who leaves Islam should be killed:

> Some Zanadiqa (atheists) were brought to `Ali and he burnt them. The news of this event, reached Ibn `Abbas who said, "If I had been in his place, I would not have burnt them, as Allah's Messenger (☝) forbade it, saying, 'Do not punish anybody with Allah's punishment (fire).' I would have killed them according to the statement of Allah's Messenger (☝), 'Whoever changed his Islamic religion, then kill him.'"[10]

As has been already mentioned, Chechens follow the Shafi'i *madhab*. The main manual for Shafi'i school of law is the *Reliance of the Traveller*, written by Ahmad ibn Naqib al-Misri. According to this manual:

> When a person who has reached puberty and is sane voluntarily apostatizes from Islam, he deserves to be killed. In such case, it is obligatory for the caliph to ask him to repent and return to Islam. If he does, it is accepted from him, but if he refuses, he is immediately killed.[11]

Although it said that the apostate should be brought to the caliph, it is also stated that there is no indemnity for killing the apostate, since "it is killing someone who deserves to die."[12]

Persecution of Christians in Chechnya

During the 1990s Christians living in Chechnya faced severe persecution. Sometimes Chechen leaders would conflate Russia with Christianity. Akhmad Kadyrov in one of his speeches in 1999 stated that Orthodox Christians brought enemies to Chechnya and that it is Christians who are fighting against Chechens.[13]

---

[10] Sahih al-Bukhari, Hadith no.6929, https://sunnah.com/bukhari:6922
[11] Ahmad ibn Naqib al-Misri, *Reliance of the Traveller: A Classic Manual of Islamic Sacred Law*, (tr.) Nuh Ha Mim Keller, (Amana Publications, Maryland: 2011), pp.595-596
[12] *Reliance of the Traveller*, p.596
[13] Akhmad Kadyrov was a Chief Mufti of Chechnya in the 1990s, and later became the President of the Chechen Republic. An excerpt of the speech is available on youtube: https://www.youtube.com/watch?v=59tb_VrAyzY. After the assassination of Akhmad Kadyrov his son, Ramzan Kadyrov, became the president of the Chechen republic.

Christian leaders were kidnapped and killed: some ministers who travelled to Chechnya received threats of abduction.[14] Even long after the end of the Chechen-Russian conflict Protestant leaders in the Caucasus believe that Chechens "are the hardest to convert and working among them is considered to be a dangerous enterprise."[15]

Persecution of Christians in Dagestan

Situation in Dagestan is less severe than in Chechnya, however Christians, and especially those who converted from Islam can be persecuted. The author of this article lived in Dagestan knew many Christians who were intimidated by Muslim neighbours, threatened, and beaten up for converting to Christianity. Several Christians were killed. In 1997 a couple of Seventh Day Adventists - Haji-Murat Gadjiev and his wife - were falsely accused by a Muslim mob in kidnapping and killing a little girl with the aim of selling her organs. These Christians were tortured to death and their bodies were burned. There was no proper investigation and none of the torturers were prosecuted.[16] Artur Suleimanov – a pastor of Pentecostals church "Hosanna" was gunned down in front of his church in Makhachkala (capital of Dagestan).[17] Suleimanov's killers were never found.

Enjoining Right and Forbidding Wrong

Enjoining Right and Forbidding Wrong – are two principles that can be found in Islamic scriptures. Below are a few examples from the Qur'an:

---

[14] Dan Wooding, "Evangelical Cleansing" in Chechnya," (June 1999), https://christiananswers.net/q-eden/persec-chechnya1.html.
See also "Dagestan, Chechnya: Christians still face kidnap, murder; now war", EA Foundation (21 September 1999), http://www.ea.org.au/ea-family/Religious-Liberty/DAGESTAN--CHECHNYA--CHRISTIANS-STILL-FACE-KIDNAP--MURDER--NO cited 10 October, 2020.
[15] Maribek Vatchagaev, "Russian Orthodox Church Redraws Its Map of the North Caucus," The Jamestown Foundation (25 January 2013), https://jamestown.org/program/russian-orthodox-church-redraws-its-map-of-the-north-caucasus-2/
[16] «Христианские мученикив Дагестане», (15 Сентября 2013), http://kavpolit.com/xristianskie-mucheniki-v-dagestane cited 10 October, 2020.
[17] «Radical Islam spreading in troubled North Caucasus», (31 May 2011), https://barnabasfund.org/AU/News/Archives/Radical-Islam-spreading-in-troubled-North-Caucasus cited 10 October, 2020.

> "Let there arise out of you a band of people inviting to all that is good, enjoining what is right, and forbidding what is wrong: They are the ones to attain felicity." Q.3:104

> "Ye are the best of peoples, evolved for mankind, enjoining what is right, forbidding what is wrong, and believing in Allah. If only the People of the Book had faith, it were best for them: among them are some who have faith, but most of them are transgressors." Q.3:110

> "The believers, both men and women, are guardians of one another. They encourage good and forbid evil, establish prayer and pay alms-tax, and obey Allah and His Messenger." Q.9:71

The same principle can be found in the hadith:

> "Messenger of Allah (ﷺ) said, "Whoever amongst you sees an evil, he must change it with his hand; if he is unable to do so, then with his tongue; and if he is unable to do so, then with his heart; and that is the weakest form of Faith"." Riyad as-Salihin 184[18]

The main idea behind these principles is that Muslims have to be proactive in forbidding deeds that are deemed evil, or un-Islamic, and force weaker Muslims into obeying Islamic laws. There are various instances where local Muslims in the North Caucasus – sometimes with the help of the local police – have endeavoured to forbid un-Islamic behaviour.

Enforcing headscarfs

In 2010 in Chechnya unidentified men who were driving around Grozny were shooting women without headscarfs with paintball guns. Several video clips were circulated where shooters were demanding the women to cover their heads. Local police at first did nothing about it. Furthermore, relatives of one of the victims stated that one of the shooters' cars belonged to a Chechen policeman. After the public outcry became more vocal Chechen police had to react. The shootings stopped,however no perpetrators were found.[19]

---

[18] Riyad as-Salihin, hadith no.184, https://sunnah.com/riyadussalihin:184
[19] Lechi Hamzatov, «Чеченский пейнтбол» (Chechen Paintball), (6 July 2010), https://www.bbc.co.uk/blogs/russian/northcaucasus/2010/07/post-30.html

Rapper's Concert

In 2018 Egor Krid – a Russian rapper – had to cancel his concert in Dagestan due to death threats. Hundreds of local Muslims, who thought that his music and lyrics are un-Islamic and lead to moral decay, left threats on social media. The cancellation of the concert was approved by Khabib Nurmagomedov – a famous UFC fighter.[20] Nurmagomedov's point of view was later supported by other Dagestani UFC and MMA fighters. Local police did not prosecute any of the people who made death threats against the rapper.

Anime fest

Also in 2018 an Anime festival AniDag that was planned to take place in Avar Theatre in Dagestan was cancelled at the last minute. Shortly before the beginning of AniDag the Theatre's administration and organisers of the festival started to receive anonymous threats. Police accompanied by unidentified men entered the Theatre, declared that the festival had to be postponed and arrested the festival's organiser. She was released several hours later without any charges. The youth that came to the festival were harassed and intimidated by local Muslims when they left the building. Again, as with the cases above – none of the people who left threats or harassed festival participants was arrested or charged.[21]

Persecution of LGBT community
Islam and homosexuality

The Qur'an mentions homosexuality in the story of Lot (Lut):

> "We also (sent) Lut: He said to his people: "Do ye commit lewdness such as no people in creation (ever) committed before you? For ye practise your lusts on men in preference to women: ye are indeed a people transgressing beyond bounds."" Q.7:80-81

It is also mentioned in the hadith that Muhammad was worried that Muslims might follow the example of the people of Lot:

---

[20] Alexandr Rassokhin, «Егор Крид обошел Махачкалу стороной», (Egor Krid bypassed Makhachkala), (10 September 2018),
https://www.kommersant.ru/doc/3737532
[21] Igor Bykin, «В Дагестане сорвали аниме-фестиваль» (Anime Festival Disrupted in Dagestan), (26 Novebmer 2018), https://info24.ru/news/v-dagestane-sorvali-anime-festival-uchastnikov-nazvali-neformalami-i-prostitutkami.html

"That the Messenger of Allah (ﷺ) said: "What I fear most from my Ummah is the behavior of the people of Lut."" Jami' at-Trimidhi, 1457[22]

Although the Qur'an does not specify a punishment for homosexuality, various hadith stated that the penalty for taking part in this behaviour is death:

"That the Messenger of Allah (ﷺ) said: "Whomever you find doing the actions of the people of Lut then kill the one doing it, and the one it is done to.""[23]

"It was narrated from Abu Hurairah that the Prophet (ﷺ) said concerning those who do the action of the people of Lut: "Stone the upper and the lower, stone them both.""[24]

Persecution of gays in Chechnya

In 2017 reports of the anti-gay purge in Chechnya emerged. The Organization for Security and Cooperation in Europe did an investigation of this report and concluded "that the allegations of unlawful detentions and torture in Chechnya were credible."[25] Two more anti-gay sweeps took place in late 2018 and early 2019, however there were no investigations or prosecutions by Russian Federal authorities.

Women

In the Qur'an it is stated that men are in charge of women:

"Men are the protectors and maintainers of women, because Allah has given the one more (strength) than the other, and because they support them from their means. Therefore the righteous women are devoutly obedient, and guard in (the husband's) absence what Allah would have them guard." Q.4:34

Generally, in Islam a woman is under the guardianship of her father until she gets married. After the marriage – her husband becomes her guardian. There are cases in the North Caucasus when young

---

[22] Jami' at Tirmidhi, hadith 1457, https://sunnah.com/tirmidhi:1457
[23] Jami' at Tirmidhi, hadith 1456, https://sunnah.com/tirmidhi:1456
[24] Sunan Ibn Majah, hadith 2562, https://sunnah.com/ibnmajah:2562
[25] Katy Steinmetz, "A Victim of the Anti-Gay Purge in Chechnya Speaks Out: 'The Truth Exists,'" Time (26 July 2019), https://time.com/5633588/anti-gay-purge-chechnya-victim/

women, who are considered independent by Russian law, tried to leave their parent's home, but were forcefully returned. We will consider a few cases.

In June 2021 Khalima Taramova, a Chechen woman who stayed in Dagestan in a shelter for domestic violence victims, was forcibly removed by Chechen police and taken back to Chechnya. Her father, Ayub Taramov is a close associate of Ramzan Kadyrov.[26] Khalima Taramova is still kept in Chechnya, despite attempts by various Human Rights groups to get her released. In this case Chechen policemen acted in the neighbouring republic and were not opposed by Dagestani police despite the fact that Khalima had recorded three videos for the Dagestani police where she stated that she left Chechnya on her own accord, fearing for her life, and asked not to disclose her location to her relatives.

Milana Magomedova lived with her parents in Tumen. Her family was originally from Dagestan. She was raised in strict Caucasian traditions – she was not allowed to leave home without permission or to work. Her family was looking for a good husband for Milana. At some point she decided to escape, and her parents declared her a missing person. Despite the fact that Milana went to the police and explained that she willingly left her parents, the police gave them her whereabouts. Milana agreed to meet with her mother, but her father with another man came as well and kidnapped her. Milana's friends called the police and told them that she has been abducted. The police apprehended Milana's father and took them both to the police station. Despite her explanation that she was not willing to go with her father, the police returned her to her father and let him go. When she asked a policeman why they are doing this, he replied: "Milana, you surely understand this – these are your customs".[27] So in this case even Russian policemen were returning a young woman to her parents, because they thought it is normal for the Caucasian Muslims. Later on, Milana escaped her parents again.

---

[26] "Chechen Woman Abducted by Police In Daghestan may Face 'Honor Killing,' Rights Groups Warn," RadioFreeEurope (11 June 2021), https://www.rferl.org/a/russia-daghestan-chechnya-shelter-attacked/31302426.html
[27] Sergei Khazov-Kassia, ««У вас так принято». Как полиция беглых девушек выдает» ("These are your customs". How police return escaped young women), (26 March 2021), https://www.svoboda.org/a/31170506.html

In July 2021 a young Dagestani girl who had lived in Sweden since she was nine was invited to a relative's wedding in Dagestan. After travelling to her home town, she found out that she was to be a bride and that her relatives had agreed to marry her to a man she never met. After she refused to marry the man, her relatives took her documents from her, she was beaten and threatened to be killed. The young girl managed to call the police who came and took her to the police station. After she was released from the station – she escaped to Moscow, and then to Sweden – she had a dual citizenship. Her relatives came to the police and declared that she was kidnapped. Despite the fact that the young woman sent her statement to Dagestani police that she was not kidnapped and left voluntarily, the police were demanding that she returns to Dagestan.[28]

Female Genital Mutilation

Out of the four Sunni Schools of Law female circumcision is practised by the adherents of the Shafi'i school of law. English translation of the Shafi'i manual of law states that:

> "Circumcision is obligatory (O: for both men and women.) For men it consists of removing the prepuce from the penis, and for women, removing the prepuce (Ar. bazr) of the clitoris (n: not the clitoris itself, as some mistakenly assert). (A: Hanbalis hold that circumcision of women is not obligatory but sunna, while Hanafis consider it a mere courtesy to the husband.)"[29]

However, this translation is incorrect, the facing Arabic text states:

> "Circumcision is obligatory (for every male and female) (by cutting off the piece of skin on the glans of the penis of the male, but circumcision of the female is by cutting out the bazr 'clitoris' [this is called *khufaadh* 'female circumcision')"[30]

Female Circumcisions is practiced in some villages of the North Caucasus despite such practices being prohibited by Russian Federal

---

[28] «18-летнюю жительницу Швеции родные в Дагестане хотели насильно выдать замуж и угрожали убийством чести» (Relatives of an 18-year old citizen of Sweden were trying to forcefully marry her and threatened her with honour killing), (2 July 2021), https://www.currenttime.tv/a/letnyaya-devushka-uehala-iz-dagestana--ubiystvo-chesti/31337790.html
[29] Reliance of the Traveller, p.59
[30] Mark Durie, The Third Choice, Deror Books, 2010, p.65

law. In 2016 *Stichting Justice Initiative* (*SJI*)– an organisation dedicated to legal protection of human right violations – published a report about female genital mutilation of girls in Dagestan.[31] This report led to heated discussions on the internet. Ismail Berdiev – the chairman of the *Coordination Centre of the North Caucasus Muslims* – stated in response to the report that it would be good to circumcise all women in order to eliminate debauchery from the Earth.[32] Later on he stated that Islam does not prescribe to circumcise women, but at the same time he confirmed that FGM is practiced in some areas of the North Caucasus and stated that there is a problem of sexual debauchery and it needs some kind of solution.[33]

Almost two years later, SJI researchers came to the conclusion that since the publishing of the first report no measures were taken in order to intervene and stop the practice of genital mutilations in Dagestan. In 2018 they published a second report on FGM in Dagestan, Ingushetia and Chechnya.[34] According to the second report by the lowest estimates in Dagestan alone 1240 girls are subjected to FGM every year. This report did not lead to any changes either. Muslim scholars from the Muftiyat of Dagestan recently posted an article discussing different types of female circumcision and stating that only skin around clitoris should be circumcised.[35] The article concludes with the words "And Allah knows best" which usually shows there is uncertainty regarding this statement.

Despite of the above-mentioned reports and the various articles written on this topic no specific measures have been taken and none

[31] *Female Genital Mutilations of Girls in Dagestan* (Russian Federation), 2017, accessible here:
https://www.srji.org/upload/iblock/c94/fgm_dagestan_2016_eng_final_edited_2017.pdf
[32] «Муфтий Северного Кавказа призвал обрезать всех женщин России» (North Caucasus Mufti called for circumcision of all women of Russia), (17 August 2016), https://www.interfax.ru/russia/524002
[33] «Муфтий Северного Кавказа оказался от призыва обрезать всех женщин» (North Caucasus Mufti took back his words to circumcise all women), (17 August 2016), https://www.interfax.ru/russia/524033
[34] Yu.A. Antonova, S.V. Siradhudinova, *The practice of genital mutilation in Dagestan: strategies for its elimination*, 2018. Accessible here:
https://www.srji.org/upload/iblock/957/The_practice_of_female_genital_mutilation_in_Dagestan_strategies_for_its_elimination_15.06.pdf
[35] «Женское Обрезание» (Female Circumcision), https://muftiyatrd.ru/fatawa/zhenskoe-obrezanie

of the persons performing FGM in the North Caucasus have been prosecuted.

Polygamy

In Islam men are allowed to have up to four wives at a time. This is based on the following verse from the Qur'an:

> "If ye fear that ye shall not be able to deal justly with the orphans, Marry women of your choice, Two or three or four; but if ye fear that ye shall not be able to deal justly (with them), then only one, or (a captive) that your right hands possess, that will be more suitable, to prevent you from doing injustice."
> Q.4:3

In the Soviet Union polygamy was a criminal offence. Modern day Russian Family Law prohibits the registration of the second marriage, however there is no criminal administrative punishment for having a de-facto second marriage. In the beginning of 2000th, Ruslan Aushev – then president of *Ingushetia* – declared polygamy legal in his Republic. This decision was in conflict with Russian Federal Law and was later overturned. In 2006, Ramazan Kadyrov called for legalising polygamy.[36]

Despite the fact that polygamy in the Russian Federation has not been legalised, a lot of Muslims do take, de-facto second or third wives. In 2016 researchers from Heinrich Boll Fund conducted interviews on the life and problems of men and women in the North Caucasus. According to their findings 14.7% of interviewed Dagestani men stated that they have a second wife, and 5.9% that they have three wives. In Chechnya 11% of interviewed men stated that they have a second wife and 2% that they have three wives. In Ingushetia – 6.7% of men stated that they have two wives.[37] Ramazan Kadyrov – the head of Chechnya reportedly have two wives.[38]

---

[36] «Многоженство в России: миф или реальность?» (Polygamy in Russia: myth or reality?), (19 May 2015),
https://www.bbc.com/russian/society/2015/05/150519_tr_russia_polygamy_discussion
[37] «На Северном Кавказе многоженство снова становится нормой? (Does Polygamy in the North Caucasus become a norm again?), (1 September 2018), https://rus.azattyq.org/a/mistresses-in-law-becomes-a-norm-in-northern-caucasus/29465336.html
[38] ««Проект» рассказал о «второй жене» Рамазана Кадырова» ("Project" reported about the "Second wife" of Ramazan Kadyrov), (7 April 2021), https://meduza.io/feature/2021/04/07/proekt-rasskazal-o-vtoroy-zhene-ramzana-kadyrova-i-novoy-lichnosti-ego-pervoy-suprugi

Blood Feuds in the North Caucasus

Various local traditions and customary practices in the Caucasus are called *Adat*. They often include pre-Islamic practices, as well as regulations regarding aspects not mentioned in the *Shari'a* law.[39] One of the pre-Islamic traditions still practiced in the North Caucasus is the Blood Feud. After the end of the first Chechen-Russian conflict, Aslan Mashadov (then president of Chechnya) attempted to established *Shari'a* law instead of the traditional *adat* system. Blood Feud traditions were supposed to be replaced by fines. However, this attempt failed. In 2010, Ramzan Kadyrov, a sitting president of Chechnya, created a *Commission for National Reconciliation* in order to resolve all the conflicts related to the Blood Feuds. One year later he disbanded the commission because it had reconciled all the cases. However, the very next day another *Commission for National Reconciliation* was created by Chechen religious leaders.[40] Interestingly, at the same time when Ramzan Kadyrov created the Commission he also declared a Blood Feud against Ahkmed Zakayev, whom he accused of organising an armed attack on Tsentoroi – Kadyrov's village.[41]

This is not the only case when Ramzan Kadyrov openly declared a Blood Feud or threatened somebody. In December 2020 representatives of Ingush clans stated that Chechen officials unlawfully detained relatives of a few Ingush men killed during attack on Chechen policemen. In response Kadyrov ordered Magomed Daudov (the Chairman of the Chechen Parliament) to meet with the representatives of the clans and to declare a Blood Feud against them.[42] In 2019 Magomed Daudov himself declared a blood feud against Tumso Abdurakhmanov – a popular blogger, for

---

[39] Г.В. Милославский, Ю.А. Петросян, М.Б. Пиотровский, «`Ада», (Adat), *Ислам: Энциклопедический Словарь*, (М.: Наука, 1991), стр. 11

[40] «Кровная Месть – как теперь убивают на Кавказе,» (Blood Feud – how people are get killed in the Caucasus nowadays), Кавказский Узел, https://www.kavkaz-uzel.eu/articles/296137/

[41] «Рамзан Кадыров стал главой Всемирного конгресса чеченцев», Кавказский Узел (13 Октября 2010), https://www.kavkaz-uzel.eu/articles/175480/

[42] Марк Ульянов, «Кадыров приказал объявить кровную месть родственникам напавших на полицейских,» (Kadyrov orderd to declare a blood feud against the relatives of the people who attacked policemen), Lenta.Ru (31 декабря 2020), https://lenta.ru/news/2020/12/31/mest/

criticizing Kadyrov's late father.[43] In 2020 two Chechens were sentences in Sweden for attempted murder of Tumso Abdurakhmanov.[44]

In May 2020 Ramzan Kadyrov threatened a person who called him "Satan" during a live broadcast. In the video posted by Kadyrov on his Instagram page he said that he would find the person who said that and would destroy him, as he has destroyed many 'Satans' before.[45] A few days later relatives of the teenager who called Kadyrov 'Satan' recorded a video where all the elders of the boy's larger family apologised on his behalf and asked Kadyrov to forgive him.[46]

Despite open death threats and declarations of blood feud made by Ramzan Kadyrov and other Chechen officials, there were no prosecutions or even investigations of these claims by the Russian Police. Very often Chechens defy the laws of the Russian Federation "considering themselves part of a legitimate if underground Chechen state."[47]

Conclusion

Despite being a part of Russian Federation, local Muslim governments in the North Caucasus often do not follow Russian Federal law. The situation in Dagestan, Chechnya and Ingushetia is different, but there are similarities as well. Local police often side with the perpetrators and sometimes even help to enforce local *adats* which are in line with Islamic tradition but contradict the laws of the Russian Federation.

---

[43] "Top Chechen Official Claims Blood Feud Against Blogger," VOA (12 March 2019), https://www.voanews.com/europe/top-chechen-official-claims-blood-feud-against-blogger

[44] Eli Moskowitz, "Sweden Sentences Two Russians for Attempted Murder of Chechen Blogger", OCCRP (12 January 2021), https://www.occrp.org/en/daily/13609-sweden-sentences-two-russians-for-attempted-murder-of-chechen-blogger

[45] "'I Will Destroy You': Chechen Leader Threatens Kid On Instagram," RadioFreeEurope (20 May 2021), https://www.rferl.org/a/chechnya-kadyrov-instagram/31265313.html

[46] «Родственники подростка, назвавшего Кадырова шайтаном, извинились на камеру,» (Relatives of the teenager who called Kadyrov shaytan apologised on tape), BBC News (20 Мая 2021), https://www.bbc.com/russian/news-57182946

[47] Caspar ten Dam, "How to Feud and Rebel: 2. Histories, Cultures and Grievances of the Chechens and Albanians," *Iran and Caucasus*, 15 (2011), p.241

Following the Chechen-Russian wars and Wahhabi insurrections in Dagestan and other places in the North Caucasus the Federal government has turned a blind eye to what is happening in the region in return for relative peace and loyalty. The Republics of the North Caucasus consistently overwhelmingly vote for Vladimir Putin and his party "Edinaya Rossia" (United Russia). In the recent Duma elections, citizens of Dagestan, Chechnya and Ingushetia voted 81%, 96%, and 85% respectively for "Edynaya Rossia" party.[48] Furthermore, Ramazan Kadyrov has been implicated in a number of assassinations of his own Chechen adversaries and also of Putin critics, such as Natalia Estimirova and Boris Nemtsov.[49] This is another possible reason why the authorities of the Russian Federal Government turn a deaf ear to the situation in Chechnya where Russian Federal law has been defied more than in the neighbouring republics.

Bibliography

Antonova, Yu.A., Siradhudinova, S.V., *The practice of genital mutilation in Dagestan: strategies for its elimination*, 2018. https://www.srji.org/upload/iblock/957/The_practice_of_female_genital_mutilation_in_Dagestan_strategies_for_its_e limination_15.06.pdf

Акаев, Вахит, «Специфика современного чеченского Ислама,» (Specificity of the Modern Chechen Islam), Россия и Мусульманский Мир, 2008, №11

Al-Bukhari, Muhammad, *Sahih al-Bukhari*, https://sunnah.com/bukhari

Bykin, Igor, «В Дагестане сорвали аниме-фестиваль» (Anime Festival Disrupted in Dagestan), (26 Novebmer 2018), https://info24.ru/news/v-dagestane-sorvali-anime-festival-uchastnikov-nazvali-neformalami-i-prostitutkami.html

---

[48] «Все за власть: почему на Северном Кавказе «поддерживают» «Единую Россию»» (Everybody for the authority, why North Caucasus "supports" "United Russia"), (22 September 2021), https://newstracker.ru/article/general/22-09-2021/vse-za-vlast-pochemu-na-severnom-kavkaze-podderzhivayut-edinuyu-rossiyu
[49] Margareta Cederfelt, "The Nemtsov Murder and Rule of Law in Russia," Organisation for Security and Co-operation in Europe, (30 July 2020), pp.27-28

Cederfelt, Margareta, *"The Nemtsov Murder and Rule of Law in Russia,"* Organisation for Security and Co-operation in Europe, 30 July 2020

"Chechen Woman Abducted By Police In Daghestan May Face 'Honor Killing,' Rights Groups Warn," RadioFreeEurope (11 June 2021), https://www.rferl.org/a/russia-daghestan-chechnya-shelter-attacked/31302426.html

«Христианские мученики в Дагестане», (15 Сентября 2013), http://kavpolit.com/xristianskie-mucheniki-v-dagestane

"Dagestan, Chechnya: Christians still face kidnap, murder; now war", EA Foundation (21 September 1999), http://www.ea.org.au/ea-family/Religious-Liberty/DAGESTAN--CHECHNYA--CHRISTIANS-STILL-FACE-KIDNAP--MURDER--NO

Дудаева, Алла, *Миллион Первый*, Ультра Культура, Екатеринбург, 2005

Durie, Mark, *The Third Choice*, Deror Books, 2010

Female Genital Mutilations of Girls in Dagestan (Russian Federation), 2017, https://www.srji.org/upload/iblock/c94/fgm_dagestan_2016_eng_final_edited_2017.pdf

Hamzatov, Lechi, «Чеченский пейнтбол» (Chechen Paintball), (6 July 2010), https://www.bbc.co.uk/blogs/russian/northcaucasus/2010/07/post-30.html

"'I Will Destroy You': Chechen Leader Threatens Kid On Instagram," RadioFreeEurope (20 May 2021), https://www.rferl.org/a/chechnya-kadyrov-instagram/31265313.html

Ibn Majah, Muhammad, *Sunan Ibn Majah*, https://sunnah.com/ibnmajah

Кадыров, Ахмат «Война среди нас самих!» (War Is Among Us!), https://web.archive.org/web/20110903225543/http://www.kadirov.ru/node/8

Кадыров, Ахмат, «Через референдум Чечня прозреет!» (Chechnya will see the light through referendum!”, https://web.archive.org/web/20110724061104/http://kadirov.ru/node/88

«Кадыров Ахмад (Ахмат-хаджи),» (Kadyrov Ahmad (Ahmat-hajji), Кавказский Узел, https://www.kavkaz-uzel.eu/articles/13679/

Khazov-Kassia, Sergei, «««У вас так принято». Как полиция беглых девушек выдает» (“These are your customs”. How police return escaped young women), (26 March 2021), https://www.svoboda.org/a/31170506.html

«Кровная Месть – как теперь убивают на Кавказе,» (Blood Feud – how people are get killed in the Caucasus nowadays), Кавказский Узел, https://www.kavkaz-uzel.eu/articles/296137/

Милославский, Г.В., Петросян, Ю.А., Пиотровский, М.Б., «`Ада», (ʻAdat), *Ислам: Энциклопедический Словарь*, М.: Наука, 1991, стр. 11

al-Misri, Ahmad ibn Naqib, *Reliance of the Traveller: A Classic Manual of Islamic Sacred Law*, (tr.) Nuh Ha Mim Keller, Amana Publications, Maryland: 2011

«Многоженство в России: миф или реальность?» (Polygamy in Russia: myth or reality?), (19 May 2015), https://www.bbc.com/russian/society/2015/05/150519_tr_russia_polygamy_discussion

Moskowitz, Eli, “Sweden Sentences Two Russians for Attempted Murder of Chechen Blogger”, OCCRP (12 January 2021), https://www.occrp.org/en/daily/13609-sweden-sentences-two-russians-for-attempted-murder-of-chechen-blogger

«Муфтий Северного Кавказа призвал обрезать всех женщин России» (North Caucasus Mufti called for circumcision of all women of Russia), (17 August 2016), https://www.interfax.ru/russia/524002

«Муфтий Северного Кавказа оказался от призыва обрезать всех женщин» (North Caucasus Mufti took back his words to circumcise all women), (17 August 2016), https://www.interfax.ru/russia/524033

«На Северном Кавказе многоженство снова становится нормой? (Does Polygamy in the North Caucasus become a norm again?), (1 September 2018), https://rus.azattyq.org/a/mistresses-in-law-becomes-a-norm-in-northern-caucasus/29465336.html

An-Nawawi, Yahya ibn Sharaf, *Riyad as-Salihin*, https://sunnah.com/riyadussalihin

«"Проект" рассказал о «второй жене» Рамазана Кадырова» ("Project" reported about the "Second wife" of Ramazan Kadyrov), (7 April 2021), https://meduza.io/feature/2021/04/07/proekt-rasskazal-o-vtoroy-zhene-ramzana-kadyrova-i-novoy-lichnosti-ego-pervoy-suprugi

«Radical Islam spreading in troubled North Caucasus", (31 May 2011), https://barnabasfund.org/AU/News/Archives/Radical-Islam-spreading-in-troubled-North-Caucasus

«Рамзан Кадыров стал главой Всемирного конгресса чеченцев», Кавказский Узел (13 Октября 2010), https://www.kavkaz-uzel.eu/articles/175480/

Rassokhin, Alexandr, «Егор Крид обошел Махачкалу стороной», (Egor Krid bypassed Makhachkala), (10 September 2018), https://www.kommersant.ru/doc/3737532

Rippin, Andrew, *Muslims, Their Religious Beliefs and Practices*, Routledge, London: 2012

«Родственники подростка, назвавшего Кадырова шайтаном, извинились на камеру,» (Relatives of the teenager who called Kadyrov shaytan apologised on tape), BBC News (20 Мая 2021), https://www.bbc.com/russian/news-57182946

Steinmetz, Katy, "A Victim of the Anti-Gay Purge in Chechnya Speaks Out: 'The Truth Exists,'" Time (26 July 2019), https://time.com/5633588/anti-gay-purge-chechnya-victim/

Ten Dam, Caspar, "How to Feud and Rebel: 2. Histories, Cultures and Grievances of the Chechens and Albanians," *Iran and Caucasus*, 15 (2011), pp.235-271

Теслова, Елена «Численность Российской Уммы достигла 25 миллионов человек,» (Russian Ummah has reached 25 million people), Anadolu Agency (07 March 2018), https://www.aa.com.tr/ru/заголовки-дня/численность-российской-уммы-достигла-25-млн-человек/1081820

At-Tirmidhi, Muhammad, *Jami' at Tirmidhi*, https://sunnah.com/tirmidhi

"Top Chechen Official Claims Blood Feud Against Blogger," VOA (12 March 2019), https://www.voanews.com/europe/top-chechen-official-claims-blood-feud-against-blogger

Ульянов, Марк, «Кадыров приказал объявить кровную месть родственникам напавших на полицейских,» (Kadyrov orderd to declare a blood feud against the relatives of the people who attacked policemen), Lenta.Ru (31 декабря 2020), https://lenta.ru/news/2020/12/31/mest/

Vatchagaev, Maribek, "Russian Orthodox Church Redraws Its Map of the North Caucasus," The Jamestown Foundation (25 January 2013), https://jamestown.org/program/russian-orthodox-church-redraws-its-map-of-the-north-caucasus-2/

«В Грозном состоялось собрание, посвященное Дню памяти и скорби народов ЧР,» (A meeting dedicated to the Day of remembrance and sorrow of the Chechen people was held in

Grozny) Грозный Информ (10 Мая 2018), https://www.grozny-inform.ru/news/politic/95935/

«Все за власть: почему на Северном Кавказе «поддерживают» «Единую Россию»» (Everybody for the authority, why North Caucasus "supports" "United Russia"), (22 September 2021), https://newstracker.ru/article/general/22-09-2021/vse-za-vlast-pochemu-na-severnom-kavkaze-podderzhivayut-edinuyu-rossiyu

Wooding, Dan, "Evangelical Cleansing" in Chechnya," (June 1999), https://christiananswers.net/q-eden/persec-chechnya1.html

«Женское Обрезание» (Female Circumcision), https://muftiyatrd.ru/fatawa/zhenskoe-obrezanie

«18-летнюю жительницу Швеции родные в Дагестане хотели насильно выдать замуж и угрожали убийством чести» (Relatives of an 18-year old citizen of Sweden were trying to forcefully marry her and threatened her with honour killing), (2 July 2021), https://www.currenttime.tv/a/letnyaya-devushka-uehala-iz-dagestana--ubiystvo-chesti/31337790.html

Chapter 7

BEDIÜZZAMAN SAID NURSI
A Politico-Religious Opponent of the Early Turkish State

Thomas Messick[1]

O my Turkish brother... Your nationhood has fused with Islam and may not be separated from it. If you do separate them, you will be finished... We do not recognize as Turks those who embrace misguidance and want to abandon Islamic nationhood, which holds all the true cause of pride of the Turks. We consider them to be Europeans hiding behind the screen of Turkishness! Because even if they claim to be Turkists a hundred thousand times over, they could not deceive the people of truth. For their actions and works would give the lie to what they claim.[2]

I   Introduction

Said Nursi was a very unique Islamic leader during a tumultuous time; witnessing the fall of the Ottoman Empire and the rise of the Republic of Turkey in the prime of his life. Nursi's life is broadly divided into three stages: the *Old Said* (1878–1922), the *New Said* (1922–1950), and the *Third Said* (1950–1960).[3] These three periods illustrate the changing context of Anatolia during Nursi's lifespan; the demise of the Ottoman Empire (1878–1923), the establishment of the Turkish Republic under the Republican People's Party (RPP) (1922–1950), and the rise of the *Demokrat Parti* (Democratic Party) (1950–1960). Colin Turner claims these three

---

[1] Thomas Messick is a PhD Candidate at Melbourne School of Theology and the Internship Director at Crescent Project.

[2] Bediuzzaman Said Nursi, *Emirdağ Letters: From the Risale-i Nur Collection-8* (Berkeley, CA: Nur Publishers, 2019), 375, 486.

[3] Students of Bediuzzaman Said Nursi, *The Author of the Risale-i Nur; Bediuzzaman Said Nursi; The Authorised Biography; His Works, Method and Approach* (Turkey: Risale Press, 2016), 33.

periods of Nursi's life also reflect three unique stages in Nursi's understanding of politics.[4] In each of these eras, Nursi acted uniquely in response to the changing times. It should not be inferred then that his theological and political ideas had no continuity over his lifespan. Even the *Risale-i Nur* itself bears the fruit of ideas which Nursi's wrote in all these periods. The division of *Old Said*, *New Said*, and *Third Said* does not completely describe the progression of Nursi's thoughts, though these were his own way of segregating the stages of his life.[5] In reality, he never let go of his 'old self' but the 'old' was simply absorbed, and at times, transformed by the 'new.' The *Third Said* was really a re-manifestation of the *Old Said* with the *New Said's* experience. Nursi often called himself the *Old Said* when he had to say something difficult; something he did not want to be associated with his 'new self' which he felt was divorced from politics and represented living for the next world as a godly Muslim. Nursi formed the *Third Said* to set himself apart from his life of bondage under the RPP (*Halk Partisi* Peoples Party) and to again openly engage in politics with the Democratic party whom he saw as a sort of 'saviour' from the RPP's aggression against Islam.

Several scholars have emphasised Nursi's 'famous' quote, "I seek refuge with God, from Satan, and from politics," to imply that Nursi's primary life's goal was apolitical.[6] It is not surprising that some scholars present Nursi's life mission as apolitical because Nursi himself and his students claimed they were not political, even while they were knee-deep in political activities. Nursi alleges, "We act solely for religion and belief and have no political aims."[7] What exactly does Nursi mean by this statement? Using the above quote from Nursi under a section heading entitled, "Avoidance of Politics," Salih Sayilgan briefly mentions Nursi's political engagement as the *Old Said* but quickly emphasises Nursi's abandonment of politics as the *New Said*.[8] What is interesting is that Sayilgan never mentions Nursi's full-blown political involvement as the *Third Said*. Other scholars such as Sükran Vahide and Turner

[4] Colin Turner, *Qur'an Revealed: A Critical Analysis of Said Nursi's Epistles of Light* (Berlin: Gerlach Press, 2013), 537.

[5] Lois W. Banner, 2009. "Biography as History." *American Historical Review* 114, no. 3 (2009): 579–586.

[6] Nursi, *Letters; 1928-1932; Collection: From the Risale-i Nur Collection-2*, 67.

[7] Bediuzzaman Said Nursi, *The Rays Collection: From the Risale-i Nur Collection-4* (Berkeley, CA: Nur Publishers, 2019), 366.

[8] Salih Sayilgan, *An Islamic Jihad of Nonviolence: Said Nursi's Model* (Eugene, OR: Cascade Books, 2019), 105.

acknowledge Nursi's involvement in politics but they, at times, soften Nursi's role and responsibility in forming a rocky relationship with Mustafa Kemal and the *devlet* (state).

In this paper, I argue that Nursi was an unyielding politico-religious opponent to Mustafa Kemal and the Republican People's Party (RPP) as they sought to reform (*inkılap*) and subjugate the religion of Islam to the *devlet*. First, we will explore how Nursi was unquestionably captivated by politics in both the beginning and last part of his life (*Old* and *Third Said*). Next, we will analyse Nursi's political-religious life under the RPP's one-party rule of Turkey from 1923-1950. Here, it will be necessary to give an overview of some of the early Turkish Republic's reforms under Mustafa Kemal and the RPP to explain how Nursi reacted to these new reforms. Last, we will demonstrate how Nursi was not only political in the first and last part of his life, but throughout his life, including the period from 1923-1950 where Nursi is called the *New Said*. Nursi's statements concerning politics are somewhat contradictory which requires an explanation.

2 The Politico-Religious Nature of Said Nursi as the Old and Third Said

2.1 *The Old Said's Political Life (1907-1922)*

Though the *New Said* would later claim to renounce political involvement, the *Old Said* was a full-fledged politician. To strengthen Islamic unity, Nursi supported the Young Turks' constitutional ideas which stemmed from Nemik Kemal.[9] Nemik Kemal promoted constitutionalism based on the *Şeriat* (Islamic Law).[10] While living in the city of Van in the late 1800s, Nursi gained significant experience in politics.[11] This increased political desire led Nursi to Istanbul in 1907 where he sought to introduce his own method of education

---

[9] Mustafa Gökhan Şahin, "Said Nursi and the Nur Movement in Turkey: An Atomistic Approach," *Digest of Middle East Studies* 20, no. 2 (2011): 230; Turner, *Qur'an Revealed*, 540.
[10] Şerif Mardin, *The Genesis of Young Ottoman Thought: A Study in the Modernization of Turkish Political Ideas* (Princeton, NJ: Princeton University Press, 1962), 313–314; See also Students of Bediuzzaman Said Nursi, *The Authorised Biography*, 69.
[11] Ian S. Markham, *An Introduction to Said Nursi* (Burlington, VT: Ashgate Publishing, 2016), 18.

reform within the Ottoman Empire, particularly in Eastern Anatolia.[12]

In 1909, Nursi was accused of politically participating in the *31 March Incident* through his alliance with the Committee of Union and Progress (CUP).[13] Before a military court, Nursi rejected the accusation and defended himself asserting,

> "If I was to be hanged unfairly, I will receive double the reward of a martyr. If I was to remain in prison under a government in which freedom [is only]...lip service..., the most desirable place must surely be prison. It is far superior to die as someone oppressed than to live as the oppressor."[14]

Nursi's statement to the court almost seems 'prophetic' as this would be the first of many occasions Nursi would defend himself before Turkish courts claiming the *devlet* was the oppressor while he was the political victim under their heavy hand.

2.2 The Third Said's Political Life (1949-1960)

At the end of his life, the *Third Said* was so engrossed in politics that he began providing political commentary on the various political parties in Turkey.[15] After denouncing the *Millet Partisi* (Nation Party) and the *Halk Partisi* (People's Party or RPP) and endorsing the *Demokrat Partisi* (Democratic Party or DP), Nursi sought to cover his previous apolitical statements by claiming,

> For the sake of the religious Democrats and particularly persons like Adnan Menderes, I have dwelt on politics for one or two days, although I have given them up for the past thirty-five years.[16]

Nursi went as far as to quote a speech made by Prime Minister Adan Menderes in Konya about secularism (*laiklik*) and religious education in his *magnum opus* collection of works called the *Risale-I*

---

[12] Sukran Vahide, *Islam In Modern Turkey: An Intellectual Biography Of Bediuzzaman Said Nursi*, ed. Ibrahim M. Abu-Rabi (Albany, NY: State University of New York Press, 2005), 214.

[13] Students of Bediuzzaman Said Nursi, *The Authorised Biography*, 90; Colin Turner and Hasan Horkuc, *Said Nursi: Makers of Islamic Civilization* (London: I. B. Tauris, 2009), 14, 115.

[14] Said Nursi, *Divan-I Örfi*, 11–12, quoted in Sukran Vahide, *The Author of the Risale-i Nur; Bediuzzaman Said Nursi* (Berkeley, CA: Nur Publishers, 2019), 97.

[15] Bediuzzaman Said Nursi, *Emirdağ Letters*, 430–432; 471.

[16] Ibid., 432.

Nur to defend Menderes from his critics.[17] Here, Nursi asserts, "The Prime Minister's speech in Konya consists of true facts rebuffing those pretexts."[18] This political speech continues to be printed in the *Risaleler* making Nursi's theological treatises fundamentally political.

In a letter written by Nursi to the DP, he says,

> Our way obliges us not to consider the world and politics as far as it is possible. But now we are obliged to consider it. We saw that the Democrats may assist us against those two fearsome currents... In this respect, we know ourselves compelled to keep the Democrats in power, for the good of the Qur'an. We expect nothing from them; rather, since with their policies they oppose the first two currents.[19]

Though Nursi and the *Nurcu* (followers of Nursi) may not have seemed as political under the RPP's majority from 1923-1950, when the time was right under the DP, the *Nurculuk* (The Nur Movement) became openly political. Nursi saw the Democrats as a 'saviour' who delivered him and the *Nurcu* from a life of suffering under the RPP.[20] The DP even invited Nursi to work as the Director of Religious Affairs.[21] Interestingly, the death of the Democratic Party corresponds with the death of Nursi. As the Turkish military took action against DP leaders, it also moved Nursi's grave from its original site in Urfa to a secret location, preventing Nursi's followers from making a pilgrimage to his tomb.[22]

Like their *üstad* (master), Nursi's students openly embraced the Democratic Party which is expressed in a letter addressed to Adnan Menderes, saying,

> Although our Master Bediuzzaman has given up politics these last thirty-five years, *we members of the Democrat Party* and Nur students are certain that *he is now working* with all his strength, *his students*, and *his teachings to keep the Democrat Party in power,*

---

[17] Ibid., 467.
[18] Ibid., 468 n170.
[19] Ibid., 473.
[20] Ibid., 313, 332; 473–474.
[21] Ibid., 475.
[22] Vahide, *Islam In Modern Turkey*, 364; M. Hakan Yavuz, *Islamic Political Identity in Turkey* (Oxford: Oxford University Press, 2005), 36, 63; Turner and Horkuc, *Said Nursi*, 37.

for the sake of the Qur'an and Islam and this country (emphasis mine).[23]

Nurcu claimed,
"With their support for Islamic unity, the Nurjus form a significant mass backing the Democrats" and "there is a revival of such marks of Islam as the call to prayer and religious instruction and work with the Qur'an, and a start has been made to repair the harms caused to the Qur'an by the former party."[24]

Apparently, the *Nurcu* believed they had such an influence in the DP that

"the Democrats were obliged to placate and gratify... the Nurjus" in order "to prevent" other political parties from "overturning the Democrats."[25]

Though Nursi claims he expected nothing in return from the DP, a debatable statement in itself, his students in fact did expect something in return from the DP for their political loyalty. In a letter written on April 15, 1957, Nursi's students signed their names, "In the name of Democrat Nur Students," indicating that the *Nurcu* had fully integrated with the DP and were openly members of the party.[26] The Nur Movement, like its founder, was not only religious, but politico-religious.

Scholars do not debate whether Nursi engaged in politics in the first and last part of his life defined as the *Old* and *Third Said*. Clearly, Nursi was a politician in the *Second Constitutional Era* of the Ottoman Empire and he was highly involved in political affairs during the rule of the Democratic Party. Essentially, the entirety of Nursi's life is couched between two periods where he was openly political, illustrating his political nature that spanned across his life. What is disputed among scholars is Nursi's involvement in politics as the *New Said* from roughly 1922–1950, sandwiched between these two political stints. Did Nursi genuinely abandon politics during this period and become a quietest? Or, were there other reasons,

---

[23] Nursi, *Emirdağ Letters*, 471.
[24] Ibid., 308–309.
[25] Ibid., 310.
[26] Ibid., 480.

stemming from the new Republic that forced Nursi into appearing politically quiet?

3 The Politico-Religious Nature of Said Nursi under RPP Single-Party Rule (1922-1950)

3.1 Overview of Early Turkish Reforms

Scholars such as Erik J. Zürcher, Marshall G.S. Hodgson, and M. Hakan Yavuz believe that Mustafa Kemal wanted the Republic of Turkey to exemplify a complete break with its Ottoman Islamic heritage; so much so that it seemed he wanted a new citizen of the Republic to "own himself a traitor to all that the Ottoman state had stood for."[27] The new Turkism conceived by Mehmet Ziya Gökalp, i.e. Turkish Nationalism, would reject Ottomanism and Islamism and narrowly define what it meant to be a 'Turk.'[28] Islam was seen as backward and a detriment to the new Republic which was to be created upon secular values.[29]

Gökalp was instrumental in establishing the *Unification of Education Act* in 1924.[30] This law further secularized Turkish citizens and removed many public Islamic presentations of faith. Şerif Mardin says the *Unification of Education Act* in 1924 brought about four things:

> It abolished the caliphate,
> it abolished the Ministry of Religious Affairs, it established the monopoly of the state overall educational activities, and it vested the power to rule on religious matters to a General Directorate of Religious Affairs, which functioned under the prime minister's office.[31]

This law gave the new Republic complete control over all educational institutions in Anatolia and the ability to successfully convey their

---

[27] Yavuz, *Islamic Political Identity in Turkey*, 47; Erik J. Zürcher, *Turkey: A Modern History* (London: Bloomsbury, 2017), 289; Marshall G. S. Hodgson, *The Venture of Islam: The Gunpower Empires And Modern Times* (Chicago, IL: University of Chicago Press, 1977), 3:264.

[28] Shaw, *History Ottoman Empire and Turkey* (Cambridge: Cambridge University Press, 1977), 2:262.

[29] Yavuz, *Islamic Political Identity in Turkey,* 46.

[30] Ibid., 50.

[31] Şerif Mardin, "The Body Corporate and the Social Body," in *Mirror for The Muslim Prince: Islam and The Theory of Statecraft*, ed. by Mehrzad Boroujerdi (Syracuse, NY: Syracuse University Press, 2013), 292, EBSCOhost.

secular ideologies to all citizens.[32] Joshua D. Hendrick argues that the Kemalists intentionally used education to train future generations of children to "protect and defend eternally Turkish independence and the Turkish Republic."[33]

In Turkey, Mustafa Kemal was chosen as the national symbol of the Republic, also known as Atatürk or 'Father of the Turks.'[34] To speak against him is a high crime, even treason, as Kemal represents the essence of the Turkish *devlet*. Andrew Mango claims that Kemal "personified the Republic that he founded" and

> is the Republic's symbol, pictured on stamps, coins and banknotes, portrayed on the walls of offices and homes, quoted in and out of seasons to buttress arguments, presented as a guiding star, an ideal to inspire and follow.[35]

Practically, many Turks idolise Atatürk in their daily lives and would never tolerate anyone speaking of him negatively. There is somewhat of a reversal of Kemal's high position under the *Justice and Development Party* (AKP) with President Erdoğan, but many Turks still highly respect Atatürk's central position in Turkish society and history.

Kemal and the Republic, taking a French understanding of secularism, namely *laïcité*, divided politics and religion in such a way that had never been seen before in the Ottoman Empire. *Laïcité* gave the *devlet* the power to control religion in whatever way it felt was healthy for the *devlet* and society. Jenny B. White clarifies the difference between *laïcité* and other forms of secularism such as what is found in the U.S., stating,

> The Turkish state's position on religion (*laiklik*) is more accurately translated as "laicism," the subordination of religion to the state, than secularism, a separation of church and state. The term 'secular' is used here to refer to a non-religious identity or one that consigns religious beliefs to the private, rather than the public realm. The laic state controls the education of religious professionals and their assignment to

---

[32] Joshua D. Hendrick, *Gülen: The Ambiguous Politics of Market Islam in Turkey and the World* (New York: NYU Press, 2013), 124–125.
[33] Hendrick, *Gülen*, 124–125.
[34] Andrew Mango, "Atatürk," in *The Cambridge History of Turkey: Turkey in the Modern World,* ed. Reşat Kasaba (Cambridge: Cambridge University Press, 2008), 4:147, 165.
[35] Ibid., 147.

mosques, controls the content of religious education, and enforces laws about the wearing of religious symbols and clothing in public spaces and institutions.[36]

Instead of an integration of *Şeriat* and *Kanun* (Ottoman law outside of the *Şeriat*), with politics informing religion and religion informing politics as it was in the Ottoman Empire, *laïcité* demanded religion to kneel to the *devlet*.

The ideology of the early Turkish state is called Kemalism, named after Mustafa Kemal. The six principles of Kemalism are Republicanism, Revolutionism/Reformism, Nationalism, Populism, Statism, and Laicism.[37] The term *inkılap* that is translated 'revolution/reform' was the primary way Kemal and the *devlet* carried out their policies and the other principles within the nation. Mesut Yeğen claims that the 'politics of *inkılap*' went hand in hand with a 'politics of oppression' to implement 'the politics of assimilation,' including controlling and Turkifying the Kurds. [38] The *devlet* under the RPP also used the 'politics of *inkılap*' to reform Islam, and thus, remove Islam's integration with the *devlet* as the foundation of Turkish society. Ahmad Feroz points out that many people

> especially resented the policy of laicism/secularism, and never understood how they had benefited from it. It was all very well for the RPP to claim that what was being done was 'for the people', but why was it being done 'in spite of the people', as the party's slogan had it?[39]

Yavuz adds,

> This attempt to disengage the Turkish state from an Islamic worldview considerably widened the gap between the elite (the center) and the masses (periphery).[40]

---

[36] Jenny B. White, "Islam and politics in contemporary Turkey," in *The Cambridge History of Turkey*, 4:4, 357.

[37] Feroz Ahmad, "Politics and Political Parties in Republican Turkey," in *The Cambridge History of Turkey*, 4:230.

[38] Mesut Yeğen, "The Kurdish Question in Turkey," in *Nationalism and Politics in turkey; Political Islam, Kemalism and the Kurdish Issue*, ed. Marlies Casier and Joost Jongerden (London: Routledge, 2010), 72.

[39] Feroz Ahmad, "Politics and Political Parties in Republican Turkey," *The Cambridge History of Turkey*, 233.

[40] Yavuz, *Islamic Political Identity in Turkey*, 48.

After the Kemalists' initial reforms, from their perspective, it seemed Islam had been conquered and controlled.

3.1.1 Rise of Islamist Movements

In reality, the Kemalists could not erase hundreds of years of Islamic culture that permeated not only the landscape of Anatolia with mosques and Islamic symbols, but also the hearts of millions of Turks. As was happening across the Muslim world, Islamic movements were springing up to respond to the impact of Westernization and authoritarian governments.[41] Groups such as the *Muslim Brotherhood* (1926) and the *Jamaat e-Islami* (1941) are influential examples of such reactionary Islamic movements.[42] Said Nursi established his Islamist movement as a direct response to the Kemalist attempt to suppress Islam from the public sphere in Turkey and his collection of works, the *Risale-i Nur* apologetically combated its reforms.[43]

Utilizing the word 'Islamist' naturally forces a definition as to what this means in the context of Said Nursi and the Nur Movement. While 'Islamism' is often characterised as militant and violent, for good reason, Roxanne Euben suggests it is better to recognize a variety of meanings in the term 'Islamism.'[44] Specifically, Euben claims Islamism is

> an interpretive framework rather than a set of propositions and strategies to which every Islamist subscribes in the same way or to the same degree.[45]

Euben goes on to say, "Islamism refers to those 20th- and 21st-century Muslim groups and thinkers who seek to recuperate the scriptural foundations of the Islamic community, excavating and

---

[41] Antony Black, *The History of Islamic Political Thought: From the Prophet to the Present*, 2nd ed. (Edinburgh: Edinburgh University Press, 2011), 308; Hodgson, *The Venture of Islam*, 3:391–392.

[42] Black, *The History of Islamic Political Thought*, 308; Hodgson, *The Venture of Islam*, 3:391–392.

[43] Yavuz, *Islamic Political Identity in Turkey*, 33; Bediüzzaman Said Nursi, *Tarihçe-i Hayat (Lügatli)* (Şahdamar Yayınları, 2013), 151.

[44] Roxanne Euben, "Fundamentalism," in *Islamic Political Thought: An Introduction*, ed. Gerhard Bowering (Princeton, NJ: Princeton University Press, 2015), under "Islamism: Origins and General Characteristics."

[45] Ibid.

reinterpreting them for application to the contemporary social and political world."[46]

Considering the above descriptions of Islamism, The Nur movement can be considered an 'Islamist' movement for several reasons. First, the Nur movement arose like other Islamist movements in the 20th century as a result of 19th-century Islamic reformist ideas from ideologues such as Jamal al-Din al-Afghani (1939–1997).[47] Thus, the Nur movement shares Islamist ambitions to save the former lands of Islam, in this case, those lands in the Ottoman Empire, from Western hegemony, which was thought to have caused moral decay in Muslim society.[48]

Second, assuming that Nursi did not primarily desire immediate political results (which he did in some ways), not all Islamist groups necessarily demand immediate political outcomes and some have long-term goals for gradual societal change. Turner separates Nursi from an Islamist framework, claiming that Nursi gave no 'blueprint' for an Islamic government and utilised a 'gradualist approach,' as opposed to insisting on immediate political results.[49] However, Paul L. Heck believes the Muslim Brotherhood, clearly labeled as an Islamist movement, has generally held a 'gradualist approach' to societal change and according to Fawaz A. Gerges, the Brotherhood has also claimed to be 'apolitical.'[50] Nursi and his Islamic movement would fit both these characteristics of the Muslim Brotherhood as they allege to be both apolitical and to use a gradualist, non-violent approach for Islamic reform. Though Nursi, like Sayyed Qutb who wrote his *Milestones* in prison, also penned the bulk of his work, the *Risale-i Nur*, while in prison and exile, Nursi did not promote or justify violence as means to rebel against state institutions.[51] Nursi did, however, justify and exemplify the need to challenge states in former Muslim lands who sought to promote secular authoritative knowledge over religious knowledge as a basis for societal norms. Though Nursi may not have communicated a

---

[46] Ibid.
[47] Ibid.
[48] Ibid.
[49] Turner, *Qur'an Revealed*, 539, 555.
[50] Paul L. Heck, "Knowledge," in *Islamic Political Thought*, under The Politics of Religious Diversity; Fawaz A. Gerges, *Making the Arab World: Nasser, Qutb, and the Clash That Shaped the Middle East* (Princeton, NJ: Princeton University Press, 2018), 62.
[51] Gerges, *Making the Arab World*, 142; Vahide, *Islam in Modern Turkey*, 214.

detailed 'blue-print' as to what Muslim society should look like, he did provide a general structure with the religion of Islam as its epicenter, categorically placing Nursi within the Islamist tradition.

3.2 Nursi on Mustafa Kemal

Scholars often reference Nursi's time in Ankara in 1922 to highlight Nursi's transition from his first stage of life (*Old Said*) to his second stage of life (*New Said*).[52] During this time, scholars, as well as Nursi himself, stipulate that a significant shift occurred in Nursi's thinking that transformed him from being a politician into a *pir* (respected religious guide), leaving behind his life of politics which primarily defined his public identity as the *Old Said*. While I challenge this assertion in the next section, here I am emphasising that Nursi's meeting with Kemal and the other parliamentarians in Ankara produced the *New Said* who was defined not only as a *pir*, but as a political opponent of the Republic who subsequently became a political prisoner.

After publishing an article named *Hutuvat-ı Sitte* (The Six Steps) as a polemic against the British occupation of Istanbul, several in the Turkish Independence movement, including Kemal, invited Nursi to Ankara.[53] Kemal's objective was to recruit Nursi to work as a religious figure in the new Republic and the two had multiple conversations. However, these conversations faltered as Nursi became angry at the many parliamentarians, including Kemal, who were not living out or promoting the religious practices of Islam. Nursi was particularly concerned that the parliamentarians were not regularly performing the *salat* (prayers).[54] Moving from attacking the British, Nursi began attacking the new Republic by writing a polemical tract targeting the parliamentarian's lack of Islamic devotion.[55] Specifically, Nursi called on the parliamentarians to repent of their nominal religious behaviour and to not only perform *salat* but to institute the religion of Islam at the foundation of the future Republic.[56] Needless to say, this polemical tract did not sit well with Kemal and he was not excited about Islam playing a key role in the forming Republic of Turkey.

---

[52] Turner and Horkuc, *Said Nursi*, 25; Vahide, *The Author of the Risale-i Nur; Bediuzzaman Said Nursi*, 188.
[53] Nursi, *Tarihçe-i Hayat (Lügatli)*, 135.
[54] Ibid., 135.
[55] Ibid., 136–138.
[56] Ibid., 136.

After Kemal's death, Nursi made several derogatory statements about Kemal, who died of cirrhosis of the liver.[57] Nursi felt he had a duty to point out Kemal's bad deeds. He opposed the idolisation of Kemal within the Turkish *devlet* stating,

> compared with the sake of the nation and government and the laws of justice, which are a manifestation of divine sovereignty, what importance has the sake of someone who is dead and no longer has any connection with the government?[58]

Writing from Denizli prison, Nursi alleges that it was Kemal who established atheism in Turkey, asserting,

> For the love of that dreadful dead man was being inculcated [indoctrinated: *telkin edilmek*] in all the schools, government departments, and in the people.[59]

At the time, even today, such strong and derogatory statements about Kemal were enough to be convicted and sentenced to prison in Turkey. With Nursi displaying such intense opposition to the *devlet's* most loved iconic figure, it is astounding that he was not executed by the *devlet*.

3.3 Nursi on Turkish Nationalism and Reforms

Concerning the RPP's reforms, Nursi said, I do

> "not accept your injurious, dangerous, arbitrary principles, which in reality are without benefit and spring from unbelief and from Europe," and I do "not accept its applications so you made me suffer it."[60]

As is implied by Nursi's statement, Nursi did not think much of 'Europe', particularly Europe's ideologies that challenged Islamic knowledge and which were now intermingling with Turkish secularism. Nursi refused to endorse the RPP, rebelled against its

---

[57] Nursi, *The Rays Collection: From the Risale-i Nur Collection-4*, 382; Mango, "Atatürk," 168; Zürcher, *Turkey, 185*.
[58] Nursi, *The Rays Collection: From the Risale-i Nur Collection-4*, 300, 407. Nursi believed that a love for Kemal, who was dead, was idolatrous.
[59] "*Çünkü bütün mekteplerde ve dairelerde ve halkta, o ölmüş dehşetli adamın muhabbeti telkin ediliyor.*" Bediüzzaman Said Nursi, *Şualar; Müellifi Bediüzzaman Said Nursi*, Risale-i Nur Külliyatından (İstanbul: RNK Neşriyat, 2015), 348; Nursi, *The Rays Collection: From the Risale-i Nur Collection-4*, 360.
[60] Nursi, *Letters*, 494–495.

reforms, and because of this, his mission was heavily regulated by the *devlet*. [61] While Nursi's mission was indeed religious, it was also political because it opposed the RPP's foundational political reforms.

With a historical perspective of Islam's integration with politics (explained in the next section), Nursi claimed that "since early times," "Turkish nationalism" was "blended and united with Islam."[62] Warning Turks, Nursi says,

> O my Turkish brother! [...] Your nationhood has fused with Islam and may not be separated from it. If you do separate them, you will be finished![63] We do not recognize as Turks those who embrace misguidance and want to abandon Islamic nationhood, which holds all the true cause of pride of the Turks. We consider them to be Europeans hiding behind the screen of Turkishness! Because even if they claim to be Turkists a hundred thousand times over, they could not deceive the people of truth. For their actions and works would give the lie to what they claim.[64]

The ideology of Turkism was seen by Nursi as a deceitful screen that had more to do with "Europeanism" than the Turkish nationality because the Turkish nation had, in Nursi's mind, been sacrificed by the innovation and the dismantlement of Islam's place in Anatolian society.[65] Nursi's Ottoman understanding of Islam's politico-religious nature defined his thinking and he was bound to politically conflict with Kemal and the Turkish *devlet*'s ideological requirement for *din* to submit to the *devlet*.

Additionally, Nursi felt Turkish Nationalism was a source of disunity and racism in Turkey. Nursi claims he was derided for his Kurdish ethnicity under the RPP and he notes how the court prosecutors called him 'Said the Kurd' as a racist remark rooted in the Kemalist understanding of Turkism.[66] Nursi addressed the racist nature of Turkish nationalism saying,

> At the promptings of Satan and suggestions of the people of misguidance, they say: "You are Turks. Thanks be to God,

---

[61] Markham, *An Introduction to Said Nursi*, 13.
[62] Nursi, *Letters*, 493–494.
[63] Ibid., 375.
[64] Ibid., 486.
[65] Ibid., 485, 487, 494.
[66] Nursi, *Emirdağ Letters*, 150.

among the Turks are religious scholars and people of perfection of every sort. Said is a Kurd. To work along with someone who does not share your nationality is unpatriotic." [...] I say to those pseudo-patriotic irreligious deviants who hide under the veil of Turkism and in reality, are enemies of the Turks: "I am closely and truly connected by means of an eternal, true brotherhood with the nation of Islam, with the believers of this country who are called Turks. On account of Islam, I have a proud and partial love for the sons of this land who for close on a thousand years victoriously carried the banner of the Qur'an to every corner of the world... Yes, according to race, I am not counted as a Turk but I have worked with all my strength, with complete eagerness, in compassionate and brotherly fashion, for the groups among the Turks of the God-fearing.[67]

Though ethnically Kurdish, Nursi believed he was a 'Turk' so to speak, based on his religion and his life experience of supporting the Ottoman Turkish *devlet*. From Nursi's point of view, contrary to Kemalism, Turkism divided the Turks and Kurds (and other ethnic groups) while Islam united the country. This was one more reason Nursi kept in his arsenal for not politically submitting to the RPP.

3.4 Nursi's Life as a Political Prisoner from (1925-1950)

As a result of his politico-religious views, Nursi spent his *New Said* life as a political prisoner where he was repeatedly prosecuted by the RPP under the law, *163'üncü madde-i kanun* (*Article 163*). According to Nursi, *Article 163* was a subjective law utilised by the *devlet* to regulate "anybody provoking religious sentiment that could threaten public order". This he refuted, "This article of the law cannot be taken as having limitless implication, without commentary and any limiting conditions."[68] Yet, this is exactly how the *devlet* used *Article 163* to control their political opponents, including Nursi.

Nursi's charges were consistent over the years under the RPP. Looking back over the charges from Eskisehir to Afyonkarahisar (Afyon), Nursi says,

I was arrested and sent to the prisons of Eskişehir, Kastamonu, and Denizli. This time they arrested me and sent me to Afyon... They accuse me as follows: 1) You have founded a political

---

[67] Nursi, *Letters*, 482, 483, 486, 487.
[68] Nursi, *Tarihçe-i Hayat (Lügatli)*, 247; Students of Bediuzzaman Said Nursi, *The Authorised Biography*, 268, 269.

society. 2) You publish ideas opposing the regime. 3) You harbor political aims.[69]

Nursi was also repeatedly accused of rebelling against Kemalism because he promoted Islamic dress such as the requirement for women to wear the Islamic veil.[70] According to Nursi, all his charges from the *devlet* were really motived by atheistic ideology, which he believed warred with the traditional Islamic society of Anatolia, stemming from the Ottoman Empire.[71]

In his last appearance in court in 1952 for writing *A Guide for Youth*, Nursi says,

> Thus, relying on hundreds of verses of the Qur'an, not only myself but all people of conscience are opposed to a temporary regime that has replaced the Qur'an's sacred laws, and on account of the anarchy of corrupt civilization and behind the screen of the liberties of the Republic is an absolute despotism, and may be used as a tool to tyrannize religious people.[72]

Nursi never gave up in his fight against Kemal and the Kemalists, and the Kemalists never surrendered in fighting him. Nursi believed his fight against Kemalism produced the fruit of the DP coming to power in 1950, claiming,

> *The Risale-i Nur's* spreading everywhere *has given rise* to the firm conviction that the Democrats support religion (emphasis mine).[73]

Nursi was a political prisoner practically until his death due to his audacious stance against the RPP reforms.

4 Said Nursi's Political Persona

While the *Tarihçe-i Hayati* presents Nursi's very life as the ideological antithesis to the Turkish *devlet* under the RPP, it also repeatedly alleges that Nursi and his students were apolitical. Nursi and his students claimed they were not political, even while they were knee-deep in political activities. Nursi alleges, "We act solely for

---

[69] Nursi, *The Rays Collection*, 494.
[70] Students of Bediuzzaman Said Nursi, *The Authorised Biography*, 270, 434.
[71] Ibid., 431.
[72] Nursi, *Emirdağ Letters*, 426.
[73] Ibid., 508.

religion and belief and have no political aims."[74] Nursi's students Sadık, İbrahim, and Zübeyier assert,

> The *Risale-i Nur* and the Nurjus have nothing to do with politics, and the *Risale-i Nur* can be the tool of nothing apart from divine pleasure, those attached to it do not want to get involved in social and political movements... [and the *Nurcu*s] have never grasped the club of politics."[75]

There is no shortage of such strong claims throughout the *Risaleler* but what is to be made of these contradictory statements and actions by Nursi and his students which clearly involved, and even promoted political involvement as an Islamic movement?

4.1 Nursi's Understanding of Politics and Religion

To understand why Nursi claimed that he was not involved in politics while also being involved in politics, we must first explore what Nursi means by the term 'politics' in opposition to his rivals in the *devlet*. Muhammad himself laid the foundation for a Muslim state.[76] Antony Black states that in the Islamic world, there was a "symbiosis" between religion and politics and there was "no clear demarcation... in Islamdom... between the political and the social."[77] In the Ottoman Empire, society was governed, influenced, and structured by religion; namely, the Islamic religion.[78] The *Şeriat* and *Kanun* (Ottoman law) determined the relationship between the sexes and what represented true *adalet* (justice) throughout society. The courts were based upon the *Şeriat* and *Kanun* and Islam was fully integrated with the *devlet* in such a way that politics was intrinsically religious and religion was fundamentally political. Black also claims that

> in the Islamic world, as in pre-modern Europe, politics and the state were not conceived as a category separate from other forms of activity, but as an integral part of religion, morality, law, or clan values... der Islam, even more than under

---

[74] Nursi, *The Rays Collection*, 366.
[75] Nursi, *Emirdağ Letters*, 318.
[76] Arthur Goldschmidt Jr., *A Concise History of the Middle East*, 6th ed. (Boulder, CO: Westview Press, 2002), 31.
[77] Black, *The West and Islam Religion and Political Thought in World History*, 17; Black, *The History of Islamic Political Thought*, 5.
[78] Judith Mendelsohn Rood, *Sacred Law in the Holy City: The Khedival Challenge to the Ottomans as Seen from Jerusalem, 1829-1841* (Leiden: Brill, 2004), 3, 212, 213.

Christianity, a great deal of political ideology was conducted in terms of *Religionspolitik*.[79]

The term *politico-religious* represents the same concept as *Religionspolitik* which we have applied to Nursi's political persona.

Nursi truly saw his mission as religious; yet, in the same way that Islam historically has not been divorced from political involvement, Nursi had no category for separating politics from religion in the way the new Turkish *devlet* required. In his defense speech for his involvement in the *31 March Incident,* Nursi asserted,

> Oh political leader! I had an honorable and good name with which I was to serve the nation of Islam; you shattered it.[80]

Here, Nursi is engaging in both political activity and fully integrating his Islamic religion, even calling the Ottoman Empire "the nation of Islam," which would have been quite natural for him in 1909. Nursi felt the 'East' was distinguished from the 'West' in that the Islamic religion consumed all areas of life and

> within the world of Islam, success in any activity can only be achieved by adherence to Islamic principles [and] there is no other way.[81]

According to Nursi, "Islam is the greatest humanity, and the Shari'a [is] the most virtuous of [all] civilizations."[82] Nursi believed "the world of Islam was destined to become the ideal city envisaged by Plato," a city where religion and politics were one in Nursi's mind.[83] Such an understanding of civilization included the integration of politics with religion which represented early Islam's model to regulate not only individuals but also social structures as well.[84] While Nursi certainly would not have used the term 'politico-religious' or '*Religionspolitik*' to define his political and religious philosophy, he held politics and Islam intertwined in the same hand within his teaching. This is why Nursi could claim in one continuous thought in his writing that he has "not become involved in politics"

---

[79] Black, *The History of Islamic Political Thought*, 5.
[80] Students of Bediuzzaman Said Nursi, *The Authorised Biography*, 79.
[81] Ibid., 111, 149.
[82] Ibid., 81.
[83] Ibid.
[84] Black, *The West and Islam Religion and Political Thought in World History*, 13.

while at the same time willingly rebelling against both Kemal and the *devlet*.[85]

4.2 Nursi's Allegiance to a Government Controlled by Islamic Knowledge

The struggle between Nursi, Kemal, and the *devlet* was one that concerned knowledge; specifically, the battle raged over authoritative knowledge which defined, then impacted society. Heck argues that as European ideas penetrated Muslim lands during the colonial period, this new knowledge then challenged traditional forms of Islamic knowledge.[86] While Turkey was never colonised so to speak, the Ottomans, then Turkey, were impacted by modernisation proceeding from the West. According to Heck, Islamic reformers met the challenge of Westernization by extending Islamic knowledge to "all spheres of life, including political and economic no less than ritual and moral."[87] The political realm became the stadium where secular and Islamic actors fought over authoritative knowledge.[88] Yet, as we learned above, Islam had been claiming to possess authoritative knowledge over all of society, including politics, since its inception. Nursi intrinsically had a *politico-religious* understanding of society proceeding from his Ottoman Islamic heritage.

In Anatolia, Kemalism's form of secularism based on France's *laïcité* clashed with Islam's traditional politico-religious nature and neither Nursi nor the ideologically driven *devlet* had any plans of backing down before their opponent. The *devlet* claimed superiority over Islamic knowledge to regulate society, for example, in the areas of dress and the relationship between the sexes, and Nursi continued to raise Islam's banner, refusing to let the *devlet*'s voice replace what he believed was Islam's rightful position as the designer and controller of a just society.[89] Nursi reprimanded the "heads of the Pharaoh-like society" for using "innovation" and "deviating from the straight path of religion."[90] Nursi was chastised by government officials for not implementing their reforms such as carrying out the *kamet* (call to prayer) in Turkish instead of Arabic.[91] Such conflicts

---

[85] Nursi, *The Rays Collection*, 416.
[86] Heck, "Knowledge," under "Introduction."
[87] Ibid.
[88] Heck, "Knowledge," under "Defining the Scope of Religious Knowledge."
[89] Zürcher, *Turkey*, 193.
[90] Nursi, *Letters*, 493.
[91] Ibid.

illustrated that there were irreconcilable differences between *laïcité* and Islam's politico-religious nature, of which the *devlet* and Nursi were the chief representatives.

The battle between the RPP and Nursi's Islam was primarily ideological but there was also a struggle for 'power'; specifically, who would hold the right to define what laws the state should legislate and implement in Turkish society. In the struggle between the Muslim Brotherhood and Egyptian President Gamal Abdel Nasser (1918-70), Gerges argues that conflicting ideologies were a background issue when compared to the raw struggle for power in Egypt.[92] The difference between Nursi's struggle with the RPP and the Brotherhood's struggle with Nassar is that when the RPP and Nursi began their ideological war, at the time, Nursi was not leading a massive Islamic movement with many loyal followers like the Brotherhood. In fact, Nursi built his base as a result of his struggle with the RPP over his years in exile and imprisonment. For Nursi, ideology was at the forefront of his retaliation against the *devlet*. The RPP was motivated by a pursuit of power.

Kemalism provided an ideological framework for the new Republic that contended with Nursi's modernist Islamic framework. Though Nursi was not necessarily motivated by seeking political power, the RPP believed that Nursi's Islamic ideology could be detrimental to their reformation plan. In this way, the struggle was over power because knowledge is a means of power and control. Controlling the flow of authoritative knowledge was especially important for the RPP in the early days of forming the Republic from the ruins of the Ottoman Empire. The ulema in the Ottoman Empire, as in other Muslim societies, knew that knowledge was attached to authority and authority gives power.[93] As politics and religion were intertwined in the Ottoman Empire, the Sultans could not ignore the influence of the ulema, who, according to Black, were powerful enough to stifle any intellectual development within society that did not conform with Islamic teaching.[94] Essentially, the Republic sought to accomplish what the Tanzimat attempted, that is, to remove the

---

[92] Gerges, *Making the Arab World*, 22–78.
[93] Black, *The West and Islam Religion and Political Thought in World History*, 107.
[94] Ibid., 155.

Islamic establishments' power over the state so the *devlet* could then have the freedom to control and regulate society by its own means.[95]

Though Nursi's very life was the antithesis of the Turkish *devlet's* ideology under the RPP, it important to acknowledge that Nursi was not opposed to the essence of the *devlet* during the early Republic. Nursi stood against the secular ideologies (secular knowledge) within the *devlet*; what he called 'Atheistic,' and later, 'Communistic' and 'Mason' parties within the *devlet* that opposed the ideological system of Islam.[96] Nursi frequently referred to those in the government who persecuted him as 'atheists,' and later on, 'anarchists' and 'communists,' but he continued to support the essence of the Turkish *devlet* as an institution to be regulated by Islam and instituted by God.

As a Muslim, Nursi felt that he had the right to stand upon the historical Islamic interpretation of the Qur'an and Hadith which held, in his mind, authority over the Turkish courts and the *devlet*.[97] Nursi followed the Shafi'i and Hanafi schools of Islamic Law above the *devlet*'s Islamic institutions (*diyanet*) and rejected the *devlet*'s Islamic reforms.[98] In his defense to the Afyon court, Nursi says:

> Unfair committee! The Qur'an of Miraculous Exposition has every century been the sacred, heavenly guide of three hundred and fifty million people, the program of all their happiness, and the sacred treasury of the life of this world and the next. If it is possible to deny numerous of its explicit verses, which do not bear interpretation, about the veiling of women, inheritance, polygamy, the recollection of God, instruction in religious knowledge and its dissemination, and the preservation of the marks of religion, and to make guilty of crimes all the authoritative Islamic interpreters of the law and all the Shaykh al-Islam's, and if you can annul the passage of time, quash the numerous court acquittals, and the legal pardons, and abolish confidentiality and the private side of things, and freedom of conscience and freedom of thought, and intellectual and scholarly opposition, and remove them from this country and its governments, you can make me

---

[95] Richard Bulliet, "Eqypt and the Ottoman Empire in the 19th Century," Columbia University, YouTube, 1:15:11, published October 19, 2011, https://youtu.be/i_5aDaUae58?t=2112.
[96] Nursi, *Emirdağ Letters*, 308, 310.
[97] Nursi, *The Rays Collection*, 428.
[98] Nursi, *Letters*, 493 (https://dergi.diyanet.gov.tr).

guilty of these things. Otherwise in the court of truth, the reality, and justice you will be awesomely guilty![99]

Undoubtedly, Nursi's choice for ultimate authority rested with Islam over the *devlet*. Nursi's allegiance to Islam's politico-religious authority as represented by the Qur'an and Hadith is clearly seen throughout the *Risale-i Nur* and in all periods of his life. There is no reason to think he ever changed his understanding that the religion of Islam should regulate the entirety of society, believing that even secular institutions such as the *devlet* were subjugated to Allah's *Şeriat*. In this way, Nursi's politico-religious teaching in the *Risaleler* was a political threat to the RPP.

5   Conclusion- Evaluating the Claim that Nursi was Apolitical

As noted in the introduction, several scholars have emphasised Nursi's 'famous' quote, "I seek refuge with God from Satan and from politics," to imply that Nursi's primary life's goal was apolitical.[100] Nursi made this statement first in Barla in one of his letters to his students during his first eight years of exile and then he quotes this again later in Emirdağ.[101] Nursi genuinely meant this statement as he spent much of his time in solitude reflecting upon the Qur'an, his life, and what he believed was the detrimental role of politics under the RPP. Nursi also sincerely intended other similar statements such as "the Old Said gave up cigarettes together with the newspapers, politics, and worldly conversation about politics."[102] As we have already seen, we know that Nursi's definition of politics proceeded from an Ottoman Islamic context that did not separate politics from religion. To use Black's language, there was a 'symbiosis' between politics and religion in Nursi's mind.[103] Considering this, along with the other considerations from this paper, we can summarise the following about Nursi's political persona.

First, Nursi's 'conversion experience' from the *Old Said* to the *New Said* after his meeting in 1922 with Kemal is often cited as Nursi 'turning his back on politics' and embracing a quietest lifestyle, but Nursi continued to make political statements in his writing as the *New Said*. Turner asserts that

---

[99] Nursi, *The Rays Collection*, 428.
[100] Nursi, *Letters*, 67.
[101] Ibid.
[102] Nursi, *Emirdağ Letters*, 81; Nursi, *The Rays Collection*, 458.
[103] Black, *The West and Islam Religion and Political Thought in World History*, 5.

after the First World War, Nursi was no longer interested in politics as a means of safeguarding Islam: he thought that the future of Islam depended not on someone ruling in its name, but in people reviving the faith in their hearts.[104]

In the context of Turner's statement, he implies that Nursi had a 'change of heart' or conversion that caused him to abandon political reform which then elevated the need to revive Muslims internally. Likewise, Vahide claims Nursi voluntarily chose to focus on reforming Turkish society from the inside out by teaching the truths of the Qur'an to Muslims after realising the direction of the Turkish Republic was headed for disaster.[105] According to these and other scholars, Nursi's voluntary choice to abandon politics as the *New Said* principally defines Nursi life's mission as a pious Muslim leader who *chose* not to attempt to use a socio-political framework to reform Turkish society, similar to other Islamists like the Muslim Brotherhood.[106] Yet, even if we account for Nursi's conversion experience from the *Old* to the *New Said*, he continued to remain politically engaged in Turkish society.

Nursi promoted political engagement as the *New Said* and as he was on the verge of transitioning into the *Third Said*. After being released from Afyon Prison and returning to Emirdağ, Nursi states,

> We do not exploit religion for politics. Our duty in the face of those who in bigoted fashion exploit irreligion for politics to the awesome harm of this country and nation is—when the definite necessity arises that we do consider politics—to make politics the tool and friend of religion so that it may lead to winning the brotherhood of three hundred and fifty million brethren for the brothers in this country.[107]

Undoubtedly, Nursi and the *Nurcu* were political when they felt they needed to be and Nursi had no issue with using his pen to communicate his political ideas.

Nurcu and scholars are incorrect to focus only on the *New Said's* apolitical statements since Nursi had no other choice but to be

---

[104] Turner, *Qur'an Revealed*, 556.
[105] Vahide, *Islam In Modern Turkey*, 223.
[106] Ibid.; Turner, *Qur'an Revealed*, 539, 545, 553, 555.
[107] Nursi, *Emirdağ Letters*, 301.

apolitical as he was jailed by the RPP. Turner acknowledges that an interpretation that considers Nursi as only apolitical and a quietest is a "simplistic view of Nursi."[108] In answering "Why does the New Said avoid politics with such vehemence?" Nursi himself concedes that "in these stormy times it is *not possible* to perform such service. Therefore, I left aside that aspect [political involvement] and chose the aspect of service to belief soundly" (emphasis mine).[109] Here, Nursi implies that he made a forced decision to retreat from politics. Nursi's statement reflects a lack of options to be involved in politics, as well as a heart that is piously seeking refuge in religion from the evils of politics. If Nursi could have been more openly involved in politics as the *New Said*, he probably would have been. If this were the case, there may have been more similarities between the *Nurculuk* and the Muslim Brotherhood, as well as other Islamist movements. The RPP saw through Nursi's apolitical claims and continued to regulate Nursi and the *Nurculuk*, viewing them not only as apolitical but as political in their core mission.

Second, when Nursi opposed Mustafa Kemal, the emblem of the Turkish nation, his interaction with Kemal was inherently political. A Turk reading Nursi statements about Kemal recognises the weight of Nursi's opinions of Kemal who is considered the *Halāskar Gazi* (Saviour and Conqueror) of Turkey starting in the *Turkish War for Independence*.[110] An attack against Kemal is an attack against the 'ethos' of Turkey and many people who have desecrated pictures of Atatürk or his image have been imprisoned.[111] Whether or not Turkish children were and are 'indoctrinated' to love Kemal or not, as Nursi asserts, does not change the reality that an attack on Kemal is an attack on the Turkish state. Criticising the Prime Minister or President of any country, including Turkey, is forbidden.

Third, Nursi's opposition to Kemalism placed him in political disagreement with the *devlet* because it provided an alternative ideology based upon Islam. Nursi was vocal until his death that true civilization must be based upon the teachings of Islam, not *laïcité*. To oppose Kemalism, whether or not Kemalism was a 'good' ideology, was to engage in Turkish politics.

---

[108] Turner, *Qur'an Revealed*, 540.
[109] Said Nursi, *The Rays Collection*, 459.
[110] Zürcher, *Turkey*, 160.
[111] See https://www.hurriyetdailynews.com/turkish-author-gets-15-months-jail-for-defaming-ataturk-121715, accessed September 2, 2020.

Fourth, as Nursi opposed Turkish nationalism, he repudiated the essence of the RPP's reforms as they built the Turkish state. Again, while Turkish nationalism had 'racist' tendencies as Nursi claimed, it does not change the reality that Nursi's counter-narrative was highly politicized. When Nursi spoke against Turkish nationalism, he exited the realm of 'religion' from a Western perspective and entered the realm of politics, which he knew very well.

Fifth, Nursi's life as a political prisoner moving from prison to prison and city to city is the greatest evidence of his political persona. Nursi was not only a religious prisoner but a political prisoner because he was a political rival of the RPP. The RPP continued to pursue and to control Nursi because Nursi continued to politically oppose Kemalism. If at any moment, Nursi had ceased from making politically charged statements against Kemal, Kemalism, and the RPP, the *devlet,* he may have been released. Nursi knew what he was doing and he chose to remain an unyielding politico-religious opponent of the RPP until his death.

I have argued that Nursi's life ambition was not only religious but inherently political. Nursi openly postured himself as the politico-religious adversary of Mustafa Kemal and the Republican People's Party. He criticised their efforts to force their secularizing reforms on the Turkish people. Nursi not only engaged in politics as the Old and Third Said but also as the New Said as evidenced by his many political statements contained in the *Risale-i Nur.* Nursi's thousands of students printed and distributed the 'Risaleler,' along with its political ideology, throughout Turkey. Nursi fought a battle to preserve authoritative Islamic traditions based upon the Qur'an and Hadith. As a result of his politico-religious stance, Nursi remained a political prisoner of the RPP from 1925–1950. After his death, his grave was moved and hidden by the Kemalist factions within the military to prevent his followers from making pilgrimages to his grave. This was the final chapter in Nursi's story of fighting, suffering and dying for what he believed as a revered religious and political leader in Turkey.

Bibliography

Abu-Rabi', Ibrahim M., ed. *Spiritual Dimensions of Bediuzzaman Said Nursi's Risale-I Nur.* Albany, NY: Suny Press, 2008.
_____. *Theodicy and Justice in Modern Islamic Thought: The Case of Said Nursi.* 2016.

Çoruh, Hakan. "Tradition, Reason, and Qur'anic Exegesis in the Modern Period: The Hermeneutics of Said Nursi." *Islam and Christian–Muslim Relations* 28, no. 1 (2017): 85–104.
_____. *Modern Interpretation of the Qur'an: The Contribution of Bediuzzaman Said Nursi.* London: Palgrave Macmillan, 2019.

Markham, Ian S. and Sayilgan, Zeyneb, eds. *The Companion to Said Nursi Studies.* Eugene, OR: Pickwick Publications, 2017.

Mardin, Serif. *Religion and Social Change in Modern Turkey: The Case of Bediuzzaman Said Nursi.* Albany, NY: Suny Press, 1989.

Şahiner, Necmettin. *Bilinmeyen Taraflarıyla Bediüzzaman Said Nursi.* Nesil Basım Yayın Gıda Ticaret ve Sanayi A.Ş, 2004.

Turner, Colin. *Qur'an Revealed: A Critical Analysis of Said Nursi's Epistles of Light.* Berlin: Gerlach Press, 2013.

Turner, Colin, and Hasan Horkuc. *Said Nursi: Makers of Islamic Civilization.* London: I. B. Tauris, 2009.

Vahide, Sukran. *The Author of the Risale-i Nur; Bediuzzaman Said Nursi.* Reset Edition. Berkeley, CA: Nur Publishers, 2019.

Chapter 8

RESTORATION TRAGEDY:
I.S., Jihad and the Second Coming of the Caliphate

Anthony McRoy[1]

Introduction

The 'Restoration' refers to the return of the Stuarts under Charles II in 1660. The previous Interregnum Parliament banned theatres in 1642. King Charles was a patron of the Arts, including theatres, which reopened in 1660. *Comedies* flourished during the Restoration: "...comedy was by far the preferred theatrical genre with audiences."[2] Farce was also popular.[3] There were also Restoration *Tragedies*, e.g. by Aphra Behn, such as *Abdelazer, Or the Moor's Revenge*, about a depraved Moor who is a murderer and attempted-rapist "who richly earns his death."[4] Marx saw the 1851 coup by Louis Bonaparte as a pale reflection of that by his uncle Napoleon on 9 November/18 Brumaire 1799: "Hegel says somewhere that that great historic facts and personages recur twice. He forgot to add: 'Once as tragedy, and again as farce.' The identical caricature marks also the conditions under which the second edition of the eighteenth Brumaire is issued."[5] This is relevant to the Islamic State Caliphate (IS); IS saw itself as fulfilling Islamic eschatology, as in its Restoration of the Caliphate, in its restoration of slavery, and its waging of a genocidal *jihad.*

---

[1] Dr Anthony McRoy has dual Eire/UK citizenship, married with three adult children. He has lectured at several colleges, and contributed to both Muslim and Christian publications, and various academic works.
[2] Brian Corman, "Comedy," in *The Cambridge Companion to English Restoration Theatre*, ed. Deborah Payne Fisk (Cambridge: Cambridge University Press, 2000), 56.
[3] Peter Holland, "Farce," in *The Cambridge Companion to English Restoration Theatre*, 107.
[4] Christopher J. Wheatley, "Tragedy," *The Cambridge Companion to English Restoration Theatre*, 72.
[5] Karl Marx, *The Eighteenth Brumaire of Louis Bonaparte*, 2nd ed., trans Daniel De Leon (Chicago, IL: Charles H. Kerr and Co., 1907), 5.

I The Caliphate in Theology and History

The Sunni concept of the successor to the Prophet is present in the *Hadith* and *Fiqh*. Sunni traditions suggest various appointment methodologies, e.g. popular election or acclamation, related to '*ijma* (consensus):

> Narrated by Aisha
> Sahih Al-Bukhari Hadith 5.19
> Allah's Apostle died while Abu Bakr was at a place called As-Sunah (Al-'Aliya)... 'Umar said (to Abu Bakr), "No but we elect you...". So 'Umar took Abu Bakr's hand and gave the pledge of allegiance and the people too gave the pledge of allegiance to Abu Bakr...

> Narrated by Abdullah ibn Abbas
> Sahih Al-Bukhari 8.817a
> ...Abu Bakr himself gave a speech... '... this question (of Caliphate) is only for the Quraysh... so take the oath of allegiance to either of them as you wish... So I said, 'O Abu Bakr! Hold your hand out.' He held his hand out and I pledged allegiance to him, and then all the emigrants gave the pledge of allegiance and so did the Ansar... Umar added, '...So, if any person gives the pledge of allegiance to somebody (to become a Caliph) without consulting the other Muslims, then the one he has selected should not be granted allegiance, lest both of them should be killed.'

That the loser would be killed suggests that the 'election' is really a matter of popular acclamation of the obvious candidate. There is, however, no absolute consensus among the *madhabs* on this:

> Imamate comes into being in two ways: the first of these is by the election of those of power and influence, and the second is by the delegation of the previous Imam. As for... election of the people of power, the 'ulama, according to the different madhabs, have different opinions as to the number of persons needed in the formation of the Imamate. One group says that it can only be conferred by way of the majority of those of power and influence in each country, such that acceptance is general and submission to the Imamate is by a consensus... Another group say that the minimum number of persons that should gather for the formation of the Imamate is five or that

it should be formed by one of them with the agreement of four others.[6]

The *Shafi madhab* lists several qualifications for the Caliphal post:

(a) Muslim (H: so that he may see to the best interests of Islam and the Muslims...
(d) male...
(e) of the Quraysh tribe (K: because of the (H: well-authenticated (hasan)) hadith related by Nasa'i: "The Imams are of the Quraysh." ...this qualification being obligatory when there is a member of Quraysh available who meets the other conditions) (H: though when there is not, then the next most eligible is a qualified member of the Kinana tribe, then of the Arabs, then of the non-Arabs).[7]

As for the means of appointment, the *Shafi madhab* allows both election and even *coup d'état*:

(1)   by an oath of fealty (H: like the one sworn by the prophetic Companions to Abu Bakr...) ... of the scholars, leaders, and notables able to attend...
(2)   ... by the caliph appointing a successor...
(3)   ... through seizure of power by an individual possessing the qualifications of a caliph...[8]

The *Shafi* jurist Imam Nawawī (1234–1277) demonstrated the juridical basis of such a constitutional *coup* in the following *hadith*:

The Messenger of Allah... said as:
Narrated by Ali: 'The Prophet... said: "There should not be obedience to a creature if it comprises an act of disobedience to Allah..."'
The first words of Abu-Bakr [on his appointment as the caliph] were: "Obey me as long as I obey Allah... If I disobey Allah..., I am not entitled to your obedience." Omar ibn Al-Khattab asked the Muslims to correct his conduct if he deviated.... One of the Muslims said: "Were we to find a defect in your

---

[6] Abu'l-Hasan 'Ali ibn Muhammad ibn Habib al-Basri al-Baghdadi al-Mawardi, *al-Ahkam as-Sultaniyyah: The Laws of Islamic Governance* (London: Ta-Ha, 2000), 12–13.
[7] Nuh Ha Mim Keller, ed., *Reliance of the Traveller: The Classic Manual of Islamic Sacred Law 'Umdat al-Salik by Ahmad ibn Naqib al-Misri'* (Beltsville: MD: Amarna, 1997), 640–641.
[8] Ibid., 643–644.

behavior, we would correct it with our swords." At that he said: "Praise be to Allah that there is one to correct our behavior with swords."[9]

Nawawī comments: "This means that there is no obedience if the ruler's order contradicts the Law of Allah as presented in the Noble Koran and Sunna."[10] This becomes important when we consider the revolutionary/insurrectionist nature of IS in relation to the governing authorities they oppose, even if Sunni. However, the Caliph, if Islamically-righteous, commands total obedience:

> Narrated by Abdullah ibn Amr ibn al-'As
> Sahih Muslim 4546
> ...He who swears allegiance to a Caliph should give him the pledge of his hand and the sincerity of his heart (i.e. submit to him both outwardly as well as inwardly). He should obey him to the best of his capacity.

Ibn Taymiyyah, associated with the Hanbali school, observed: "...monarchy is essentially unlawful, and our duty is to set up a government on the pattern of the prophetic government (*khilāfat nubūwwah*)."[11] The limits of authority are the laws of Islam: "...unqualified submission is for the Prophet only and for no one else."[12] As for appointment to the post, he says:

> Appointment to a position of authority or caliphate becomes valid when the decision-makers swear allegiance and the majority of the people give their consent, even if one or two or ten object to that.[13]

Shura (consultation) whether as *majlis* in the sense of a Parliament, or, more often, an advisory Cabinet, is part of Caliphal governance:

---

[9] Al-Imâm Abū Zakariyya Yaḥyā bin Sharaf Ad-Dimshqi An-Nawawī, *Riyâd-us Sâliheen* (Riyadh: Darussalam, 2003), 2:520–521.

[10] Ibid, 2:520.

[11] Muhammad 'Abdul-Haqq Ansari, ed., *Ibn Taymiyyah Expounds on Islam: Selected Writings of Shaykh al-Islam Taqi ad-Din Ibn Taymiyyah on Islamic Faith, Life, and Society* (Riyadh: General Administration of Culture and Publication/ Islam Future, 2000), 497.

[12] Ibid., 519.

[13] Huda Khattab, ed., *The Essential Pearls and Gems of Ibn Taymiyyah* (Riyadh: Darussalam, 2013), 18.

When the person in authority consults people and as a result comes to know the will of God's Book or the Prophet's Sunnah or the consensus of the Muslims, he should follow it and act upon it.[14]

Also, the Caliph appoints *Wazirs* (based on Surah 20:29-32): "Wazirate (ministry) is of two types: ministry of delegation and ministry of execution. The ministry of delegation is where the Imam appoints a minister to whom he delegates authority for the organisation of affairs in accordance with his judgement such that he effects them properly by his own efforts."[15] The Caliph also appoints Amirs over provinces, with responsibility for security, local judiciary, tax-collection, etc., including "Protection of the deen."[16] In the *Hanafi* school, Imam al-Nasafi (1067-1142) presented the Caliphate as obligation and necessity:

The Muslims must have an Imam, who will carry out the administration of their decisions, the maintaining of their restrictive ordinances, the guarding of their frontiers, the equipping of their armies, the receiving of their alms, the subjugation of those who get the upper hand and robbers and highwaymen, the performance of worship on Fridays and Festivals, the settlement of disputes which take place among creatures, the receiving of evidence based on legal rights, the giving in marriage young men and maidens who have no guardians, and the division of the booty... he must be of the tribe of Quraysh.[17]

This list indicates that the Caliph must engage in both *Defensive* ('guarding of... frontiers') and *Offensive Jihad* ('booty'). This was also the position of al-Mawardi:

1. He must guard the deen (Islam) as it was established in its original form...
5. He must fortify the border posts against attack and defend them with force against an enemy which might... violate what is sacred or shed the blood of Muslims or dhimmis protected by a pact.

[14] Ansari, *Ibn Taymiyyah Expounds on Islam*, 509.
[15] al-Mawardi, *al-Ahkam as-Sultaniyyah*, 37.
[16] Ibid., 48.
[17] Earl Edgar Elder, *A Commentary on the Creed of Islam: Sa'd Al-Dīn Al-Taftāzānī on the Creed of Najm Al-Dīn Al-Nasafī* (New York: Columbia University Press, 1950), 172.

6. He must make jihad against those who resist Islam after having been called to it until they submit or accept to live as a protected dhimmi-community...[18]

In short, the Amir must implement the *Shari'ah* – *in toto*. Unending *Jihad* is an obligation of the Caliphate, including raiding (*razzia*): "it is incumbent upon him to renew the raiding whenever he is able... The least amount of time which may pass without his mounting a jihad is a year."[19] Again, "...continual perseverance in fighting is among the duties of jihad, it is binding until one of four things occurs," i.e. conversion, tribute, or truce.[20] The other possibility is that the vanquished foe may be slain or enslaved:

> ...their women and children are taken prisoner, and their wealth is taken as booty, and those who are not made captive are put to death. As for the captives, the amir has the choice of taking the most beneficial action of four possibilities: the first, to put them to death by cutting their necks; the second, to enslave them and apply the laws of slavery regarding their sale or manumission.[21]

Among the means of *Jihad*, the *Amir* may "destroy their homes, make night raids against them and cause fires."[22] A *mujahid* may have sexual intercourse with a captive-woman "after she has been allotted to him in his share."[23] We must remember these rulings when analysing IS policy.

Sunnis refer to the *Khulafah Rashidun* – 'the rightly-guided Caliphs,' e.g. the Hanbali scholar Zayn ad-Deen Ibn Rajab al-Hanbali:

> The Rightly-Guided Caliphs are Abû Bakr, 'Umar, 'Uthmân and 'Aly bin Abî Tâlib... These Caliphs are described as rightly-guided because they know the truth and act in accordance with it, contrary to the deviant who know the truth but do not act in accordance with it.[24]

---

[18] al-Mawardi, *al-Ahkam as-Sultaniyyah*, 27–28.
[19] Ibid., 82.
[20] Ibid., 75–78.
[21] Ibid., 76.
[22] Ibid., 79.
[23] Ibid., 81.
[24] Ibn Rajab, *Jami' al-Ulum wal-Hikam: A Collection of Knowledge and Wisdom* (Al Mansura: Umm Al Qura, 2002), 362–363.

Thereafter, were a succession of Caliphates – Umayyads (661–750), Abbasids (750–1258), and Ottomans, who asserted their claims from 1517 and held it until 1924. It is significant that the regime (or dynasty) changes occurred through violence. The first formal external reference to the Ottoman Sultan as Caliph was in the Treaty Kutchuk Kainardji with Russia, 1774: "His Highness, in his capacity of Grand Caliph of Mahometanism."[25] Imber, however, states that: "From the 1540s, Süleyman I promulgated the notion that the Ottoman Sultan was Caliph."[26]

The gaps in the list are theologically problematic, since Sunnis are not supposed to be without a Caliph for more than three days:

> If the Muslims did not appoint a Khalifah within three days they would all be sinful until they had appointed a Khalifah.[27]

This is based on the experience of Abu Bakr's appointment and more specifically what 'Umar enjoined:

> When I am dead, hold your consultations for three days... Before the fourth day comes you should have your commander from among you.[28]

It is an urgent concern for Sunni Islamists that since 1924, more than three days have elapsed without a Caliph. A further problem is that the Ottomans were neither Quraish nor Arab. The Ottomans countered by pointing to their success in *jihad* and implementation of *Shari'ah*:

> Beyazid II (r. 1481–1512)... stated that he was entitled to be caliph because he was the best fighter in the cause of Islam... service to Islam and to the Muslim community... emerged as the chief legitimizing condition for the claim to the caliphate, supplanting the view that the caliph should descend from the Prophet's tribe – the Qureyish... practical considerations now... became central to Ottoman arguments for the legitimacy of their hold on the caliphate. Jalaladdin Dawwani (ca. 1427–

---

[25] A. L. Macfie, *The Eastern Question 1774–1923*, Rev. ed. (New York: Routledge, 2014), 81.
[26] Colin Imber, *The Ottoman Empire, 1300–1650: The Structure of Power* (New York: Palgrave Macmillan, 2002), 116.
[27] Taqiuddin an-Nabhani, *The Islamic State* (London: Al-Khilafah Publications, 1998), 221–222.
[28] G. Rex Smith, trans., *The History of al-Tabari* (Albany, NY: Suny, 1994), 14:146.

1502)... argued that... a righteous ruler could hold the caliphate if he... enforced the Şeriat.[29]

Within the dynasties listed previously, the Caliphate effectively became hereditary, to one degree or another, which was also theologically problematic in the light of *ahadith*:

> Narrated by Hudhayfah ibn al-Yaman
> Mishkat Al-Masabih 5378
> ...Allah's Messenger ... said, "...there will be a caliphate according to the manner of prophecy... then Allah... will remove it. Then there will be a distressful kingdom... then Allah... remove it. Then there will be a proud kingdom which will remain as long as Allah wishes... Then there will be a caliphate according to the manner of prophecy."

The establishment of dynastic rule in the Caliphates, and the subsequent dynasties in the monarchies and even republics of the modern Muslim world (e.g. Syria, Pakistan, Bangladesh), often characterised by corruption, despotism and servility to Western hegemony, has led Islamists to see their contemporary situation as evidence of fulfilled prophecy. This became acute after the failed 1683 Ottoman siege of Vienna, which effectively ended land-based *Offensive Jihad* against Christendom, and the 1816 British bombardment of Algiers, which decimated its maritime version (involving the centuries-long enslavement of Europeans). This intensified as the Ottomans could not successfully engage in *Defensive Jihad*, with the acceleration of Balkan independence, leaving only Eastern Thrace under their control by 1914, and the loss of North Africa to European powers by the same date.

The Ottoman argument that their lack of descent from the Quraish was irrelevant since they engaged in *Jihad* and implemented the *Shari'ah* was thus hollow by 1914. Indeed, during the 1915 Hussain-MacMahon correspondence, both Arab nationalists and Britain desired "resumption of the Khalifate by an Arab of true race."[30] The situation became more pressing with Ataturk's abolition of the Caliphate in 1924. Hussain did advance his claim, taking *bayah*

---

[29] Kemal H. Karpat, *The Politicization of Islam: Reconstructing Identity, State, Faith, and Community in the late Ottoman State* (Oxford: Oxford University Press, 2001), 242.

[30] Timothy J. Paris, *Britain, the Hashemites and Arab Rule, 1920–1925: The Sherifian Solution* (London: Frank Cass, 2003), 26.

from his followers.[31] However, there was little other support, and his betrayal by Britain through the Sykes-Picot Agreement, then the Mandate system, and finally the loss of Hijaz to Ibn Saud undermined his dreams. The 1926 Cairo conference, where Egypt's King Fu'ad aimed for the title also failed. Movements such as the *Muslim Brotherhood* and *Hizb ut-Tahrir* have campaigned for the Caliphate's restoration, essentially to establish a single Sunni State and overthrow Western hegemony. Often, they accessed the clause in the last-mentioned *hadith* which predicted the restoration of a true Caliphate. It is in this context we examine IS.

2 Al-Qaida, Zarqawi and the emergence of IS

Interviewed by Al-Jazeera in October 2001, Osama bin Laden stated:

> So I say that, in general, our concern is that our *umma* unites either under the Words of the Book of God or His Prophet, and that this nation should establish the righteous caliphate of our *umma*, which has been prophesised by our Prophet in his authentic *hadith*.[32]

Al-Qaida's goal was to destroy Western hegemony over the *Ummah*. The founder of what became *Tanzim al-Jihad*, Mohammed Abd al-Salam Faraj, held:

> "fighting the near enemy must take priority over that of the far enemy" and so prioritised the overthrow of the "apostate" Egyptian regime, hoping to establish an Islamic system (which could become the nucleus of a future Caliphate).[33]

This was the dominant idea among the global *jihadi* movement. However, terrorist actions against one's own people tended to alienate local support, without which no successful insurrection is possible, as demonstrated by an action led by a successor of Faraj, Ayman al-Zawahiri, who merged his group into Al-Qaida:

> Zawahiri attempted to kill Egypt's prime minister, Atef Sidqi. A car bomb exploded as the minister was driven past a girls'

---

[31] Reza Pankhurst, *The Inevitable Caliphate? A History of the Struggle for Global Islamic Union, 1924 to the Present* (Oxford: Oxford University Press, 2013), 5, 52.

[32] Bruce Lawrence, ed., *Messages to the World: The Statements of Osama Bin Laden*, trans. James Howarth (London: Verso, 2005), 121.

[33] Fawaz A. Gerges, *The Far Enemy: Why Jihad Went Global* (New York: Cambridge University Press, 2005), 10–11.

school in Cairo. The minister, in his armored car, was unhurt, but the explosion injured twenty-one people and killed a young schoolgirl, Shayma Abdel-Halim, who was crushed by a door blown loose in the blast. Her death outraged Egyptians... When her coffin was borne through the streets of Cairo, people cried, "Terrorism is the enemy of God!"[34]

The innovation of Bin Laden, to assault the 'far enemy,' the USA, avoided the alienation caused by attacking compatriots, and recognised that in a globalised world, with 'apostate' regimes being essentially US client states, the concept of 'near' or 'far' enemy was redundant. He noted that one superpower—the USSR—got fatally embroiled in Afghanistan, and wanted to draw America into the Afghan imbroglio – a second Vietnam to make Washington bleed in bodies and money.

America followed its invasion of Afghanistan with that of Iraq in 2003, which enabled Al-Qaida to establish a franchise there through a Jordanian *jihadi*, Abu Musab al-Zarqawi, who pledged his group, *al-Tawhid wal Jihad* to Bin Laden.[35] However, Zarqawi pursued a militant *takfiri* practice against the Shia, and also Sunni 'collaborators' with the American occupation, his strategy resembling that of previous anti-regime groups rather than Bin Laden:

> Zawahiri and Bin Laden pushed for a focus on US targets, while Zarqawi (and those who took his place after his death in 2006 from a US air strike) emphasized sectarian war and attacks on Sunni Muslims they deemed apostates, such as those who collaborated with the Shi'a-led Iraqi regime.[36]

After Zarqawi's death, leadership eventually fell to Abu Bakr al-Baghdadi in May 2010:

> Abu Bakr al-Baghdadi was a member of the Albu Badr tribe, which claims descent from the Quraysh, the tribe of the Prophet Mohammed. Baghdadi held a doctorate in Islam, religious

[34] Lawrence Wright, *The Looming Tower: Al-Qaeda and the Road to 9/11* (New York: Alfred A. Knopf, 2006), 186.
[35] Gerges, *The Far Enemy*, 257f.
[36] Daniel Byman, *Al Qaeda, The Islamic State, and the Global Jihadist Movement: What Everyone Needs to Know* (New York: Oxford University Press, 2015), 166.

credentials that few Iraqis could match. Under his leadership, AQI gained a deeper legitimacy.[37]

It was at this point that serendipity came to his aid – the rising against the quasi-Shia Alawite regime of Assad in Syria:

> Baghdadi took advantage of the civil war in Syria that had started in 2011 and escalated in 2012. The regime lost much of the country, including the territory next to Anbar. Those regions became safe havens for AQI. Baghdadi relocated portions of AQI to the Euphrates river valley in eastern Syria. AQI had long had cells and operatives in Syria. The enhanced presence amid the civil war allowed AQI to attract more Syrians and larger numbers of foreign fighters. Fighters located in Syria traveled back and forth into Iraq, launching raids and suicide bombing missions.[38]

As the group consolidated control over areas, they renamed themselves "the Islamic State of Iraq and al- Sham (Syria)... By claiming to form a new state across existing borders—tied together by the universal Islamic faith—the Islamic State appeared to be succeeding where others had failed."[39] Finally, "on the first night of Ramadan in 2014, al-Baghdadi proclaimed the return of the caliphate, with himself as leader."[40]

3   IS Interior Politics/Governance: Caliphate and *Shari'ah*

The first edition of the IS magazine *Dabiq* was entitled *The Return of Khilafah*: "the revival of the Khilafah was announced by the spokesman for the Islamic State, Shaykh Abu Muhammad al-'Adnani ash-Shami (hafidhahullah). The good news was followed by the first official speech of Amirul-Mu'minin Abu Bakr al-Husayni al-Qurashi al-Baghdadi (nasarahullah)."[41] Caliphal qualifications included 'uprightness,' and Al-Qurtubi was quoted:

---

[37] Carter Malkasian, *Illusions of Victory: The Anbar Awakening and the Rise of the Islamic State* (Oxford: Oxford University Press, 2017), 174.
[38] Ibid., 175.
[39] Ibid., 175–176.
[40] Byman, *Al Qaeda*, 165.
[41] *Dabiq* 1, Ramadan 1435, 6, downloaded from both the Clarion Project (Islamic State's [ISIS, ISIL] Horrific Magazine, Clarion Project) and Internet Archive.

...the imam must be a man of justice, good conduct, and virtue, and have the strength to fulfill his role... the sinful, unjust, immoral tyrant... doesn't qualify for this position.[42]

Justification for al-Baghdadi's rule is given in terms of IS establishing *Shari'a* and political control:

It established the religion in the areas where it exists and continues to pursue this effort vigorously.

All this, after Allah had granted the imam of The Islamic State the blessing of performing hijrah and fighting jihad in His cause, on top of already having been characterized by his noble lineage, sound intellect, and a prestigious level of knowledge and religious practice.[43]

Thus, the justifications for IS Caliphal claims are: establishment of *Shar'ia* (rather than the Islamist bug-bear of 'man-made law'), including governance - effectively acting as the Constitution and law-code of the Caliphate; and Al-Baghdadi's knowledge, piety, performance of *jihad*; and Quraishi ancestry. Moreover, we saw that it is permissible for someone to claim the Caliphal role by force. The 1924 abolition of the Caliphate left a politico-theological hole that IS was able to fill, since its proclamation did not even involve a coup or deposition. The *takfiri* practice of Zarqawi was continued:

...anyone who rebels against its authority inside its territory is considered a renegade, and it is permissible to fight him.[44]

It follows therefore that the democratic-Parliamentary concept of 'loyal opposition' common to Britain, Australia, and other such democracies, is rejected – opponents of the government are traitors, indeed apostates, whose blood may be shed, rather than simply refuting them, as demonstrated by its quote of *Sahih Muslim* (q.v.) about the Caliph: "...if another man comes forward disputing his legitimacy, then strike that other man's neck."[45]

---

[42] Ibid., 23.
[43] Ibid., 27.
[44] Ibid.
[45] Ibid., 28.

The issue quoted the *hadith* about the prophesied restoration of the Khilafah, e.g., "Then there will be Khilafah on the prophetic methodology [Ahmad]."[46] Eschatology plays a major role in IS ideology and propaganda, and presenting its Caliphal claims as the fulfilment of prophecy was a means of undermining opposition and gaining universal support. *Dabiq* asserted that nationalism 'tainted' the Afghan jihadis, and we should remember that the Taliban called their regime 'The Islamic Emirate of Afghanistan.'[47] Not only was this geographically/demographically circumscribed, its nature as an 'Emirate' further localised its appeal. IS, declaring itself a *Caliphate*, by contrast asserted *global* ambition.

In 2016 the entity's *al-Furqan Media* issued a video entitled 'The Structure of the Khilafah':

> The governing structure consists of the *khalifa,* the Shura Council, the Delegated Committee, the *dawawin* [ministries/bureaus], the *wilayat* [provinces], and the committees and offices.[48] We previously noted Ibn Taymiyyah on *Shura*, and what al-Mawardi stated about Wazirs and Amirs; the IS *dawawin* included: "...Bureau of Hisbah [religious compliance police]... Bureau of the Soldiery, Bureau of Public Security... Bureau of Spoils and Plunder" so the structure of IS mirrored this.[49]

The functions of the different offices are explained thus:

> The head of its affairs is *Amir al-Mu'minin*... the *khalifa.* He upholds and spreads the religion, defends the homeland, and fortifies the fronts. He prepares the armies, implements the *hudud*, enforces the people's adherence to the *shari'a* rulings, and governs their worldly affairs. He is aided in all this by... *ahl al-hal wa al-'aqd* [those qualified to elect or depose the caliph on behalf of the *umma*] and his shura council. The task of communicating orders... and ensuring their execution, is delegated to a select group... So it's necessary for there to be a body of individuals that supports him, and that body is the Delegated Committee. The Delegated Committee supervises

---

[46] Ibid., 34.
[47] Ibid., 35.
[48] Haroro J. Ingram, Craig Whiteside, and Charlie Winter, *The ISIS Reader: Milestone Texts of the Islamic State Movement* (Oxford: Oxford University Press, 2020), 236.
[49] Ibid., 236–237.

the following branches of state: firstly, the *wilayat;* secondly, the *dawawin;* thirdly, the offices and committees.[50]

4   IS Caliphate citizenship

Among the *dawawin* committees was

> The Hijra [migration] Committee: It is an office concerned with receiving those who immigrate to the Islamic State.

This brings us to the issue of citizenship. *Hijrah* was a major concern of IS, underlying its claim to be a universal Caliphate, as opposed to religious nationalist groups like HAMAS or the Taliban, as indicated by al-Baghdadi's call during the announcement of the restoration:

> Amirul-Mu'minin said: "Therefore, rush O Muslims to your state... The State is a state for all Muslims. The land is for the Muslims, all the Muslims. O Muslims everywhere, whoever is capable of performing hijrah (emigration) to the Islamic State, then let him do so, because hijrah to the land of Islam is obligatory... We make a special call to the scholars, fuqaha' (experts in Islamic jurisprudence), and callers, especially the judges, as well as people with military, administrative, and service expertise, and medical doctors and engineers of all different specializations and fields.[51]

Whilst the Caliphate did not have an Australian-style points system to encourage the immigration of skilled personnel, IS recognised its need of such people to build a genuine state. However, there was a general call to boost numbers, the Caliphate being the *universal* state of Sunnis:

> It is a state where the Arab and non-Arab, the white man and black man, the easterner and westerner are all brothers. It is a Khilafah that gathered the Caucasian, Indian, Chinese, Shami, Iraqi, Yemeni, Egyptian, Maghribi (North African), American, French, German, and Australian. Allah brought their hearts together, and thus, they became brothers by His grace, loving each other for the sake of Allah, standing in a single trench, defending and guarding each other, and sacrificing themselves for one another. Their blood mixed and became one, under a single flag and goal, in one pavilion, enjoying this blessing, the blessing of faithful brotherhood.[52]

---

[50] Ibid., 237.
[51] *Dabiq* 1, Ramadan 1435, 11.
[52] Ibid., 7.

Apart from natural concerns of increasing their numbers, *Hijrah* was also part of their 'prophetic methodology', given that Muhammad migrated to Yathrib to assume leadership there. So important was this matter to IS that the third issue of *Dabiq* was entitled 'A call to Hijrah,' which examined its practical and theological aspects. In IS ideology, *Hijrah* involved not only physical motion, but also theological rejection. If, as the *Shahadah* declares, there is only one deity worthy of worship, and Muhmmad is his Messenger, and 'worship' includes political allegiance (given that Muhammad was a Ruler, and the Caliphs are his successors in governance), it follows that no man may serve two (State) masters – dual citizenship is impossible. This explains the destruction of passports by those who made *Hijrah* – they were renouncing their previous citizenship. An IS video, *Saleel al-Sawarim,* or *Clanging of the Swords*, displayed "A preacher brandishing a machete proclaims the Islamic State and warns the kuffar and Jews of Jerusalem that the jihadists are coming for them. He then leads the tearing up of passports."[53] In an article about American racism, *Dabiq* 11 stated:

> Here in the Islamic State, all affiliations are null and void when they conflict with one's allegiance to Islam and the Muslims. So the Syrian mujāhid doesn't hesitate to trample on the Syrian flag, and the American mujāhid doesn't think twice about setting fire to the "star-spangled banner.[54]

Hijrah was not the only means of population increase – normal reproduction figured too. On 23 July, 2015, female IS supporters – apparently from the Al-Khanssaa Brigade, which policed women's attire outside the home, and was purportedly involved in the enslavement of Yezidi girls – issued *Women in the Islamic State: Manifesto and Case Study*. Whilst declaiming official sanction, it clearly represents IS attitudes towards women and their citizenship. The starting point is that "woman, as with man, was created to populate the Earth."[55] IS, with none of the embarrassment of Western Muslim *dawah* on the subject, quoted several *ahadith* about the position of women:

---

[53] Michael Hassan Weiss, *ISIS: Inside the Army of Terror* (New York: Regan Arts, 2016), 174.
[54] *Dabiq* 11, 1436 Dhul Qa'dah, 20.
[55] Ingram et al., *The ISIS Reader*, 201.

And that is the great right of the husband: "Were I to order someone to prostrate before another, I would order the woman to prostrate before her husband." But regretfully women today do not realise this, in general, except those upon whom Allah has mercy. If all the men were to be men, then the women would all be women!

...The correct place for woman in society is one of serenity, among her children and family, nurturing, teaching, preserving, and raising the future generations.[56]

Immediately we can predict what follows – the woman's place is in the home, in a sense beyond the 1950s Western housewife:

It suffices those considering the issue to be aware of the Prophetic hadith that encourages women not to go out [for prayer]... And stay in your homes: This divine command is no longer welcomed among some women, whose hearts have been pierced by the arrows of Iblis' temptations. The silence of the home is no longer Paradise, and the heat of the Sun outside is no longer fire.[57]

With this comes the deriding of women seeking education above the three 'Rs' and religious knowledge:

...as our eminent 'ulama have stated, if woman learns to read and write, and to understand the commands of her religion alongside some worldly knowledge, that is sufficient for what is required of her – for her to fulfil the role for which she was created. There is no need to jump from here to there, attaining qualifications and titles.[58]

IS did allow for exceptional circumstances where women may leave the home for *jihad* (as some IS women did), or to act as medical personnel, etc.:

The fundamental position for the woman... is in her home with her husband and children. But sometimes, some may be required to go out and serve the Muslim society...

1. Obligatory jihad. If the enemy attacks her country and the efforts of the men are not sufficient, and if the lordly 'ulama

---

[56] Ibid., 202.
[57] Ibid., 204.
[58] Ibid., 204–205.

authorise it, as some of the distinguished women did in the jihad of Iraq and Chechnya...

2. Most often a woman goes out to seek knowledge, and the most important is the knowledge of religion.

3. A woman may go out as a doctor or teacher to benefit other women, but this must be done within the regulations of the law, without exception.[59]

Since the qualification for the Caliph—and thus all governmental positions—is masculine gender, women were excluded from senior governance. Obviously, the Caliph must be a Sunni. IS provided a secondary citizenship for non-Muslims. In a statement by IS *Diwan al-Qaḍa*, 17 July 2014, *Jizyah* was imposed on Christians:

After informing the heads of the Christians and their followers of the appointment for a meeting to affirm their status in the shadow of the state of the Caliphate in Wilayat Ninawa, they avoided it and failed to attend on the intended appointment...and it had been decided that we offer them one of these three choices:

1. Islam.
2. Dhimmi pact (and it is taking the jizya from them) [cf. Qur'an 9:29].
3. If they refuse that, only the sword for them.

But The Commander of the Believers, Caliph Ibrahim... has given them the blessing of allowing them to get themselves out of the borders of the state of the Caliphate at the latest by Saturday 21 Ramadan 1435 AH at noon. After this, there is only the sword between us and them.[60]

In Raqqa province in 2014, the following conditions were proclaimed:

This is what the servant of God, Abu Bakr al-Baghdadi, the Commander of the Faithful... has given to the Christians concerning the pact of protection. He has given them security for themselves, their wealth, their churches and the rest of their property in the province of Raqqa: their churches should

---

[59] Ibid., 205–206.
[60] Aymenn Jawad Al-Tamimi, *Archive of Islamic State Administrative Documents*, January 27, 2015, https://www.aymennjawad.org/2015/01/archive-of-islamic-state-administrative-documents (accessed July 24, 2020).

not be attacked, nor should anything be taken [by force] from them, nor from their domain, nor anything from their wealth, and there should be no compulsion against them in religion, and none of them should be harmed.

He has imposed these conditions on them:

1. That they must not build in their town or the periphery a monastery, church or monk's hermitage, and must not rebuild what has fallen into disrepair.

2. That they must not show the cross or any of their scriptures in any of the roads or markets of the Muslims and they must not use any means to amplify their voices during their calls to prayers or similarly for the rest of their acts of worship.

3. That they must not make Muslims hear recital of their scriptures or the sounds of their bells, even if they strike them within their churches.

4. That they must not engage in any acts of hostility against the Islamic State...

5. That they must not engage in any displays of worship outside the churches.

6. That they must not stop any of the Christians from embracing Islam if he so wishes.

7. That they must respect Islam and Muslims, and not disparage their religion in any way.

8. The Christians must embrace payment of the jizy[ah] - on every adult male...

9. They are not allowed to bear arms.

10. They are not to deal in selling pork and wine with Muslims or in their markets; and they are not to consume it [wine] publicly – that is, in any public places.

11. They should have their own tombs, as is custom.

12. That they must accept the precepts imposed by the Islamic State like modesty of dress, selling, buying, and other things.[61]

---

[61] Aymenn Jawad Al-Tamimi, *The Islamic State of Iraq and ash-Sham's dhimmi pact for the Christians of Raqqa province*, February 26, 2014,

These provisions resemble the so-called 'Pact of Umar.' In practice, most Christians fled, and later reports indicated forcible 'cleansing,' not least because IS wanted their homes for the *muhairun*.[62] Their fate was arguably less tragic than that of the Shia and Alawites – whom IS derided with the pejorative term 'Rafidah'; their publication *This is our Aqeeda and This is our Manhaj* was clear on the issue:

> The Rafidite Shi'a are… a sect of idolatry, apostasy and *hiraba* [a people waging war on Islam and sowing corruption in the land: cf. Qur'an 5:33–34].[63]

As such, they could not be even *subjugated* citizens – or even left alive. IS was a definite Tragedy for the Yezidis, who 'belonged' to the Caliphate – but as *slaves*, not citizens. *Dabiq* 4 stated:

> Upon conquering the region of Sinjar… the Islamic State faced a population of Yazidis, a pagan minority… there was no room for jizyah payment. Also, their women could be enslaved.[64]

The article referred to various eschatological *ahadith*, so presenting this action as fulfilment of prophecy. We saw that Al-Mawardi depicted enslavement as a legitimate consequence of *Jihad*.

5   'Foreign'/'Defence' Policy: Jihad

Caliphates did not have fixed 'borders,' but rather *frontiers* – the limits of Caliphal territory were only provisional, until they could be extended. In this sense, Caliphates were like Mirabeau's comment on Prussia, 'an army with a state,' rather than the reverse. IS policies on external relations and 'war' were identical: *Jihad* against infidels – not 'States,' since IS recognised no legitimate authority but its own. Its military policies were openly expansionist – infidels could hope at

https://www.aymennjawad.org/14472/the-islamic-state-of-iraq-and-ash-sham-dhimmi (accessed July 24, 2020).

[62] James Seidel, "Christmas under ISIS is a time of tension throughout the Middle East," *News*, published December 26, 2014, https://www.news.com.au/world/e57ec60b66496e62f388074ebd496508.

[63] Aymenn Jawad Al-Tamimi, "This is our Aqeeda and This is our Manhaj: Islam 101 according to the Islamic State," October 27, 2015, https://www.aymennjawad.org/2015/10/this-is-our-aqeeda-and-this-is-our-manhaj-islam#_edn27 (accessed July 25, 2020).

[64] *Dabiq* 4, 1435 Dhul-Hijjah, 14–15.

best for 'a temporary truce.'[65] Traditionally, jurists have distinguished between Defensive and Offensive *Jihad*, the latter expansionist or to raid for slaves. IS did not clearly differentiate between the two, although certain comments point to the distinction. IS listed their 'legitimate targets.' 'Ash-Shafi'i said,

> And the kafir's blood is not spared until he becomes a Muslim... Muslims currently living in Dar al-Kufr must be reminded that the blood of the disbelievers is halal, and killing them is a form of worship to Allah. This includes the businessman riding to work in a taxicab, the young adults (post-pubescent "children") engaged in sports activities in the park, and the old man waiting in line to buy a sandwich. Indeed, even the blood of the kafir street vendor selling flowers.[66]

IS saw Defensive *jihad* as anti-colonial liberation:

> ...the mujahidin of the Khilāfah delivered yet another blow to... the Sykes-Picot-inspired borders.[67]

Dabiq quoted az-Zarqāwī and his successors:

> We perform jihād here while our eyes are upon al-Quds... They strive to reestablish a khilāfah expanding from Spain to Indonesia.[68]

Again:

> O Americans, and O Europeans, the Islamic State did not initiate a war against you, as your governments and media try to make you believe. It is you who started the transgression against us.[69]

Offensive *Jihad* is also present:

> ...our goal is Rome... we will not rest from our jihād until we are under the olive trees of Rome, after we destroy the filthy house called the White House... "This prompted the enemy of

---

[65] *Dabiq* 15, 1437 Shawwal, 31.
[66] *Rumiyah* 1, Dhul-Hijjah 1437, 35–36.
[67] *Dabiq* 4, 18.
[68] Ibid., 4.
[69] Ibid., 8.

Allah – Bush – to say… 'They strive to establish an Islamic State stretching from China to Spain.' He spoke the truth although he is a liar."[70]

An official statement in the issue declared:

> We will conquer your Rome, break your crosses, and enslave your women.[71]

IS issued a pamphlet on enslavement, especially sexual, indicating that all non-Muslim women—including pre-pubescent girls—could be captured for enslavement, impregnated, passed around, and beaten:

> …it is permissible to capture unbelieving women who are characterized by Kufr Asil (original unbelief), such as the al-Kitabiyat (women from among the People of the Book, i.e. Jews and Christians) and polytheists… It is permissible to have sexual intercourse with the female captive… If she is a virgin, he (her master) can have intercourse with her immediately after taking possession of her. However, if she isn't, her uterus must be purified first… It is permissible to buy, sell, or give as a gift female captives and slaves, for they are merely property… It is permissible to have intercourse with the female slave who hasn't reached puberty if she is fit for intercourse… It is permissible to beat the female slave.[72]

A practical exemplar of this was 'Jihadi John,' whose reported 'kindness and generosity' included passing on 'a sabiyyah (concubine)' he received "as a gift… to an unmarried injured brother."[73] The open threat of enslavement was part of the IS psychological warfare of inducing terror:

> The State revels in gore and wants everyone to know it… Because violence and gore work.[74]

---

[70] Ibid., 4.

[71] Ibid., 8.

[72] Diwan al-Buhouth wal-Iftaa (Departments of Scholarly Research and Verdicts in the Islamic State), *Questions and Answers on Taking Captives and Slaves* (n.p.: al-Himma Library, 2014), 2–5.

[73] *Dabiq* 13, 23.

[74] William McCants, *The ISIS Apocalypse: The History, Strategy, and Doomsday Vision of the Islamic State* (New York: St. Martin's Publishing Group, 2015), 148.

IS threats and goals—especially enslavement and sexual exploitation—were deliberately chilling, contrasting how IS would have treated certain historical enemies or victims of Western war or oppression:

> The Japanese... would have been forcefully converted to Islam... and if they stubbornly declined, perhaps another nuke would change their mind. The Vietnamese would likewise be offered Islam or beds of napalm. As for the Native Americans – after the slaughter of their men... then the Muslims would have taken their surviving women and children as slaves, raising the children as model Muslims and impregnating their women to produce a new generation of mujahidin. As for the treacherous Jews of Europe and elsewhere... their post-pubescent males would face a slaughter that would make the Holocaust sound like a bedtime story, as their women would be made to serve their husbands' and fathers' killers... the lucrative African slave trade would have continued.[75]

Against dismissing this as propagandistic bravado rather than serious intent, consider the IS rape of Yezidis, terrorist massacres of Westerners and slaughter of Shia/Alawites, including the 2017 Tehran massacre of seventeen people by IS Iranian-Kurdish Sunnis. This unique existential threat to Shia meant they had no option of *Jizyah* or enslavement, as open to *Ahl-ul-Kitab* and pagans:

> The Rafidah are a disease which cannot be cured except with the sword.[76]

Again:

> It was also the verdict of Ibn Taymiyyah and others upon the Bātiniyyah including the Druze, the Nusayriyyah, and the Ismā'īliyyah... the Rāfidah are to be treated with the sword against riddah... the Rāfidah are mushrik apostates who must be killed wherever they are to be found.[77]

The annihilation of Shia (and Alawites, Druze, etc.), was a *declared* policy of genocide. This explains the extensive military involvement by Iran and Shia militia/volunteers from Pakistan, Afghanistan, etc.

---

[75] *Dabiq* 14, 1437 Rajab, 80.
[76] *Rumiyah* 9, Sha'ban 1438, 39.
[77] *Dabiq* 13, 1437 Rabi' Al-Akhir, 43, 45.

– whilst Westerners, Christians, etc. battled to preserve their *freedom*, Shia-related groups fought for their *physical* existence.

In World War II, the British Special Operations Executive (SOE) supported what was termed 'fifth column' elements in Nazi-occupied Europe, e.g. the Polish Resistance, and "the encouragement and supply of secret armies."[78] IS similarly saw Western Sunnis as potential *local* jihadis:

> As for the Muslim... unable to perform hijrah... there is much opportunity for him to strike out against the kāfir enemies of the Islamic State... In addition to killing crusader citizens... what... prevents him from targeting Rāfidī communities in Dearborn (Michigan), Los Angeles, and New York City?[79]

Though incapable of supplying weapons to such people, IS gave explicit direction on their usage – specifically the best knives or vans and the *modus operandi* with which to kill infidels.[80]

During *Operation Greif* in the Battle of the Bulge, 1944-1945, Waffen-SS fighters donned US uniforms, spoke American-accented English, etc., to deceive the Allies, aiming to seize "one or more of the bridges over the Meuse between Liege and Namur."[81] Similarly, Kim Philby, the British MI6 traitor who spied for the Soviets, before the War joined the pro-Nazi Anglo-German Fellowship, as instructed by his Soviet handler, to play down his previous Leftist sympathies.[82] IS has the same strategy – often referencing the hadith "War is deception."[83] Jihadi John was an exemplar:

> On his last attempt to leave the UK for his homeland of Kuwait, Abū Muhārib was stopped at the airport and kept for questioning by MI5... During the interrogation, Abū Muhārib would present himself as unintelligent... The Prophet said, "War is deception."[84]

---

[78] David Stafford, *Britain and European resistance, 1940-1945: A Survey of the Special Operations Executive, with Documents*, (London: Macmillan, 1980, 1983), 32, 132.

[79] *Dabiq* 11, 54.

[80] *Rumiyah* 2, Muharram 1438, 12–13; *Rumiyah* 3, Safar 1438, 10–11.

[81] Samuel W. Mitcham, *Panzers in winter: Hitler's army and the Battle of the Bulge* (London: Praeger, 2006), 30–31.

[82] Ben Macintyre, *A Spy Among Friends: Kim Philby and the Great Betrayal*, (London: Bloomsbury, 2014), 22, 41.

[83] *Dabiq* 7, 1436 Rabi' Al-Akhir, 13; *Dabiq* 13, 22; *Rumiyah* 9, 49.

[84] *Dabiq* 13, 22.

This was also applied to terrorism in non-Muslim countries:

> ...using deception as a tactic of warfare in order to lure one's target or trick them into believing that they are safe before killing them... is divinely approved... It is likewise one of the most appropriate methods to apply for the one seeking to slaughter large numbers of the kuffar while armed with something as simple and easily attainable as a knife.
>
> Those residing in the lands of disbelief will surely note the ease and simplicity in achieving the confidence and trust of a disbeliever. Portraying oneself to them as harmless gives them the impression that they are secure and free from danger.[85]

Perhaps this explains IS recruits who attempted *jihad* in their home countries or those who made *Hijrah* to the Caliphate (often inciting massacre against their former compatriots), but now in Western prisons or Kurdish camps, suddenly announcing their 'disillusionment' and 'remorse.' In the light of the IS directive "War is deception," it could be inferred that this is a tactic aimed at dispelling suspicion to get 'behind enemy lines,' free to strike at some future point:

> The issue of false compliance has recently come to prominence following a succession of jihadists who deceived authorities before carrying out attacks... Usman Khan, the 2019 London Bridge attacker, had participated in rehabilitation and disengagement programmes and was considered a success story of an extremist turning their life around.[86]

Khan, sentenced for terrorist offences in 2012, had deceived his Cambridge University rehabilitation ('Learning Together') mentors in prison into believing he had repented, and was due to speak at the event where he murdered two people, one being his rehabilitation mentor Jack Merrit.

Conclusion

The analytical historian not being the moral philosopher, ethical criticism is outside our brief – the facts speak for themselves. In terms of its pretensions to global conquest, and after so brief a

---

[85] *Rumiyah* 9, 49.
[86] Rajan Basra and Peter R. Neumann, *Prisons and Terrorism: Extremist Offender Management in 10 European Countries* (London: King's College, 2020), 28–29.

Reign of Terror (another French analogy), the IS Caliphate ended in Farce. However, it was certainly a Tragedy for its victims in every sense. This was especially true of its enslavement of Yezidis and attempted genocide against the Shia. At the time of writing, IS territorial control has been decimated, but it remains an active terrorist entity, with franchises – and volunteers – across the world. The IS Caliphate Restoration Tragedy has yet to reach its epilogue.

Bibliography

al-Mawardi, Abu'l-Hasan 'Ali ibn Muhammad ibn Habib al-Basri al-Baghdadi.
> *al-Ahkam as-Sultaniyyah: The Laws of Islamic Governance.* London: Ta-Ha, 2000.

Al-Tamimi, Aymenn Jawad.
> *Archive of Islamic State Administrative Documents*, January 27, 2015, https://www.aymennjawad.org/2015/01/archive-of-islamic-state-administrative-documents.
> _____. *The Islamic State of Iraq and ash-Sham's dhimmi pact for the Christians of Raqqa province*, February 26, 2014, https://www.aymennjawad.org/14472/the-islamic-state-of-iraq-and-ash-sham-dhimmi.
> _____. *This is our Aqeeda and This is our Manhaj: Islam 101 according to the Islamic State*, October 27, 2015, https://www.aymennjawad.org/2015/10/this-is-our-aqeeda-and-this-is-our-manhaj-islam#_edn27.

an-Nabhani, Taqiuddin.
> *The Islamic State.* London: Al-Khilafah Publications, 1998.

An-Nawawī, Al-Imâm Abū Zakariyya Yaḥyā bin Sharaf Ad-Dimshqi.
> *Riyâd -us Sâliheen.* Vol. 2. Riyadh: Darussalam, 2003.

Ansari, Muhammad 'Abdul-Haqq, ed.
> *Ibn Taymiyyah Expounds on Islam: Selected Writings of Shaykh al-Islam Taqi ad-Din Ibn Taymiyyah on Islamic Faith, Life, and Society.* Riyadh: General Administration of Culture and Publication/Islam Future, 2000.

Basra, Rajan and Neumann, Peter R.

Prisons and Terrorism: Extremist Offender Management in 10 European Countries. London: King's College, 2020.

Byman, Daniel.
Al Qaeda, The Islamic State, and the Global Jihadist Movement: What everyone needs to know. Oxford: Oxford University Press, 2015.

Dabiq 1, Ramadan 1435 downloaded from both the Clarion Project (Islamic State's [ISIS, ISIL] Horrific Magazine, Clarion Project) and Internet Archive.
Dabiq 4, 1435 Dhul-Hijjah.
Dabiq 7, 1436 Rabi' Al-Akhir.
Dabiq 11, 1436 Dhul Qa'dah.
Dabiq 13, 1437 Rabi' Al-Akhir.
Dabiq 14, 1437 Rajab.
Dabiq 15, 1437 Shawwal.

Diwan al-Buhouth wal-Iftaa (Departments of Scholarly Research and Verdicts in the Islamic State).
Questions and Answers on Taking Captives and Slaves. (n.p.): al-Himma Library, 2014.

Elder, Earl Edgar.
A Commentary on the Creed of Islam: Saʻd Al-Dīn Al-Taftāzānī on the Creed of Najm Al-Dīn Al-Nasafī. New York: Columbia University Press, 1950.

Fisk, Deborah Payne, ed.
The Cambridge Companion to English Restoration Theatre. Cambridge: Cambridge University Press, 2000.

Gerges, Fawaz A.,
The Far Enemy: Why Jihad Went Global. New York: Cambridge University Press, 2005.

Ibn Rajab.
Jami' al-Ulum wal-Hikam (A Collection of Knowledge and Wisdom). Al Mansura: Umm Al Qura, 2002.

Imber, Colin.

The Ottoman Empire, 1300–1650: The Structure of Power. New York: Palgrave Macmillan, 2002.

Ingram, Haroro J., Craig Whiteside, and Charlie Winter.
The ISIS Reader: Milestone Texts of the Islamic State Movement. Oxford: Oxford University Press, 2020.

Karpat, Kemal H.
The Politicization of Islam: Reconstructing Identity, State, Faith, and Community in the late Ottoman state. (Oxford: Oxford University Press, 2001.

Keller, Nuh Ha Mim, ed. and trans.
Reliance of the Traveller (The Classic Manual of Islamic Sacred Law 'Umdat al-Salik by Ahmad ibn Naqib al-Misri). Beltsville, MD: Amarna, 1997.

Khattab, Huda, ed.
The Essential Pearls and Gems of Ibn Taymiyyah. Riyadh: Darussalam, 2013.

Lawrence, Bruce, ed.
Messages to the World: The Statements of Osama Bin Laden. Translated by James Howarth. London: Verso, 2005.

Macfie, A. L.
The Eastern Question 1774–1923. Rev. ed. New York: Routledge, 2014.

Macintyre, Ben.
A Spy Among Friends: Kim Philby and the Great Betrayal. London: Bloomsbury, 2014.

Malkasian, Carter.
Illusions of Victory: The Anbar Awakening and the Rise of the Islamic State. Oxford: Oxford University Press, 2017.

Marx, Karl.
The Eighteenth Brumaire of Louis Bonaparte. 2nd ed. Translated by Daniel De Leon. Chicago, IL: Charles H. Kerr and Co., 1907.

McCants, William,
    *The ISIS Apocalypse: The History, Strategy, and Doomsday Vision
    of the Islamic State*. New York: St. Martin's Publishing Group,
    2015.

Mitcham, Samuel W.
    Panzers in Winter: Hitler's army and the Battle of the Bulge.
    London: Praeger, 2006.

Pankhurst, Reza.
    *The inevitable caliphate? A History of the struggle for global Islamic
    union, 1924 to the present*. Oxford: Oxford University Press,
    2013.

Paris, Timothy J.
    *Britain, the Hashemites and Arab rule, 1920–1925: The Sherifian
    solution*. London: Frank Cass, 2003.

Rumiyah 1, Dhul-Hijjah 1437, downloaded from both the Clarion
Project (Islamic State's [ISIS, ISIL] Horrific Magazine, Clarion
Project) and Internet Archive.
    Rumiyah 2, Muharram 1438.
    Rumiyah 3, Safar 1438.
    Rumiyah 9, Sha'ban1438.

Seidel, James.
    "Christmas under ISIS is a time of tension throughout the
    Middle East," *News*, published December 26, 2014,
    https://www.news.com.au/world/christmas-under-isis-is-
    a-time-of-tension-throughout-the-middle-east/news-
    story/e57ec60b66496e62f388074ebd496508.

Smith, G. Rex, trans.
    The History of al-Tabari. Vol. 14. Albany: Suny, 1994.

Stafford, David.
    *Britain and European resistance, 1940-1945: A Survey of the Special
    Operations Executive, with Documents*. London: Macmillan,
    1983.

Weiss, Michael Hassan.
    ISIS: Inside the Army of Terror. New York: Regan Arts, 2016.

Wright, Lawrence.
   The Looming Tower: Al-Qaeda and the road to 9/11. New York:
   Alfred A. Knopf, 2006.

Further Reading

Al-Britani, Abu Rumaysah.
   A Brief Guide to the Islamic State. (n.p., no stated publisher, but
   probably IS, 2015).

Atwan, Abdel Bari.
   Islamic State: The Digital Caliphate. Oakland, CA: University
   of California Press, 2015.

Cockburn, Patrick.
   *The Age of Jihad: Islamic State and the Great War for the Middle
   East.* London: Verso, 2016.

Filiu, Jean-Pierre.
   *From Deep State to Islamic State: The Arab Counter-Revolution
   and its Jihadi Legacy.* Oxford: Oxford University Press, 2015.

Hosken, Andrew.
   Empire of Fear: Inside the Islamic State. London: Oneworld,
   2015.

Kepel, Gilles, with Jardin, Antoine.
   Terror in France: The Rise of Jihad in the West (Princeton, NJ:
   Princeton University Press, 2017.

Mohamedou, Mohammad-Mahmoud Ould.
   *A Theory of ISIS: Political Violence and the Transformation of the
   Global Order.* London: Pluto Press, 2018.

Rogers, Paul.
   Irregular Warfare: ISIS and the new threat from the margins.
   London: I. B. Tauris, 2016.

Roy, Oliver.
   Jihad and death: The global appeal of Islamic State. Translated by
   Cynthia Schoch. Oxford: Oxford University Press, 2017.

Van Damme, Laurens.
   Contemporary Islamic Apocalyptic Thought: An Analysis of ISIS'
   Dabiq and Rumiyah. Ghent: University of Ghent, 2017–2018.

Chapter 9

A STATE OF 'UN-REALIZED ESCHATOLOGY':
Shi'ism, Iranian Constitutionalism, Regency and Khomeini's Theory of the Vilayet-i-Faqih

Anthony McRoy[1]

Introduction

Biblical scholar C. H. Dodd famously defined the ministry of Jesus as "realized eschatology," the impact upon this world of the "powers of the world to come" in "a series of events now in actual process."[2] G. E. Ladd stated:

> "The future Kingdom has invaded the present order to bring... the blessings of the age to come."[3] The eschatological consummation arrives with the *Parousia*: "...the final perfect realization of God's rule would be accomplished only by a supernatural, world-transforming act of God... the Second Coming of Christ."[4]

This is the 'already/not yet' tension of the Kingdom of God – inaugurated/unconsummated. This helps to clarify the self-image of the Islamic Republic of Iran and its constitutional guiding theological/ideological principle—the *Vilayet-i-Faqih*—the 'Guardianship of the Jurist.' Iran is governed on an eschatological dogma – the future manifestation of the Twelfth Imam as Mahdi. In one sense, for Iranian constitutionalism, the Mahdi's rule has *already* begun with the success of the 1979 Islamic Revolution; his advent completes the process. Hence, the Islamic Republic is a regime with

---

[1] Dr Anthony McRoy has dual Eire/UK citizenship, married with three adult children. He has lectured at several colleges, and contributed to both Muslim and Christian publications, and various academic works.

[2] C. H. Dodd, *The Parables of the Kingdom*, rev. ed. (Glasgow: Collins, 1978), 41.

[3] George E. Ladd, *The Presence of the Future* (Grand Rapids, MI: Eerdmans, 1974), 298 (originally published as *Jesus and the Kingdom* in 1964).

[4] Ibid., 335.

a built-in future constitutional *obsolescence*, occurring with the Mahdi's manifestation. Until then, it is in a state of *un*-realized eschatology.

Another way to consider Iranian constitutionality is as a *Regency*. In British history, this occurred because of *incapacity* – sometimes illness (e.g. George III from 1811, power being exercised by his son, designated Prince Regent); usually because of the Sovereign's *minority*, until he/she came of age, as with Mary, Queen of Scots, acknowledged as Sovereign after her birth in 1542; aged five sent to France (following her betrothal to the Dauphin) until 1561, during which, for most of the time, her mother, Mary of Guise, acted as Scots Regent. Regents usually enjoyed most, if not all the powers of the Sovereign, but again, there was a built-in anticipatory constitutional obsolescence – when the Sovereign attained maturity or returned from absence to reign (as with Mary), the Regency terminated.

In examining the *Vilayet-i-Faqih*, several factors must be recognised. Firstly, Shia political theology and the congruity of Religion and State in Islam in general. Secondly, it must be recalled that for much of their history, Shi'ites have been a minority or at least second-class citizens among Sunni-dominated societies, often persecuted. Thirdly, Iran is an ancient nation, with a proud history, but since the colonial era has suffered domination by non-Muslim entities – Russia, Britain and America:

> Iran's imperial legacy remains important to Iran's contemporary narrative. There is a strong sense among Iranians that Iran is a great civilization that deserves to be treated as a great power.[5]

Linked to this, Iran's domestic rulers have often been from outside the ethnic Persian majority. Many Shahs were weak, tyrannical and/or corrupt. As part of both the anti-imperialist struggle and a demand for constitutional rights, we must consider the 1906 Revolution and its contemporary influence. Finally, it must be remembered that the 1979 revolution was enacted by a *de facto* coalition of Islamists, democrats, secular nationalists and Leftists, and so the immediate constitutional arrangements following the Revolution partly reflected this.

---

[5] Patrick Clawson and Michael Rubin, *Eternal Iran: Continuity and Chaos* (New York: Palgrave Macmillan, 2005), 11.

Alid lineage as a central factor in Shia politics[6]

The central distinction between Sunni and Shia concerns the succession to Muhammad – as Amir, rather than Prophet. According to Shi'ism, the community is not to be led by communally-elected Caliphs, but by divinely-designated Imams:

> In Shi'i usage... *the term acquires a specialized sense as the person placed* in charge of all the political and religious affairs of the Islamic nation... the *Imam* is a person appointed by God and nominated first by the Prophet and then by each succeeding Imam, through explicit designation *to lead the Muslim community, to interpret* and safeguard both religion and law (shari'ah) and to guide the community in all its concerns.[7]

Shia believe that the first Imam was Ali.[8] All his successors should be of his family – the *Ahl-ul-Bayt*:

> Usul al-Kafi H 1373, Ch. 125, h 11
> "Amir al-Mu'minin Ali said to ibn 'Abbass, "...the Leaders with Divine Authority after the Messenger of Allah."
> Ibn 'Abbass then asked, "Who are they?" He said, "I and the eleven persons from my descendants who all are Imams."

Shi'ite traditions also present the election of Abu Bakr as the first Caliph as being essentially an illegitimate usurpation and *coup d'etat* – indeed, since Ali is held to be divinely-selected as the successor to Muhammad, as an act of apostasy:

> Usul al-Kafi H 1375, Ch. 126, h 13
> Ali took the hand of Abu Bakr and showed the Holy Prophet (s.a) to him, who said to him, "O Abu Bakr, believe in Ali and in the eleven Imams from his descendants. They are all like me except prophethood. Repent before Allah because of what you are involved in. You have no right in it."

Thus, religio-political authority in Shia Islam is held to lie with the Alid Imams. Therefore, in Shia theology, all other rulers are

---

[6] Parts of this section previously appeared in my paper "Shia Eschatology in Contemporary Politics," in *Islam and the Last Day*, ed. Brent J. Neely and Peter G. Riddell (Melbourne: MST Press, 2014), 91ff.
[7] Mohammad A. Shomali, *Shi'i Islam: Origins, Faith, and Practices* (London: ICAS, 2003), 93.
[8] Ibid., 16.

usurpers. Khomeini lamented the early history of Islam which perpetuated the defection from Alid legitimacy:

> After the death of the Most Noble Messenger (s), the obstinate enemies of the faith, the Umayyads... did not permit the Islamic state to attain stability with the rule of 'Ali ibn Abi Tālib ('a). They did not allow a form of government to exist that was pleasing to God... The form of government of the Umayyads and the Abbasids, and the political and administrative policies they pursued, were anti-Islamic. The form of government was thoroughly perverted by being transformed into a monarchy... this non-Islamic form of government has persisted to the present day.[9]

This holds true for *all* non-Muslim political authority, not just in terms of the religious identity of the rulers, but also of their constitutional structure – it must be according to Shia *Shari'a*, and led by Alids. Even *Shia* rulers who do not meet these criteria are guilty of apostasy. The Shia *must* be ruled by the Imam of the Age. It follows that any other regime is inherently illegitimate and oppressive. Shi'ism places a particular emphasis on justice ('*adl*):

> This emphasis on divine justice has influenced not only the theoretical aspect of Shi'ism, for the Shi'a regard justice as such so fundamental an aspect of Islam that they have often called for its implementation in society.[10]

Justice is defined as being what Allah has revealed:

> ...He never commits any injustice towards His servants and never oppresses anyone.[11]

Hence, to appoint someone as ruler who has not been so-designated by Allah is unjust and thus sinful/heretical, and anyone who governs by other than the Shia *Shari'a* is unjust – an oppressor.

Significantly, Muhammad's grandson Hussein is said to have journeyed to Iraq in response to an agonised plea by the people of Kufa in 680 AD:

---

[9] Ayatollah Khomeini, *Islamic Government*, trans. Hamid Algar (Tehran: The Institute for Compilation and Publication of Imam Khomeini's Works, 2002), 44.
[10] Shomali, *Shi'i Islam*, 93.
[11] Ibid., 91–92.

This is a letter to Husayn bin Ali from his Muslim and faithful supporters. Be quick... for the people are waiting for you, and they do not look towards anyone other than you.[12]

The usual Shia exclamation upon reference to the Mahdi is "May Allah hasten his coming (or return)." The people of Kufa urgently desired the coming of an Imam who would establish 'justice' and deliver them from 'oppression', and it was this which Hussein promised in his reply to them:

You have written that you do not have an Imam and asked me to come to you so that Allah may perhaps draw you together on truth and guidance through me... I swear by my life that a true Imam and leader is only he who takes decisions according to the Qur'an, establishes justice, promotes the Divine religion and dedicates himself to the path of Allah.[13]

British historical examples help us to comprehend this. After the death of Edward VI, there was an attempt to thwart the will of Henry VIII by enthroning Edward's cousin Lady Jane Grey ('the Nine Days' Queen') rather than the legitimate heir, Mary, but 'people power' rejected this constitutionally illegitimate move, enforcing the rightful succession. Later, in 1688 when James II was deposed in the Glorious Revolution, and his son was banned from the succession, followers of James (nicknamed 'Jacobites') fought for what they held was constitutional legitimacy, rising in 1715 and 1745. The problem they faced was the *other* side of constitutional legitimacy – the liberties of the people as enshrined in Magna Carta and subsequent laws, not least those assigned to the Anglican Church, which James, as part of his 'Catholic Design', sought to overthrow. Effectively, Magna Carta established in English law the principle of a limited monarchy/Executive, as opposed to the absolutism in Continental monarchies. This aids in understanding the *revolutionary* character of Shia political thought – insurrection is justifiable when faced with an illegitimate regime characterised by oppression, even under an ethnic Persian Shia dynasty such as the Pahlavis.

The problem for Shia politics and specifically governance is that the Twelfth Imam – Muḥammad ibn al-Ḥasan al-Mahdī, born 869 AD – disappeared from public view; he began the 'lesser occultation'

---

[12] Ibrahim Ayati, *A Probe into the History of Ashura* (Karachi: Islamic Seminary Publications, 1985), http://al-islam.org/ashura.
[13] Ibid.

in 874, during which he communicated by a succession of four deputies, and the 'greater occultation' in 941, since when there has been no direct communication: "The Shi'a believe that he is the son of Imam Hasan al-'Askari. He was born in 255 (A.H). His occultation began in the year 260 (A.H). He is still alive, but... in the state of occultation till preparations are made for his reappearance."[14] This left a constitutional hole in Shia politics – how could there be *any* legitimate governance in his absence?

The scholars as the heirs or regents of the Imam with respect to Shia dynasties

The religious scholars made their rather obvious assertion about governance while the Imam was not present:

> In his absence, community leadership has generally been held by the scholars (*'ulamā'*), since (they argue) they were delegated by the Imams (when present) to adopt this role.[15]

There is support in Shia traditions for this, for example: "Imām Alī (A.S.) said, 'The scholars are the governors over people,' (*Ghurar al-Hikam*, no. 507)."[16] Kulayni's *al-Kāfi* presents a hadith supporting this:

H 118, Ch. 14, h 5
Ali... said the following.
"The holy Prophet has said, *Al-Fuqaha*, the scholars of the *Fiqh*, Islamic laws are the trustees of the prophets until they are not involved in the worldly matters." People asked, "What is their entering in the worldly matters, O the holy Prophet of Allah?" "Their following the kings is entering in the worldly matters. When they follow the kings then you must be very careful in involving them in your religion." Replied the holy Prophet (s.a.).

Perhaps, originally, it simply implied that *ulema* should avoid political entanglements. Some suggest this *was* the situation after the martyrdom of Hussein at Kerbela:

---

[14] Ibid., 109.
[15] Robert Gleave, *Scripturalist Islam: The History and Doctrines of the Akhbārī Shī'ī School* (Leiden: Brill, 2007), 4–5.
[16] M. Mohammadi Rayshahri, *The Scale of Wisdom: A Compendium of Shi'a Hadith*, trans. N. Virjee et al. (London: ICAS, 2009), 783, 1270.

An entire series of traditions, traceable to various imams and recorded in Shi'i canonical writings, emphasises this separation of the worldly and spiritual realms. The faithful are forbidden to seek power or to collaborate with men of power: "Beware of those who command and promote themselves as leaders..." Thus the faithful are forbidden to rise up against the powers of this world... "None among the Shia has rebelled, or will rebel, even against oppression or to defend a just cause, lest a great calamity tear him up by the roots. And so shall it be until the return of the Imam of the Resurrection. The rebellion of one of us will only provoke more suffering for us, the Imams, and for our followers."

In short, these texts ban all political activity by the faithful.[17]

The phrase 'easier said than done' comes to mind as an appropriate analysis of the idea of clerical rule in the face of the historical realities that Shia faced after this period. Sachedina elaborates on this issue:

The Imamite jurists, who lived as a minority in the Sunnite circle and who were faced with challenges from within and without, had to deal with two major problems in the absence of the Imam: first, organizing the transmitted sources of the Imamite school in order to systematize the central doctrines, like the Imamate, which were under attack; secondly, organizing the community so as to ensure its survival under the Sunnite dominance.[18]

Whilst the ideal might have been a State led by Shia *fuqaha*, the reality was that as a minority and often persecuted, the aspiration was prevented from being realised. Almost concurrent with the start of the Great Occultation was the rise of the ethnic Iranian Buyid dynasty, whose empire eventually stretched from Syria to the Subcontinent. Possibly originally Zaydi Shia, they moved to the Twelver position:

In 945, a Shi'a family—the Buyids—which had grown to control much of Iran, seized control of Baghdad. While accepting the titular authority of the Abbasid caliph, these

---

[17] Mohammad Ali Amir-Moezzi and Christian Jambet, *What is Shi'i Islam? An Introduction* (Oxford: Routledge, 2018), 26.
[18] Abdulaziz Abdul Hussein Sachedina, *The Just Ruler (al-sultān al-'ādil) in Shī'ite Islam: The Comprehensive Authority of the Jurist in Imamite Jurisprudence* (Oxford: Oxford University Press, 1998), 60.

rulers assumed control as the grand *vazir* – in fact, they used the ancient Sassanian title, *Shahanshah* (Shah of Shahs).[19]

While in many ways the Shia might have welcomed the arrival of a sympathetic regime, it should be borne in mind that the Buyid dynasty was tainted by two matters. Firstly, as already observed, their attachment to the infidel Sasanian empire, which had no role in Shia thought. Secondly, they were willing to compromise with the Sunni Abbasid caliphate:

> 'Adud al-Daula observed all the prescribed ceremonial and prostrated himself before the caliph...
> Even the Samanids, though strict Sunnis, displayed considerable reverence for the Iranian royal past, especially when it came to genealogies. But 'Adud al-Daula went one step further by obtaining the approval of the caliph... and by claiming descent from the great kings of the past. He was a devout Muslim, and was undoubtedly convinced that the coexistence of caliphate and monarchy would provide a solution for the political and religious problems of the period.[20]

This showed that even a Shi'ite regime could not properly defend Shia governmental theology. Ultimately, this demonstrated that only the Heirs of the Prophets (and *de facto* Deputies of the Imams) could provide any semblance of legitimate governance during the Occultation, not the Buyids:

> In no time they put an end to the influence of the other great Shi'i families. Consequently, only the doctors of the Law remained to fill the power vacuum created by the occultation... During the Buyid period, the principal aim of the doctors of the Law seems to have been... to provide justification for power-sharing with the Buyids and, ultimately, with the Abbasids.[21]

This again suggests two factors: the role of *ijtihad*, and the problem of legitimate governance even under a Shia regime, and indeed, as far as Iran is concerned, even a Persian one. Experience demonstrated to Shia the impossibility of valid governance by those not *theologically* equipped to administer it. Shaykh al-Mufid (d.

---

[19] Clawson and Rubin, *Eternal Iran*, 19.
[20] Herbert Busse, "Iran under the Buyids," in *The Cambridge History of Iran*, ed. R. N. Frye (Cambridge: Cambridge University Press, 2008), 4:276–277.
[21] Amir-Moezzi and Jambet, *What is Shi'i Islam*, 107.

413/1022) attempted to address the issue of governance during the Occultation by arguing

> that unjust power is either illegitimate (as in the case of Abbasid power and other non-Shi'i powers in general) or it is legitimate (as in the case of Buyid power since the Buyids were stalwart Shia who were well disposed to handing over the reins of power to the Hidden Imam upon his return).[22]

Notice the qualifications therein – the need for a regime to be religiously faithful, and implicitly, the concept of temporary *regency* until the manifestation of the Mahdi. Shaykh al-Tusi (d. 460/1067) built on this:

> According to Tusi, a ruler can be considered just if he commands Good, forbids Evil and distributes religious taxes equitably in accordance with Shi'i legal injunctions ...Thus, just power is not the exclusive province of the imams. A ruler who governs in accordance with Shi'i canon law is also a just ruler. Tusi explained this notion with reference to his doctrine of divine Grace (*lutf*), according to which God in His justice cannot allow His servants to live indefinitely under the authority of unjust governments. Thus, the great theorist of the late Buyid period succeeded in introducing new ideas for the establishment of a "just power" during the occultation.[23]

The situation became more acute after the Buyids were overthrown by the Sunni Seljuk Turks in 1055, leaving Iran and the Twelver Shia in general under Sunni rule until 1501. It was then the Safavids took power until 1736:

> The historical achievement of the Safavids was to establish a strong, enduring state in Iran after centuries of foreign rule and a lengthy period of political fragmentation.[24]

The Safavids gloried in Iran's identity, but also established Iran as a Twelver Shia entity – Shah Ismā'īl "announced that the official religion of his kingdom would be Shi'ism."[25] The effect of this change was not only theological, but also political and national, in that the Shia scholars imported into Iran at this time

---

[22] Ibid., 111.
[23] Ibid.
[24] H. R. Roemer, "The Safavid Period," in *The Cambridge history of Iran*, ed. Peter Jackson and Laurence Lockhart (Cambridge: Cambridge University Press, 1986), 6:189.
[25] Elton L. Daniel, *The History of Iran* (London: Greenwood Press, 2001), 87.

were prepared to transform Shi'ism from a religion of the community to that of the state, proposing significant modifications in political theory.[26]

Internally, efforts were made to produce communal cohesion by conversion to Shi'ism:

> Soon after Shah Isma'il I ascended the throne, he mandated that all regions under Safavid control accept Twelver Shi'ism. His immediate successors also persevered in their efforts to convert Persia's numerous tribal groups and social classes to Twelver Shi'ism.[27]

Henceforth, a distinctive Shia-Iranian identity was asserted over against Sunni entities outside their borders, such as the Ottomans, Uzbeks and Mughals.

By converting Iran to Shi'ism, the country was immediately relieved of even nominal obedience to the Sunni Ottoman Caliph, but the issue of theological legitimacy remained, even though the Safavids (perhaps dubiously) claimed to be "descendants of the Prophet Mohammad through the Imam Mousa al-Kazem."[28] The Shia clerics were *Arabs* imported by the Safavids, and so the former owed their positions to the latter:

> The decision to patronize these Syrian clerics rested on the belief that the 'Amilis would provide a much-needed source of legitimacy for imperial sovereignty. For their part, the 'Amilis consented to such sovereignty, and eagerly sought Safavid patronage.[29]

Further, these scholars

> advocated a socio-political role for the jurists and had little compunction about associating with temporal rulers or receiving financial rewards from them... The new empire needed clerics like the 'Amilis who could 'invent' sources of legitimacy.[30]

---

[26] Rula Jurdi Abisaab, *Converting Persia: Religion and Power in the Safavid Empire* (London: I. B. Tauris, 2004), 4.
[27] Ibid., 8.
[28] Daniel, *The History of Iran*, 84.
[29] Abisaab, *Converting Persia*, 9.
[30] Ibid., 12.

However, Shia clerics in Iraq objected. This can be seen in the experience of a senior scholar like 'Abd al-'Ali al-Karaki (d. 940 A.H./153A.D.), also known as al-Muhaqqiq al-Thani, another 'Amili:

Shi'ite jurists, particularly in Iraq, rejected any association with temporal rule even under a Shi'ite sovereign like Shah Isma'il who claimed descent from the Seventh Imam. As long as the Twelfth Imam is in hiding, conventional jurists continued to shun involvement in governmental institutions. Al-Karaki, like succeeding 'Amili theologians, never accepted claims by Safavid followers that the Shahs were the rightful Imams, and agreed that the political state of the Mahdi is the ideal legitimate form of authority for Shi'ites. Nonetheless, they considered the religious service and support, which a cleric renders to a 'just' ruler in the absence of the Imam, necessary and spiritually rewarding. Shi'ite law differentiated between the just and unjust ruler and considered the sovereignty of the latter illegitimate. Adept and pious jurists can even assume the functions of the 'just' ruler during the period of awaiting the Mahdi, known as the Occultation (*ghayba*).[31]

Al-Karaki, in his attempt to provide legitimacy for the Safavids, arguably sowed the seeds for Khomeini's theories. This came about as a result of Safavid desire to re-institute Friday prayers to legitimise their regime:

Sovereigns normally led Friday prayer or appointed a special deputy to fulfill this duty. For the most part, however, Shi'ites viewed the rule of Sunnite caliphs and sultans as a usurpation of the rights of their Imams, the descendants of 'Ali and Fatima. Consequently, they rejected participation in Friday prayer... Al-Karaki... declared that congregational prayer must be held by a designated *mujtahid* who is qualified to act as the general deputy of the Hidden Imam. Only in the presence of such a *mujtahid* or the Imam himself is it absolutely necessary for Shi'ites to perform Friday prayer. Al-Karaki insisted the *mujtahid* does not need a special appointment from the Hidden Imam to perform Friday prayer. A general deputyship is sufficient. Nowhere did al-Karaki state that the sovereign should identify the deputy of the Imam. Only a high-ranking cleric and legal expert can determine who is qualified to be the general deputy of the Imam. In retrospect, al-Karaki extended

---

[31] Ibid., 15–16.

to the jurist a socio-political base somewhat independent from the sovereign.[32]

Further, "As early as 916AH/1510 CE... al-Karaki designated himself the deputy of the Imam. Al-Karaki was eager to awaken the political aspects of Shi'ism and resolve the paradox caused by the Occultation."[33]

Another court mullah, an 'Amili 'émigré and outstanding jurist, Husayn b. 'Abd al-Samad al-Harithi al-Juba'i (d. 984 AH/1576 CE), became a significant figure at Shah Tahmasb's court. He felt that the Shah was not equipped to evaluate claimants to *ijtihad* or safeguard society from false *mujtahids*. Husayn reminded the Shah that "divine will limits his political sovereignty and undermines his authority."[34] These were the views of someone *committed* to the Safavid dynasty, and yet we see that, for theological reasons, aspects of his opinions circumscribed the Royal authority. He later penned a poem that "showed his deep discontent with the Shah's lifestyle and his sense of alienation from Safavid society."[35] That this was no aberration can be seen in this quote from Keddie:

> In late Safavid times some mujtahids claimed that they had more right to rule than did the impious, wine-bibbing shahs. They did not yet say they should rule directly, an idea that came forth only with Ayatollah Khomeini, but that the shah should carry out their rulings when given and defend the nation militarily. The political claims of the Iranian ulama developed further from the eighteenth century on.[36]

An example of this was Shah 'Abbas, who enjoyed "wine-drinking and drugs, and various forms of entertainment like dancing and singing."[37] The Shia *ulema* merely *tolerated* the Safavids, because they enabled Shi'ism to function freely and on a State level, and because they militarily defended the only Shia state surrounded by hostile Sunnism. Their toleration was essentially *expedient*, exemplified in the words of Shaykh Ahmad Ardabīlī, who "reminded

---

[32] Ibid., 20–21.
[33] Ibid., 23.
[34] Ibid., 32, 37–38.
[35] Ibid., 41.
[36] Nikki R. Keddie (with a section by Yann Richard), *Modern Iran: Roots and Results of Revolution* (New Haven, CT: Yale University Press, 2006), 17.
[37] Abisaab, *Converting Persia*, 68.

his monarch, Shah 'Abbas, that he was ruling over a 'borrowed kingdom' (*mulk-i 'āriya*)."[38] The legitimate authority remained the Imam.

The Safavids were overthrown by the Sunni Afghan invasion in 1722, but this regime was overthrown by Nadir Shah, who declared himself Shah in 1736, and was a tyrant with a "forceful and harsh ruling style, combined with his lack of governing ability."[39] Worse, he was guilty of *bida* (innovation in religion) by advancing the idea of a *de facto* fusion of Sunnism and Shi'ism:

> He called for the integration of Shi'ism into Sunni Islam as a fifth *madhhab* (school of Islamic legal interpretation) that would enjoy the same status as the conventional four Sunni *madhhabs*.[40]

At his enthronement, he served wine, and declared:

> if the people of Persia desire that we (Nadir) should reign, they must abandon this doctrine... and (they must) follow the religion of the Sunnis.[41]

It has been questioned whether he had any real religious beliefs at all, this innovation being an attempt at reconciliation with the Ottomans.[42] This showed that the Shia could not trust the monarchy to maintain their theological stance.

After Nadir's assassination in 1747, a period of instability followed, until Karim Khan between 1751–1760 managed to assert control over most of Iran and establish the Zand dynasty. What is interesting is the title he assumed, as well as his general policies: "He never took a title such as shah and continued to act as a *vakil*, but now as *vakil-al-raaya*, regent 'for the people'... He supported Shi'ite religious practices... He rarely resorted to cruel or excessive punishments."[43] Significantly, Keddie observes:

---

[38] Hamid Algar, *Religion and State in Iran, 1785–1906: The Role of the Ulama in the Qajar Period* (Berkeley, CA: University of California Press, 1980), 22.
[39] Ernest S. Tucker, *Nadir Shah's Quest for Legitimacy in Post-Safavid Iran* (Gainesville, FL: University Press of Florida, 2006), 67.
[40] Ibid., 1.
[41] L. Lockhart, *Nadir Shah: A Critical Study Based Mainly Upon Contemporary Sources*, 2nd ed. (Lahore: Al-Irfan, 1938), 98–99.
[42] Ibid., 100.
[43] Daniel, *The History of Iran*, 98.

Their popularity and their refusal to call themselves shahs, preferring to be called "deputies" either of the Safavids or, even better, of the people, made them the only rulers whose names were not taken off streets and monuments after the 1979 revolution.[44]

The pertinent point is the implied nod to popular sovereignty. This was to come to the fore during the Qajar and Pahlavi eras, and still is present in the Islamic Republic.

The Qajars and Pahlavis: Constitutional Revolution and the *Vilayet i-Faqih*

By 1794-96, the Turcoman Qajars had overthrown the Zands. Although Persianate and Shia, they are renowned for two issues: the shrinkage of Iran's independence and borders, and the Constitutional Revolution. They claimed descent from "ancient Iranian dynasties and... the Shi'i Imams."[45] Initially, the Qajars courted the *ulema* and 'clearly felt they needed the 'ulama's consent and cooperation in order to buttress their own precarious legitimacy as successors to the Safavids', but we should also recognise "the 'ulama's ambivalence in collaborating with the Qajar shahs."[46] Boldly, the Qajars considered the Shah as the "shadow of God [*zillullah*] on earth."[47] Other titles included "'refuge of Islam" (*Islam panah*) and a "shield of the Islamic shari'a" (*shari'at panah*).[48] Such honorifics, however, were hostages to fortune.

Notably, they could not preserve Iran's borders. Russia's expansionist policies in the Caucasus led to war with Iran, settled by the Treaty of Golestan (1813) and the Treaty of Turkomanchay of 1828, which confirmed the Aras river as the border.[49] The 'Shadow of Allah' was evidently not a strong 'Shield of Islam,' and this was emphasised with Iran becoming a pawn in the Great Game between Russia and Britain up to the Great War.[50] The *theological*

---

[44] Keddie, *Modern Iran*, 37.

[45] Ervand Abrahamian, *A History of Modern Iran* (Cambridge: Cambridge University Press, 2008), 17.

[46] Abbas Amanat, *Pivot of the Universe: Nasir Al-Din Shah Qajar and the Iranian Monarchy, 1831–1896* (Berkeley, CA: University of California Press, 1997), 5.

[47] Ibid., 9.

[48] Ibid., 10.

[49] Manoutchehr M. Eskandari-Qajar, "Between Scylla and Charybdis," in *War and Peace in Qajar Persia: Implications Past and Present*, ed. R. Farmanfarmaian (New York: Routledge, 2008), 27.

[50] Ibid., 21.

consequences of this failure of Shia *jihad* is that obviously, Allah did not smile on a regime of questionable legitimacy. Effective Western/infidel domination was to be an enduring factor of Iranian politics until the 1979 Revolution, as was Western treachery – between 1801 and 1814. Iran signed various treaties with Britain and France, which they both violated:

> The nineteenth century thus introduced Iran to the inscrutable ways of Occidentals, who might break treaties within less than a year of signing them, switch allies and enemies at their own whim, and hence behave in ways that Iranians versed in politics could only consider utterly irrational.[51]

The vital point for our concerns is that Fath Ali Shah, who ruled 1797-1834, was unable to do anything about it, even at the urging of the *ulema*:

> Some preachers cited... mistreatment suffered by their coreligionists in Russian Caucasia. Influenced in part by leading and vocal ulama, some within the Iranian government encouraged the growing pressure for holy war (jihad) against Russia. Fath Ali Shah then proclaimed jihad, launching an attack on the Russians in 1826. The Iranian army, with only a minority of well-drilled and modernized forces, was decisively defeated.[52]

The obvious reason for the defeat was the relative competence and equipment of the two armies, but again, theologically, it could be interpreted that Allah withheld His blessing from an illegitimate regime. This must be considered when we analyse the nature of the 1979 Revolution – effectively, a religious uprising/*jihad* was *successful* in liberating Shia-Islamic territory from infidel domination and an illegitimate regime. Keddie shows how this domination was also economic, to the detriment of Iranian manufacture and exports.[53] However,

> the numerous Iranian merchants and workers who travelled to India, Russian Transcaucasia, and Turkey could witness reforms and hear liberal or radical ideas suggesting ways that governments could change and could undertake self-

---

[51] Keddie, *Modern Iran*, 38.
[52] Ibid., 41.
[53] Ibid., 51–53.

strengthening policies of a kind that might better Iran's condition and free it from foreign control.[54]

Simultaneously, the propaganda of the pan-Islamist anti-imperialist Sayyed Jamal ad-Din al-Afghani (1839–97), an Iranian Shi'ite despite his name, along with other reformers and traders, opposed Shah Naser al-Din's monopoly concession of tobacco to a Briton in 1891, which, with clerical involvement, led to mass protests, and national boycott of tobacco, successfully overturning the concession.[55] This demonstrated the success of 'people power' (as opposed to armed insurgency), anti-imperialism and the power of *taqlid*, where the pious imitate a senior *mujtahid* – in this case against their regime's collaboration with infidel domination. Naser al-Din— who was infamous for "his lifelong interest in women and young boys"—was assassinated by one of Afghani's followers.[56]

The new Shah, Mozaffar ad-Din, was inept and extravagant, and under him Russian and later British economic influence (notably the D'Arcy oil concession) increased at the expense of Iranian businesses. An act by the Tehran governor provoked the Revolution:

> The Iranian constitutional revolution is usually dated from December 1905, when the governor of Tehran beat the feet of several sugar merchants... A large crowd of ulama then decided, at the suggestion of the prominent liberal mujtahid, Sayyed Mohammad Tabataba'i, to retire to the shrine of Shahzadeh Abd al-Azim and formulate demands for the shah. The crucial demand was for a representative *adalatkhaneh* (house of justice) of which the meaning and composition were left unclear — perhaps in order to maintain the unity of modernizers and traditional ulama.[57]

However, the Shah procrastinated, and protests continued, until a *sayyed* was killed, leading to further tumult and the demand for a *majles*. Eventually, this was granted. The resultant constitution was an amalgam of Belgian law with restrictions based on Shia *Shari'a*. Being partly based on a European constitutional-monarchy arrangement, it necessarily *limited* the power of the Shah, and provided for a measure of *popular* sovereignty – problematic in Islam,

---

[54] Ibid., 58.
[55] Ibid., 61–62.
[56] Ibid., 63–64.
[57] Ibid., 67.

especially Shi'ism, which asserts *divine* sovereignty. However, the caveat to this is the problem of the absence of the Imam. The preamble to 'The Fundamental Law [*Qānūn-e Āsāsī-e Mashrūteh*] of the Iranian Empire of December 30, 1906' included the *bismillah*, so asserting divine sanction for the constitution. It proceeded to state:

> We issue a Command for the establishment of a National Consultative Assembly [and a Senate] to... give effect to the enactments of the Sacred Law of His Holiness the Prophet; and whereas, by virtue of the fundamental principle [therein laid down], we have conferred on each individual of the people of our realm, for the amending and superintending of the affairs of the commonwealth, according to their degrees, the right to participate in choosing and appointing the members of this Assembly by popular election.[58]

This was an amalgam of sacred law and secular principle – the assembly would effect *Shari'a*, yet this is qualified by Article 17:

> The National Consultative Assembly shall, when occasion arises, bring forward such measures as shall be necessary for the creation, modification, completion or abrogation of any Law, and, subject to the approval of the Senate, shall submit it for the Royal Approval, so that due effect may thereafter be given to it.[59]

This allowed for extra-*Shari'a* legislation, but 'The Amendment of the Fundamental Law of the Iranian Empire of October 7, 1907' qualified this by stating:

> Art. 1. The official religion of Iran is Islām, according to the orthodox *Ja'farī* doctrine of the *Ithnā 'Ashariyya* ... which faith the *Shāh* of Iran must profess and promote.
> Art. 2. At no time must any legal enactment of the sacred National Consultative Assembly... be at variance with the sacred principles of Islām... it is for the 'ulamā'... to determine whether such statutory laws are or are not conformable to the principles of Islām.[60]

---

[58] Tilmann J. Röder, "The Separation of Powers in Muslim Countries: Historical and Comparative Perspectives," in *Constitutionalism in Islamic Countries: Between Upheaval and Continuity*, ed. Rainer Grote II and Tilmann J. Röder (Oxford: Oxford University Press, 2012), 359.
[59] Ibid., 361.
[60] Ibid., 365–366.

However, Art. 26 stated: "The powers of the realm are [all] derived from the people."[61] So, both Allah and the Iranian people were sovereign. This was expressed in the latter case by the Assembly, elected by restricted male suffrage, and in the former by the clerical Council of Guardians, which had the power of veto over any laws enacted by the *Majles*:

> The decision of this Ecclesiastical Committee shall be followed and obeyed, and this article shall continue unchanged until the appearance of His Holiness the Proof of the Age, may God hasten his glad Advent![62]

There was thus a built-in obsolescence of the Council. Likewise, the powers of the Shah depended on popular sovereignty and divine blessing: "Art. 35. The sovereignty is a trust, which in Divine blessing, has been conferred by the people to the person of the King."[63]

The Constitution was overthrown by the next Shah, with foreign support, and during the Great War, Ottoman, Russian and British forces violated Iran's borders. The Qajars, having demonstrated their impotence in defending Iran, were overthrown by Reza Khan in 1925, after he, as Commander of the Cossack Brigade, had mounted a coup in 1921. An admirer of Atatürk, he initially wanted to declare a republic, but clerical pressure, eager to avoid Kemalist secularism, resulted in his taking the throne instead.[64] Significantly,

> He took the dynastic name Pahlavi, an ancient term meaning "heroic" that consciously evoked Iran's pre-Islamic past.[65]

Iran quickly became an authoritarian dictatorship where the *majlis* became a *façade*. Ideologically,

> Official nationalism propagated an emphasis on Iranian history and literature, with stress on the pre-Islamic empires and de-emphasis of Islam.[66]

---

[61] Ibid., 367.
[62] Ibid., 366.
[63] Ibid., 368.
[64] Touraj Atabaki and Erik J. Zürcher, *Men of Order: Authoritarian Modernization under Atatürk and Reza Shah* (London: I. B. Tauris, 2004), 21.
[65] Richard Foltz, *Iran in World History* (Oxford: Oxford University Press, 2016), 96.
[66] Keddie, *Modern Iran*, 99.

In 1935, the attack on religious identity included enforcing men to wear Western headgear, which led to protests in Mashad, which was brutally suppressed.[67] Western dress was obligated on women in 1936.[68] However, Reza was unable to resist the Anglo-Soviet invasion in 1941 which de-throned him in favour of his son, Mohammad Reza, displaying that not only was he an impious tyrant, but that he could not even safeguard the country against infidel conquest.

The young Mohammad Reza owed his position – weak as it was – to the British. Despite being married (successively) to three beautiful women, Mohammad Reza was a serial, open philanderer.[69] The impression Iranians gained was of an impious playboy. His best friend and companion, Ernest Perron, who followed him from Switzerland to Tehran, was a flamboyant homosexual.[70] The new Shah, under Allied encouragement, moved to respect the constitution.[71] However, this led to the rise of nationalist and leftist bodies, the former being best represented by the National Front and its leading politician, Mohammad Mosaddeq. Appointed Prime Minister in 1951, he pushed for the nationalisation of the Anglo-Iranian Oil Company (now BP) which largely owned Iran's oil. This eventuated in the Anglo-American coup (Operation Ajax) in 1953, notably through the CIA agent Kermit Roosevelt, and involving the Shah.[72] A dictatorship under the Shah himself was established, and brutal oppression became the hallmark of the regime:

> The coup seriously undermined the legitimacy of the monarchy... It identified the shah with... the imperial powers... It destroyed the National Front and the Tudeh Party – both suffered mass arrests, destruction of their organizations, and even executions of their leaders... the coup helped replace nationalism, socialism, and liberalism with Islamic "fundamentalism."[73]

Once again, the State's Crisis of Legitimacy was exposed. The Shah and the military had colluded with infidel powers to overthrow

---

[67] Atabaki and Zürcher, *Men of Order*, 33.
[68] Ibid., 34.
[69] Ibid., 78.
[70] Ibid., 158.
[71] Ibid., 92; Keddie, *Modern Iran*, 106, 109.
[72] Daniel, *The History of Iran*, 153. See Kermit Roosevelt's own account, *Countercoup: The Struggle for the Control of Iran* (New York: McGraw-Hill, 1979).
[73] Ervand, *A History of Modern Iran*, 122.

the legitimate government and maintain control of Iran's key resource. Democratic nationalism and Communism (the Tudeh) had proved incapable of resisting this. The obvious client-state character of the Shah was displayed in SAVAK:

> He received technical assistance from the Israeli intelligence service, as well as from the CIA and the FBI, to establish in 1957 a new secret police named Sazmani Ittila'at va Amniyat-i Keshvar (National Security and Information Organization), soon to become notorious under its acronym SAVAK.[74]

Effective economic and intelligence relations with Israel were established between 1950-58.[75] This was despite popular pro-Palestinian sentiment – a contingent of Iranian volunteers fought in the Arab-Israeli War in 1948.[76]

The Shah also moved to culturally de-Islamise Iran – not just by normal secularism in dress, cinema, etc., but by harking back to its pre-Islamic past by the hugely expensive 1971 Persepolis celebrations, supposedly commemorating 2,500 years of Iranian monarchy (but which largely excluded Iranians themselves, and their Shia heritage), and by instituting "a new calendar that was supposedly based on the date of Cyrus's coronation instead of Mohammad's hegira."[77] In the eyes of pious, patriotic Iranians, the Shah was a tyrannical U.S. puppet/quisling – in religious terms, an apostate. Yet neither the nationalists nor the Left were able to overcome the regime:

> ...the shah's regime became more repressive... SAVAK had a new target in those years – radical movements prepared to use violence against the regime. This notably included the Marxist Feda'i and the Mojahedin-e Khalq Organization (MKO), both of which fused Islam and Marxism. SAVAK expanded, and its use of torture became routine. In 1975 Amnesty International pronounced the shah's government to be one of the world's worst violators of human rights.[78]

[74] Abrahamian Ervand, *Iran Between Two Revolutions* (Princeton, NJ: Princeton University Press, 1982), 419.

[75] Roham Alvandi, *Nixon, Kissinger, and the Shah: The United States and Iran in the Cold War* (Oxford: Oxford University Press, 2016), 71.

[76] Abbas Amanat, *Iran: A Modern History* (New Haven, CT: Yale University Press, 2017), 527.

[77] Javier Gil Guerrero, *The Carter Administration and the Fall of Iran's Pahlavi Dynasty: US-Iran Relations on the Brink of the 1979 Revolution* (New York: Palgrave Macmillan, 2016), 17.

[78] Michael Axworthy, *Iran: Empire of the Mind* (New York: Basic Books, 2008), 250.

The other factor is that neither element could present an alternative constitutional order *religiously* legitimate. Khomeini addressed both issues – by utilising Shia traditions of self-sacrifice, he turned the protests into martyrdom 'people power' operations which the military could not vanquish, and with his dogma of the *vilayet i-faqih*, he could present a valid *religious* answer to the issue of legitimacy. Yet we must remember that the 1979 Revolution was effected by a coalition of democrats, leftists, liberal clerics and Islamists, but obviously led by Khomeini as a *marja i-taqlid*, and eventually the Islamist cuckoo was able to eject the others from the nest. The hybrid democratic-Islamic nature of the Iranian constitution reflects the mixed character of the 'people power' forces that staged the Revolution, and the heritage of the 1906 Constitution, and indeed, Iran's Shia history.

Khomeini's theory of the *Vilayat i-Faqih*

Khomeini asserted that Islam was a comprehensive religion, with a form of government.[79] This is an essential point: He was claiming that all that was necessary for life and society was divinely-revealed: "...there are laws, practices, and norms for the affairs of society and government."[80] That his point was polemical can be seen in his dismissal of the Constitutional Revolution's use of the Belgian legal code, which implied that Islam was 'defective' – lacking.[81] The next step was the need for an Executive to implement divine law.[82] He elaborated about this:

> Their execution and implementation depend upon the formation of a government, and that it is impossible to fulfill the duty of executing God's commands without there being established properly comprehensive administrative and executive organs.[83]

In the light of this, Khomeini addressed the Crisis of Legitimacy during the Occultation by quoting the *hadith*

---

[79] Khomeini, *Islamic Government*, 2–3.
[80] Ibid., 4.
[81] Ibid., 5.
[82] Ibid., 15.
[83] Ibid., 25.

The *fuqahā* are the trustees of the prophets ('a), as long as they do not concern themselves with the illicit desires, pleasures, and wealth of the world.[84]

This means establishing Qur'anic social relations through "government and implementing laws, whether this is accomplished by the prophet himself... or by the followers who come after him."[85] The latter are thus the *fuqahā*:

...are the trustees who implement the divine ordinances in levying taxes, guarding the frontiers, and executing the penal provisions of the law.[86]

Khomeini invoked traditions by:

'Ali indicating that the Ruler must be supremely knowledgeable about Islam – which in terms of Shia, points to a *Marja i-taqlid* (e.g. a Grand Ayatollah).[87]

He must also:

possess excellence in morals and belief; he must be just and untainted by major sins.[88]

This is in obvious contrast to

the tyrannical ruling family and the libertines that associate with them. It is these rulers who establish centers of vice and corruption, who build centers of vice and wine-drinking.[89]

We have already noted the Shahs' womanising, and the reputation of 'wine-bibbing Shahs,' and also their oppressive characters, so clearly, they were unqualified to rule by this standard. Further, previous Shahs had failed in 'guarding the frontiers,' reducing Iran to a US client state.

Two points need to be recognised: firstly, the terminus of the trusteeship of the *Faqih* – he rules

---

[84] Ibid., 61.
[85] Ibid., 62.
[86] Ibid., 65.
[87] Ibid., 41 n57 for the list of *ahadith*.
[88] Ibid., 43.
[89] Ibid., 40.

during the Occultation' – until the Mahdi returns, demonstrating eschatological future obsolescence.[90]

Secondly, in this work, Khomeini seemed to have no place for a normal Parliament:

> No one has the right to legislate and no law may be executed except the law of the Divine Legislator. It is for this reason that in an Islamic government, a simple planning body takes the place of the legislative assembly.[91]

However, the post-revolutionary *Majlis* does in fact operate like a normal Parliament, within certain limits – Article 72 of the original constitution stated:

> The Islamic Consultative Assembly cannot enact laws contrary to the official religion of the country or to the Constitution. It is the duty of the Guardian Council to determine whether a violation has occurred, in accordance with Article 96.[92]

A Western analogy is the Federal Republic of Germany, whose constitution bans

> Parties which, by reason of their aims or the behavior of their adherents, seek to impair or abolish the free democratic basic order or to endanger the existence of the Federal Republic of Germany are unconstitutional. The Federal Constitutional Court decides on the question of unconstitutionality.[93]

Article 93 delineates that the Court considers whether a State or Federal law is compatible with the German *Constitution,* whereas Iran's Guardian Council considers if a law is truly Islamic. Hence, in Iran, there is a 'constitution' *above* the Constitution – the former being the *Shari'a* and its sources. The German Court banned Communist and Neo-Nazi groups as unconstitutional; Iran's Council bans *Majlis* candidates as un-Islamic.

---

[90] Ibid., 70.
[91] Ibid., 37.
[92] M. Mahmood, *The Political System of the Islamic Republic of Iran* (Delhi: Kalpaz, 2006), 155.
[93] A. Tschentscher, trans., *The Basic Law (Grundgesetz) 2016: The Constitution of the Federal Republic of Germany (May 23rd, 1949) – Introduction and Translation*, 4th ed. (Würzburg: Jurisprudentia, 2016), https://ssrn.com/abstract =1501131.

This hybrid theocratic-democratic character of the State reflects its religio-political history, and the diversity of the forces which overthrew the Shah. Arguably, this is one reason it has survived against a backdrop of local dictatorships, who struggle against both democratic and Islamist elements, yet internally, the balancing act has occasionally caused protests such as the Green Movement, who emphasise democracy over theocracy. Further, it should be remembered that "Khomeini's theory was not accepted by the Shi'a ulema as a whole; indeed initially, it was not accepted by very many at all."[94] It is *one* answer to the Crisis of Legitimacy during the Occultation, not the decisive one, but certainly the practically successful offering.

Conclusion

Reflecting Iran's historic democratic constitutional tendencies, it has elections, but theocratic limitations on who can stand. It has a popularly-elected President – but his power is limited by the clerical domination of the *Rahbar* (Leader) and the Guardian Council. The constitutional checks are not based on American-style considerations of 'separation of powers', but on the balance between Theocracy and Democracy. The mixed nature of the Revolution ensured this result. The *vilayet i-faqih* has its own constitutional terminus in Article 5, which refers to the Occultation, and limits the rule of the *Faqih* for as long as it lasts. It has long been the dream of US right-wingers to see 'regime change' in Iran. Ironically, the Iranian constitution itself desires this, when, referring to the Mahdi, it urges, "may Allah Hasten his reappearance." Ultimately, all regencies conclude.

Bibliography

Abisaab, Rula Jurdi. *Converting Persia: Religion and Power in the Safavid Empire*. London: I. B. Tauris, 2004.

_____. *A History of Modern Iran*. Cambridge: Cambridge University Press, 2008.

_____. *Iran Between Two Revolutions*. Princeton, NJ: Princeton University Press, 1982.

---

[94] Axworthy, *Revolutionary Iran*, 97.

Algar, Hamid. *Religion and State in Iran, 1785-1906: The Role of the Ulama in the Qajar Period* (Berkeley, CA: University of California Press, 1980.

Alvandi, Roham. *Nixon, Kissinger, and the Shah: The United States and Iran in the Cold War*. Oxford: Oxford University Press, 2016.

Amanat, Abbas. *Iran: A Modern History*. New Haven, CT: Yale University Press, 2017.
_____. *Pivot of the Universe: Nasir Al-Din Shah Qajar and the Iranian Monarchy, 1831-1896*. Berkeley, CA: University of California Press, 1997.

Amir-Moezzi, Mohammad Ali and Christian Jambet. *What is Shi'i Islam? An Introduction*. New York: Routledge, 2018.

Atabaki, Touraj and Erik J. Zürcher. *Men of Order: Authoritarian Modernization under Atatürk and Reza Shah*. London: I. B. Tauris, 2004.

Axworthy, Michael. *Iran: Empire of the Mind*. New York: Basic Books, 2008.

Ayati, Ibrahim. *A Probe Into the History of Ashura*. Karachi: Islamic Seminary Publications, 1985, http://al-islam.org/ashura.

Busse, Herbert. "Iran under the Buyids." In *The Cambridge History of Iran*. Vol. 4, *From the Arab Invasion to the Saljuqs*, edited by R. N. Frye. Cambridge: Cambridge University Press, 2008.

Clawson, Patrick and Michael Rubin. *Eternal Iran: Continuity and Chaos*. New York: Palgrave Macmillan, 2005.

Daniel, Elton L. *The History of Iran*. London: Greenwood Press, 2001.

Dodd, C. H. *The Parables of the Kingdom*. Rev. ed. Glasgow: Collins, 1978.

Eskandari-Qajar, Manoutchehr M. "Between Scylla and Charybdis." In *War and Peace in Qajar Persia: Implications Past and Present*, edited by Roxane Farmanfarmaian. New York: Routledge, 2008.

227

Gleave, Robert. *Scripturalist Islam: The History and Doctrines of the Akhbārī Shīʿī School.* Leiden: Brill, 2007.

Guerrero, Javier Gil. *The Carter Administration and the Fall of Iran's Pahlavi Dynasty: US-Iran Relations on the Brink of the 1979 Revolution.* New York: Palgrave Macmillan, 2016.

Keddie, Nikki R. *Modern Iran: Roots and Results of Revolution.* New Haven, CT: Yale University Press, 2006.

Khomeini, Ayatollah. *Islamic Government.* Translated by Hamid Algar. Tehran: The Institute for Compilation and Publication of Imam Khomeini's Works, 2002.

Ladd, George Eldon. *The Presence of the Future.* Grand Rapids, MI: Eerdmans, 1974.

Lockhart, L. *Nadir Shah; A Critical Study Based Mainly Upon Contemporary Sources.* 2nd ed. Lahore: Al-Irfan, 1938.

Mahmood, M. *The Political System of the Islamic Republic of Iran.* Delhi: Kalpaz, 2006.

Neely, Brent J. and Peter G. Riddell. *Islam and the Last Day.* Melbourne: MST Press, 2014.

Rayshahri, M. Mohammadi. *The Scale of Wisdom: A Compendium of Shiʿa Hadith.* Translated by N. Virjee, A. Kadhim, M. Dasht Bozorgi, Z. Alsalami, and A. Virjee. London: ICAS, 2009.

Röder, Tilmann J. and Rainer Grote II, eds. *Constitutionalism in Islamic Countries: Between Upheaval and Continuity.* New York: Oxford University Press, 2012.

Roemer, H. R. "The Safavid Period." In *The Cambridge History of Iran.* Vol. 6, *The Timurid and Safavid Periods,* edited by Peter Jackson and Laurence Lockhart. Cambridge: Cambridge University Press, 1986.

Sachedina, Abdulaziz Abdul Hussein. *The Just Ruler (al-sultān al-ʿādil) in Shīʿite Islam: The Comprehensive Authority of the Jurist in Imamite Jurisprudence.* Oxford: Oxford University Press, 1998.
228

Shomali, Mohammad A. *Shi'i Islam: Origins, Faith, and Practices.* London: ICAS, 2003.

Tschentscher, Axel, trans. *The Basic Law (Grundgesetz) 2016: The Constitution of the Federal Republic of Germany (May 23rd, 1949) – Introduction and Translation.* 4th ed. Würzburg: Jurisprudentia, 2016, http://ssrn.com/abstract=1501131.

Tucker, Ernest S. *Nadir Shah's Quest for Legitimacy in Post-Safavid Iran.* Gainesville, FL: University Press of Florida, 2006.

Further Reading

Adib-Moghaddam, Arshin. *A Critical Introduction to Khomeini.* Cambridge: Cambridge University Press, 2014.

Azimi, Fakhreddin. *The Quest for Democracy in Iran: A Century of Struggle against Authoritarian Rule.* (Cambridge, MA: Harvard University Press, 2008.

Boozari, Amirhassan. *Shi'i Jurisprudence and Constitution: Revolution in Iran.* New York: Palgrave Macmillan, 2011.

Buchan, James. *Days of God: The Revolution in Iran and Its Consequences.* New York: Simon and Schuster, 2013.

Dabashi, Hamid. *Theology of Discontent: The ideological Foundations of the Islamic Revolution in Iran.* New York: Routledge, 2017.

Davari, Mahmood T. *The Political Thought of Ayatullah Murtaza Mutahhari: An Iranian Theoretician of the Islamic State.* New York: Routledge, 2005.

Gheissari, Ali. *Contemporary Iran: Economy, Society, Politics.* Oxford: Oxford University Press, 2009.

Kamaly, Hossein. *God and Man in Tehran: Contending Visions of the Divine from the Qajars to the Islamic Republic.* New York: Columbia University Press, 2018.

Khomeini, Imam. *Islam and Revolution.* Translated by Hamid Algar. New York: Routledge, 2010.

Lafraie, Najibullah. *Revolutionary Ideology and Islamic Militancy: The Iranian Revolution and Interpretations of the Quran*. London: Tauris Academic Studies, 2009.

Majd, Hooman. *The Ayatollah Begs to Differ*. New York: Anchor, 2009.
_____. *The Ayatollahs' Democracy: An Iranian Challenge*. New York: W. W. Norton and Co., 2010.

Mirsepassi, Ali. *Democracy in Modern Iran: Islam, Culture, and Political Change*. New York: New York University, 2010.

Moazami, Behrooz. *State, Religion, and Revolution in Iran: 1796 to the Present*. New York: Palgrave Macmillan, 2013.

Mottahedeh, Roy P. *The Mantle of the Prophet*. New York: Simon and Schuster, 1985.

Salemson, Harold, trans. *The Little Green Book: Selected Fatawah and Sayings of the Ayatollah Mosavi Khomeini*. New York: Bantam Book, 1985.

Chapter 10

ISLAM AND POLITICS, POLITICS AND ISLAM
Pakistan's Ongoing Conundrum

Ruth J Nicholls[1]

Throughout the ages, religion and politics have been variously wedded. At one end, there is the anti-religious stance of communism where religion and politics are kept as distant from each other as governments can achieve. At the other end, countless leaders have turned to religion to validate or give credence to their political aspirations. From the early history of Islam, the Prophet's move to Medina was ultimately political, hopefully to bring validity and a future to his persecuted and at that time floundering religious movement. From then on, religion and politics were married into the foundations of Islam. The prophet of Islam became both a religious prophet and a political leader, albeit within the tribal context of the Arabia of his day. Those very foundations have not only become the launching place but also the underlying heartbeat of Islam with the consequence of it being both a religious and a political identity. To divorce the two is like trying to deny that there are two sides to a coin.

For many years I lived in the Islamic Republic of Pakistan. As my facility with the local language developed I could hear the Friday *kutbah* (sermons) broadcast with passionate earnestness at full volume out over the speakers from the nearby mosques. Most sermons appeared politically focused, religiously based deliveries in which the local Imam was waxing eloquent, emotionally fostering the devotion of his listeners. The subjects were often some

---

[1] Ruth Nicholls was until recently the Administrator of the Arthur Jeffery Centre for the Study of Islam, Melbourne School of Theology and is currently an honorary Research Fellow with the Centre. Ruth lived and worked for many years in a Muslim country where she became particularly interested in Sufism and folk Islam.

local/national/international political event that had gained media attention. Not surprisingly it seemed, that many a political protest usually chanting religious slogans followed the Friday prayers (cf. Salem, 1962, p285). Interestingly come Ramadan (Ramzan) – a time of religious fervour – many local imams were placed under house arrest, barred from their mosque pulpit. Living there it became eminently clear that Islam was not only a religion but also intensely political. Also during my stay, General Zia ul-Haq took over the reign of Government and promulgated *Nazam e-mustafa* – rule by Shari'a law. Then I witnessed and experienced the conjunction of religion and politics. It was both obvious and experiential. Religion became enforced by political decree.

The very name Pakistan incorporates both a religious and political identity. *Pak* means holy or pure, religiously pure – as defined Islamically that is – and *istan* means place: the place of the holy or pure which is also reflected in the choice of the colour green for the flag and the incorporated symbol of the crescent moon. Even the notion underlying the conception of the state of Pakistan incorporated religion and politics. The official name adopted by the country in 1963 also cements these two concepts together – Islamic Republic of Pakistan. Both the philosopher, or spiritual father of the nation as he is known, Mohammad Allama Iqbal and the founding father of the nation, Qaid e-Azam, Mohammad Ali Jinnah understood the importance of both religious and political mechanisms in their striving for a political settlement for their understanding of the practical problem facing the Muslim minority of pre-partition India.

In this paper, my focus is on Pakistan. In doing this, I will first examine the Islamic position that posits Islam as a religio-political identity with its own agenda and goals. As Salem writes,

> In Islam the association between the political and the religious is traditional. Almost every movement in Islam that started as a religious and reform movement ended in becoming also intensely political.[2]

---

[2] Elie Salem, "Nationalism and Islam," *The Muslim World* 52, no 4 (1962): 284.

Tibi claims that "Islam is both a religious faith and a cultural system, but not a political ideology."[3] While 'ideology' may be too strong a word—for there is no document like *The Communist Manifesto*—the Qur'an and its exegesis, the Hadith, and the Sira of the Prophet provide sufficient basis for both religious practice and political preferences. Then, I will merely outline the factors that gave rise to the concept of Pakistan and how this was fostered by both Iqbal and Jinnah and others through the All India Muslim League. In conclusion, I will consider very briefly, the continuing interplay of religion and politics as it affects Pakistan.

Understanding Islam

In the West, because God has been dismissed and religion is considered to have passed its used-by date, the religious dedication and commitment of Muslims and their allegiance to and obedience to their Scriptures is often ignored, rejected or relegated to the inconsequential. To understand Islam, however, it is important to recognise Muslims' allegiance to their God, Allah. The Islamic understanding of Allah's nature, especially his 'oneness' is an underlying factor in their belief of his superiority and that of their religion. Such suras as 3.5 and 48:28 say it clearly.

> It is He Who has sent His Messenger with guidance and the religion of truth, that He may make it prevail over all religion. And God suffices as witness (48:28).[4]

clearly delineates the Prophet's position and Jalalayn's *tafsir* on this verse reinforces that understanding.

> It is He Who has sent His Messenger with guidance and the religion of truth that He may make it that is the religion of truth prevail over all religion over all the other religions (underlining mine).[5]

In another sura also from the Medina period, uttered in a similar context of berating the Jews and Christians, the Prophet's message was:

[3] Bassam Tibi, *Islam between Culture and Politics*, 2nd ed. (New York: Palgrave McMillian, 2005), ix.
[4] All quotes from *The Holy Qur'an: A New English Translation of Its Meanings* in this essay are taken from 2020 Royal Aal al-Bayt Institute for Islamic Thought, Amman, Jordan (http://www.aalalbayt.org).
[5] Tafsir al-Jalalayn, trans. Feras Hamza (2017 Royal Aal al-Bayt Institute for Islamic Thought, Amman, Jordan, http://www.aalalbayt.org).

> He it is Who has sent His Messenger with the guidance and the religion of truth, that He may manifest it over every religion, even though the disbelievers be averse (9:33).

Al-Jalalayn's tafsir once again echoes the Prophet's sentiments:

> He it is Who has sent His Messenger Muhammad (s) with the guidance and the religion of truth that He may manifest it make it prevail over every religion all the religions which oppose it even though the disbelievers be averse to this.[6]

This belief in the superiority of Allah also impacts the Muslim understanding of the demands of Allah's revealed will: it is superior: it must be obeyed. This emphasis on the superiority of Allah and his religion also translates into the demand that everyone on earth become a Muslim (Sura 3:110). In order to achieve that end, force may be necessary and any resultant deaths are secondary to the demands of the Will of Allah.[7]

Still the question remains, how can one understand Islam? There are those who would claim that Islam is a religion of Peace while on the other hand there are those whose actions portray Islam as a religion of War, crying *Allah hu akhbar* as they move forward in their violent advance.[8] Any study of Islam, from my perspective, seems riddled with inconsistencies, seeming as if it is a religion in internal conflict. Writing from an anthropological perspective, Salzman speaks of 'balanced opposition'[9] which is the underlying means by which Arab tribal society operates and is organised: the 'us' and 'them'; Muslim and infidel; 'for which no central official organisers are required'. This balanced opposition is also reflected in the later development of the notion of *Dar al-Islam,* where Islam is in control and the law of Allah is fully operational. This is opposed to

---

[6] Tafsir al-Jalalayn, trans. Feras Hamza (2017 Royal Aal al-Bayt Institute for Islamic Thought, Amman, Jordan, http://www.aalalbayt.org).

[7] Richard Shumack (commenting on Shabir Akhtar's understanding of divine law), *The Wisdom of Islam and the Foolishness of Christianity* (Sydney: Island View Publishing, 2014), 203.

[8] One might ask what is the implied message in the flag of Saudi Arabia with its quotation of the Islamic *shahadah* which is underlined by a sword and on its coat of arms 'two swords'?

[9] Philip Carl Salzman, "Balanced Opposition: The Tribal Foundations of Arab Middle Eastern Islamic Culture," in *Political Islam from Muhammad to Ahmadinejad: Defenders, Detractors and Definitions*, ed. J. M. Skelly (Santa Barbara, CA: ABC-CLIO, 2010), 16.

Dar al-Harb which is any area not under Muslim authority and which must be brought under that control either through coercion, be that war and violence if required, or conversion, even if forced. So, depending on the position of the particular Muslim community in any given context, that significantly influences whether Islam is a religion of peace or of war. If the context is similar to a Mecca-like situation—a minority facing rejection and ridicule—it is acceptable to appear 'peaceful' while angling for supremacy. A derivative of this belief of supremacy is the unmistakable injunction 'to fight in the cause of Allah' (sura 9:29) with its promise of 'paradise' should one die in the effort. So whether Muslims find themselves either in a Meccan or Medina type situation, *jihad* is not only a moral obligation but an act of obedience for the sake of Allah to achieve Islamic supremacy.[10] Sura 8:39 says it clearly as does Ibn Abbas's tafsir which follows:

> And fight them until sedition is no more and religion is all for God; then if they desist, surely God sees what they do.

> (He it is Who hath sent His messenger) Muhammad (pbuh) (with the guidance) with the Qur'an and faith (and the Religion of Truth) the religion of Islam, and with it the confession that there is no deity except Allah, (that He may cause it to prevail over all religion) that He may Cause the religion of Islam to prevail over all religions which came before it until the Day of Judgement, (however much the idolaters may be averse) that this should be so.[11]

While Kirmanj[12] has pointed out that some of this interpretation and consequent action is subsequent to the life of the Prophet, it forms part of the accepted and valued Muslim tradition which provides the foundational understandings of the Sheikhs and Imams who are the teachers in the madrassas and preachers from the mosques. While some Imams do theological training, many are untrained leaders of the prayers who all hold fast to the received traditions making them the subject of their mosque sermons and the topics of their face to face interactions.

---

[10] p204, Shabir Akhtar as reported in Shumack, *The Wisdom of Islam*, 204. See also Sura 9:29, "Fight those who do not believe in Allah."

[11] Tafsir Ibn 'Abbas, trans. Mokrane Guezzou (2017 Royal Aal al-Bayt Institute for Islamic Thought, Amman, Jordan, http://www.aalalbayt.org).

[12] Sherko Kirmanj, "Challenging the Islamists Politicization of Islam: The Non-Islamic Origins of Muslim Political Concepts," in *Political Islam from Muhammad to Ahmadinejad*, 35–50.

It would appear that the Prophet's initial intentions were to reform the religious life of his fellow Arabs, Jews (or were they Judaized Arabs?) and Christians by promulgating a monotheistic religion.[13] His attempts won few followers in Mecca where he started his campaign. Even the Jews and the Christians whom he had hoped to win over generally failed to respond to his messages. Rejection, ridicule and persecution meant that the invitation from leaders in Yathrib (later Medina) to assume an essentially political role while still being a religious leader must have seemed eminently attractive. Given the tribal nature of Arabia and the fact that Muhammad was from the Quraysh tribe, who at that time was responsible for the supervision and protection of the Ka'ba with its associated religious pilgrimages and festivals, having both a religious and political role would have seemed natural and no doubt desirable. Moreover, knowing, even unconsciously, that there was the authority of divine revelation to authenticate his decisions and the paths he chose to adopt would have added weight to his decision.

Islam in India

The history of Islam in India begins with Arab traders who had been visiting its coastal areas and beyond even before Islam emerged. Having adopted Islam these Arab traders took their newly acquired faith to those places where they traded. It is believed that they settled permanently in these regions, intermarried and developed communities such as the Mappillas (Malabar Muslims). In fact some of the earliest mosques in India are said to date from about the 620s CE. As a result of the missionary efforts of these traders and others, Muslim communities developed in various parts of the Indian subcontinent. In some areas, local rulers adopted Islam as their religion.

By the 700s, Muslim armies were marching into the Sindh and establishing a Muslim identity in the Indus valley. In the late 900s Ghaznavids exercised control over the Punjab and Sind, extending Islam in those areas.[14] However, it was in the 12th century

---

[13] Page 221 in a currently unpublished manuscript by Arthur Jeffery, *Prolegomena to the Study of Islam*, n.d., held by Arthur Jeffery Centre for the Study of Islam, Melbourne School of Theology, Australia, with permission from Columbia University, New York.
[14] Ghaznavids were of Turkish military slave background who adopted Islam, came to power and ruled an area extending from the east of Persia, through Afghanistan and into India.

under Ghurids, that Muslim rulers established their control through the north of what is Pakistan today, expanding down into the Sind and along the Ganges valley of India and into Ganges delta area – especially Bengal. Varying Muslim dynasties rose and fell, exercising fluctuating degrees of power and influence till 1483 when Babur became the founder of the Moghul empire which continued basically until 1857–1858 (The Indian Mutiny/First War of Independence).

While it is not possible to go into a detailed history of Islam in India, India is now the home of the largest Muslim minority community in the world. Currently it ranks as having the third highest Muslim population after Indonesia and Pakistan. However, the Muslim population is not only linguistically, economically, educationally and regionally diverse but also scattered and unevenly distributed with Kashmir being the only Muslim state. Not surprisingly, at various times during the history of India, in numerous regions, both north and south, various Muslim rulers have exerted power. Many of the early Muslims in India were foreigners—Arabs, Turks, Persians, and Afghans—who came either as traders or associated with the conquering armies. Their descendants eventually become an elite within the country where the strength of the caste system found its way into the Indian Muslim way of life. Many of these Muslims retained their foreign identity while also claiming descent from the Prophet or from his companions. On the other hand, over time, Hindus converted to Islam: for some it was a deliberate choice, for others it was forced. Yet for the majority Hindu population, the conquering Muslims were considered foreign invaders deliberately attempting to impose on them the Muslim religion and way of life. That is, these Muslim rulers were operating a Muslim minority government in a primarily Hindu context. Aurengzeb, with his 'Fatawa Alamgiri' was possibly the most deliberate of these Muslim Moghul emperors who tried to extend Islamic influences on the population, destroying a number of Hindu temples and especially through the 'dhimmi' tax which was not well received and later was rescinded. Generally speaking, though, Muslims and Hindus lived together in an uneasy harmony.

While the Moghul emperors were able to extend their empires in a variety of directions during their rules, none of them was able to take complete control of the subcontinent and make India a Muslim country. The constant warfare needed to either extend their influence or retain their extent weakened the Moghul control.

237

Following Aurengzeb's death, the Moghul position was further weakened by internal fighting over succession. When Bahadar Shah II finally took control, the Moghul empire had virtually collapsed. The Indian Mutiny/War of Independence, in which Muslim soldiers played a role, led the British Government to intervene with the corresponding demise of the Empire. As a consequence, the British distrust of the Muslim community increased and British policy formulated around the 'two groups': the Hindus and the Muslims. Also, by this time Hindu voices turning anti-British were on the rise, demanding independence which was fanned by the recognition of the growing weakness of the Moghul Empire.

With the evident decline of the Moghul empire, the increasing weakness of the Moghul rulers, the extending power and influence of the West, the subjection of India under the British meant that there was growing unrest in India. Both Muslims and Hindus were becoming resistive. Worldwide voices of dissent in countries where foreign rulers were in control, including India, were growing louder as the calls for nationalisation were becoming stronger. From the 1920s Hindu nationalist groups began developing with decidedly anti minority sentiments and louder calls for independence with an Indian Government. Following the 1923 riot between Hindus and Muslims, the distrust between the communities began to increase. With the Hindu voices becoming even stronger and as the plans for developing an 'Indian government' grew, leaders within the Muslim community began to be concerned – how were the rights of the Muslim community going to be protected? How were Muslims going to be able to 'live as Muslims'? Current studies would tend to support that original concern, for though the Muslim community in India is large, it still remains a minority, experiencing life as a minority.[15] For Indian Muslims, World War I, in particular, was a turning point. Muslim soldiers, virtually conscripted into the war, found themselves fighting co-religionists on some of the war fronts, which for them was a conflict of interests. Yet, Muslims in India were divided: some were beginning to champion for change: some were content to live as a minority within a Hindu majority.

---

[15] Nathelene Reynolds, "Hindu Nationalism and the Muslim Minority in India," in *Corridors of Knowledge for Peace and Development*, ed. Sarah S. Aneel, Uzma T. Haroon, and Imrana Niazi (Islamabad: Sustainable Development Policy Institute, 2020), 279–303.

For the Muslim community in the Indian subcontinent, and indeed all Muslims everywhere, events on the international scene were disturbing. With the end of World War I, the Ottoman empire was on the brink of collapse which led to the rise of the *Khalifat* movement. In India, though supported by Ghandi, it was not supported by either the British or Jinnah. This lack of British support for its continuance suggested to the Muslims that it brooded ill for their future in India. For them the Ottoman empire was the symbol and centre of Islam and the restoration of pre-war boundaries paramount. While there were also growing voices for a Pan Islamic movement, it never became a significant force, though its aim for raising the profile of Islam became the agenda of individual countries.

As early as 1906, in Dhaka, now the capital of Bangladesh, the All India Muslim League came into existence. It was this organisation that was to play a significant role in the creation of Pakistan. Originally it was one of the political parties in Pakistan, though it faulted after Jinnah's death. Initially the All India Muslim League had little political voice or played any major political role, though its origin was the treatment of the Muslim community in Bengal state at the time. From the 1930s Mohammad Iqbal's voice rallied the League. Having studied in the West and seen its weaknesses, he began to extol Islam both as a religious and a political force. It was a sentiment that gained a positive response, especially among those members of the League who had graduated from that Aligarh University. Apparently it was Iqbal who encouraged Mohammad Ali Jinnah to join the League and use his skills to unite it and to foster its political voice and energies in advocating for the Muslim community. Among the growing number of supporters was Liaqat Ali Khan who was to become the first Prime Minister together with a number of others who held government positions in the newly created state of Pakistan.

Even before the formation of the League, Muslims in India were conscious not only of the Moghul Empire's fading glory but the challenge to Islam worldwide. Moreover, the Indian context was a fertile ground for the development of mystical Islam, especially during the Moghul period of which the Chishtiyah, Suhrawardiyah, Qadiriyah, and Naqshbandiyah are the most prominent. Sufism, for many, is essentially a way of entering into the heart of Islam and living with greater devotion to the Prophet and his message. As early

239

as the 1700s Shah Wali Allah (1703–1762), a Naqshbandi, recognising

> the need for renewal to the political confusions of his day and expect[ing] religious reform to usher in a worldly order as well[16]

focused on renewal within Islam. While his tariqa was located in Dehli, he also used the printed page to spread his interpretations and ideas. Keen that people should understand Islam, he translated the Qur'an into Urdu.[17] Those who were influenced by Shah Wali Allah took the movement in several directions. One of those was influential in the founding of Dar ul Uloom in Deoband, now a key centre of Islamic learning, which advocates a conservative view of Islam. It demanded the expulsion of the British and was also campaigning against the Sufis. While it advocated for a united India, thereby opposing Jinnah, the Deoband, through both its 'tariqa' and political arms, continues to have significant influence not only in Pakistan but also elsewhere. Ahmad Raza Khan of Barelwi (Barreilly)[18] (1856–1921) took the movement in the other direction: primarily countering the Deobandi position while advocating Sufi practices, expounding their development from the Qur'an and Hadith. He also "sought to carve out a state where Muslim life could flourish."[19] As a movement it supported the formation of Pakistan. The Barelwi like the Deobondi have their madrassas and political wings which are operative in Pakistan. In addition around this time there was the growth of the Ahmadiyya movement, instigated by Mirza Ghulam Ahmad (1838–1908). Branded as a heretical group by those following more conservative interpretations of Islam, their ire was played out dramatically in the new state of Pakistan, with ongoing consequences.

Syed Ahmad Khan (1817–1898) was also influenced by Shah Wali Allah. Though not formally educated in Islam, he was another important 'reformer' who realised that Islam needed to meet the

---

[16] Barbara D. Metcalf, "India," in *The Oxford Encyclopedia of the Modern Islamic World*, ed. John L Esposito (Oxford: Oxford University Press, 1995), 2:189.
[17] Percival Spear, *A History of India* (London: Penguin Books, 1966), 2:225. He says it was Persian.
[18] There are a number of ways in which this name has been transliterated.
[19] Metcalf, "India," 190.

challenges of the times: calling for a modern interpretation of Islam.[20] While initially he wrote from a Sunni perspective against the Shi'a, after the Indian Mutiny he focused on education, establishing what became the Aligarh University (1875). A number of significant leaders within the Indian Muslim community were products of this University. His emphasis though, strengthened 'the separatist Muslim politics in India.'[21] Other voices were also championing the Islamic cause. One of these was Maulana Abu al-A'la Maududi (1903–1979) who initially was for Muslims staying in India but after separation moved to Pakistan, becoming a significant voice there. Another was Maulana Abdulbari of Farangi Mahal.

One voice that was gaining significant attention was that of Mohammad Iqbal who was not only a student of the Qur'an but also a lawyer, a philosopher and writer, especially of poetry. This latter medium seems to have an irresistible appeal within India-Pakistan.[22] In furthering his education in the West, especially in philosophy, as a Muslim he contrasted his belief with the Christianity he saw there and became an even more dedicated advocate for Islam.

> Islam, as a polity, is only a practical means of making this principle (tauhid) a living factor in the intellectual and emotional life of mankind. It demands loyalty to God, (which) virtually amounts to man's loyalty to his own ideal nature (Secrets of Self).[23]

While Iqbal briefly entered politics, it was his association with Jinnah that was to have lasting effect. However, it was his call for a separate Islamic state incorporating the Sindh, Baluchistan, the Northwest frontier province and the Punjab that gained the momentum.

The role of Jinnah, however, is somewhat of an enigma. Questions are often raised as to the extent of Jinnah's devotion to Islam. It is believed that he was a Twelver Shi'ite though at his death it was claimed he was a Sunni – he had two funerals, one Shi'a: the

---

[20] Hafeez Malik, "Ahmad Khan, Sayyid," in *The Oxford Encyclopedia of the Modern Islamic World*, 57.
[21] Ibid., 58.
[22] On any occasion in Pakistan, the words of poets always seemed to be quoted. Special poetry reciting events (*mushira*) were popular and were usually conducted in a formal manner. Even the uneducated were often heard quoting poetry and any recitation always seemed to result in genuine and fervent applause.
[23] As quoted by Richard S. Wheeler, "The Individual and Action in the Thought of Iqbal," *The Muslim World* 52, no 3 (1962): 198.

other Sunni. It is also said that he was unable to say the *namaz* in Arabic and even his grasp of Urdu, the language of the Muslims at least in north India and also a rallying point for them, was limited. Initially it would also appear that Jinnah was for a united India in which the rights of Muslims were guaranteed. However, as events in Congress unfolded and Jinnah's interactions with the British left him uncertain of the Muslim position, he began to agitate, along with Iqbal and the more educated members of the All India Muslim League, for a separate state. Jinnah, it is said, championed Urdu as the Muslim's language, chose their dress, fostered their Islamic identity and promoted their Islamic destiny.[24] There is continuing controversy as to how Jinnah conceived of the state of Pakistan. There are those who claim that it was to be a place where minorities were welcome and could be safe,[25] and "where freedom of religious practice was the undisputed right of every citizen."[26] However, there are those that claim that Jinnah advocated for a truly Islamic one.[27] Sadly, for Pakistan the truth is, as Willox puts it is that,

> [The] largely secular and western educated Indian middle class... used Islam as a uniting ideology without having given much thought to what this Islamic state might look like.[28]

Pakistan today

Pakistan was born in violence. The real number of Hindus and Muslims who died trying to cross the borders when India was divided and Pakistan was created will never be known. The number often cited is horrific. Since then, violence has marked Pakistan's existence. Presidents have been assassinated or killed. Sectarian

---

[24] Akbar Ahmad, "Jinnah and the Quest for Muslim Identity," *History Today* 44, no. 9 (1994): 38. He quotes Jinnah as saying, "I am going to constitute myself the Protector-General of the Hindu Minority in Pakistan."

[25] Ibid. "Yet it's tragic that no one in Pakistan is ready to discuss that why Jinnah, the country's founder, appointed an Ahmadi Muslim as his foreign minister and a Hindu as his law minister if he wanted to create a state that would accept an Islamic faith preached by the majority of the population while rejecting the ones preached and practiced by other minority Islamic groups." Umair Jamal, "The Politics of Religious Exclusion in Pakistan," *The Diplomat*, published October, 18, 2017.

[26] Tahir Kamran, "Pakistan: A Failed State?" *History Today* 67, no. 9 (2017): 24–35.

[27] Akbar Ahmad writes, "Islamists (notably from the time of General Zia's regime) paint out Jinnah's genuine humanism, universal tolerance and affection for English culture concentrating entirely on his more 'Islamic' statements." Ahmad, "Jinnah and the Quest for Muslim Identity," 34.

[28] Alexander Willox, "Voices of Political Islam in Pakistan," Australian Institute for International Affairs, published May 26, 2014, http://www.internationalaffairs. org.au/news-item/voices-of-political-islam-in-pakistan.

violence occurs at regular intervals – targeting both Islamic groups and non-Muslims, Christians and Ahmadiyya being the main targets, though Hindus are not exempt. Governments have been overthrown. Politicians and political aspirants are put under home arrest, in prison, or charged with some offence or escape the country to live in exile. It seems almost a regular process.

The Prophet was certainly not averse to using violence and indeed recommended it. His followers, at least in Pakistan, seem very willing to adopt it and use it. Moreover, since there is no 'authoritative' structure within Islam itself, and government decrees and religious fatawa appear to lack any compelling force for demanding obedience, this allows anyone to use violence, and 'get away' with it. Even those in power adopt the same strategy. The result – an unstable and insecure Pakistan. The basis, it would seem, is the very reason for Pakistan's existence: Islam.

From the very moment of its creation, Pakistan plunged into a 'religious' war over Kashmir, a north India Muslim majority state. The Kashmir issue is constantly 'bubbling' in Pakistan. It is one that the leaders of the country, the Army and religious parties frequently use as an issue of contention and to increase religious fervour. Some of the religiously based groups were formed deliberately to take a violent stand on the question. However, several of these have been declared illegal because of their overt emphases and expressions of violence. On the other hand, the Army frequently appears to take a significant lead in perpetuating the cause. India claims Kashmir as its only Muslim state (though there are more Muslims in other states) and therefore representative of the significant number of Muslims in India. Pakistan's claim is based on religious grounds. Because it is a Muslim state, Pakistan claims that it should be part of Pakistan and so represents to Pakistan 'unfinished business'. Underlying this claim is the belief that Muslims can only truly be Muslims when they are under Islamic rule, which theoretically, at least, should be Pakistan.

Pakistan, even as it was originally conceived, included ethnically, linguistically, socially and economically diverse people groups, each with their own expression of Islam as well as a significant number of religious minorities. Those along the western border with Iran tended towards Shi'ism[29]; those in the north western provinces are a mixture of Shi'ites and Ismailis while what is today Bangladesh is largely a homogenous population of Bengalis. However, the shared belief in Islam was not enough to hold these peoples together. This belief was shattered during the Indo-Pakistan War of 1971 when East Pakistan gained its independence and became Bangladesh. While the disintegration is largely attributed to how the West Pakistani Muslims treated, rather mistreated, their Eastern co-religionists, Prime Minister Bhutto's response was to turn to 'religion' claiming the split was "a failure to sustain an Islamic ethos."[30] However, it is both the ethnic, linguistic and religious differences within current Pakistan that are constant sources of unrest and acts of violence.

During my time in Pakistan (1975-2000), it seemed that when there was an election (that is when there wasn't a coup d'état) whichever party had the most votes still needed the support of any number of smaller more locally based religious parties, often quite conservative, to assume government. As Christine Fair notes,

> Both parties have made tactical and strategic alliances with religious parties to expand their political base. Both parties have made serious concessions to the Islamists to co-opt their agenda and secure their political position.[31]

This has meant that the smaller religiously based parties have been able to exert significant influence even though they may represent only a small percentage of the total population of Pakistan. However, with the passage of time, and when favoured by the leader in power, the number of religious political parties have grown, especially after they were allowed elected representation. What that means is that whoever is in power, even if claimed via a coup d'état, has to accommodate the demands of these smaller religious parties. Also, irrespective of whether these religious groups have a voice in government or not, their voices are loud, either through their militant wings acting in violence, or their student wings holding

---

[29] There are current rumbles in Baluchistan towards an independent state, cf. Umair Jamal, "Amid a Pandemic, Pakistan Focuses on a Baloch Insurgency," *The Diplomat*, published June 16, 2020.
[30] C. Christine Fair, "Islam and Politics in Pakistan," in *The Muslim World After 9/11*, ed Angel M. Rabasa et al. (Santa Monica, CA: Rand Corporation, 2004), 272.
[31] Ibid., 257.

demonstrations or their political wings instigating agitation and strikes.

The 'power' of the religious parties, especially the Majlis-e-Ahrar-e-Islam and Jamaat-e-Islami, was certainly very evident in the case against the Ahmadiyya. Even though, just before I arrived in Pakistan, Prime Minister Zulfiqar Ali Bhutto had declared the Ahmadiyya non-Muslims, there were still calls for them to be outlawed. My arrival coincided with continued violent anti-Ahmadiyya riots – people were killed, mosques were burnt, business attacked and hate campaigns against Ahmadiyya based industries and businesses were promulgated by posters and attacks on properties. These attacks are still continuing and though there is some attempt to change this law, Imran Khan's party, Pakistan Tehreek-e-Insaf, is opposed to it.[32]

These religious parties, having achieved their goal, have been enpowered to 'fight' against other groups they consider 'deviant'. On the other hand, General Musharraf banned the anti Shi'a, Siphah-Sahaba Pakistan (SSP) and the Siphah-e-Mohammed Pakistan (SMP) a Shi'te extremist group. However, the former group, SSP, re-established itself and is currently known as the Ahle-Sunnat Wal-Jamaat (ASWJ) which apparently assisted the Pakistan Muslim League-Nawaz to gain power.[33] Benazir Bhutto also attempted to curb their power. On the other hand, Zia had his favourites and was significantly influenced by them. Imran Khan had to play the religious card very carefully because he was seen in the religious circles to have been a profligate. However, the religious parties are often in opposition to each other, and don't hesitate to use violence against each other. Trying to achieve common ground and move forward for the seeming benefit of the country and people means that progress (at least as seen through western eyes) is rarely if ever

---

[32] "Imran Khan's political party, the Pakistan Tehreek-e-Insaf, last week claimed that the ruling party is trying to remove the constitutional clause that declares Ahmadis as non-Muslims. To counter the opposition's pressure, the ruling party said that 'Ahmadis can only be equal citizens of Pakistan if they admit they are non-Muslim.' In response, Khan's party termed the government's response as 'pro-Ahmadi' and said that even calling Ahmadis as brothers amounts to hurting the feeling of majority Muslim population in the country." Umair Jamal, "The Politics of Religious Exclusion in Pakistan."

[33] Michael Kalin and Niloufer Siddiqui, *Religious Authority and the Promotion of Sectarian Tolerance in Pakistan* (Washington, DC: United States Institute of Peace, 2014), 354.

achieved.[34]   In addition, the Council of Islamic Ideology and the Federal Shari'at Court play a significant role in determining if any proposed legislation is in agreement with Islamic (usually Sunni) principles.   While in 2002, the Muttahida Majlis-e-Amal (MMA) as an alliance of religious parties did well in that election, since then it has faltered and weakened.

These religiously oriented groups represent a particular religious interpretation and were usually established to counter or be in direct conflict with the religious interpretation of the group they oppose on the basis of 'bida' (innovation) or 'sherk' (association). The result is purposely formed sectarianism which is expressed in deliberately focused sectarian violence.   Because the opposed position is in their opinion against the will of Allah, they consider the opposition worthy of death and therefore the use of force and violence is justified.   For example, Ulema-e-Pakistan (JUP) represents the Barelwi tradition, though it has splinted into various groups, one of which, Sunni Tehreek is committed to using violence. While the JUI (Jamiat-ul-Ulema-e-Islam) is the political arm of the Deobandi, several of their related madrassas have given rise to violent groups such as the Sipha-e-Sahaba Pakistan (SSP) and the Lashkar-e-Jhangi (LeJ) which more recently has also developed strong ties with the Tehreek-e-Taliban Pakistan (TTP)[35] which, to quote Willox,

> represent the largest problem for Pakistani nationalism, as they remain primarily an ethno-religious organisation intent on enforcing strict Wahhabi Islam in a nation that has both little experience and interest in it.[36]

So, the Shi'a too, often felt (and still do) the violent force of their Sunni compatriots.   Ashura and Muharram celebrations in particular are regular targets. Ismailis, too, feel the contempt. Many a time when I ventured into the bazaar, one side of the street would be closed because the other side had led an attack, usually with fatal

---

[34] Immunisation of children is one of the areas which is opposed by some of the religious groups, claiming that it is an 'innovation,' because it was not observed during the Prophet's lifetime. Often there seems to be lots of misinformation that is also circulated and used to oppose any change of direction.

[35] According to Mhd Feyyaz, "Facets of Religious Violence in Pakistan," *Counter Terrorist Trends and Analyses* 5, no. 2 (2013): 10. LeJ "remains the most ferocious militant group engaged in full scale sectarian war in Pakistan."

[36] Alexander Willox, "Voices of Political Islam in Pakistan."

consequences. Always it seemed that it was based on some 'religious issue.' It was during Zia's time that the Shi'a felt particularly threatened by his increasing Islamisation which reflected his favouring of the Shari'a interpretations of the Deobandi and Ahl-e-Hadith. In response, the militant Shi'a Tehrik-e-Nifaz-e-Fiqha-e-Jafria (TNFJ) was formed. Not surprisingly the Shi'ite groups look towards Iran and are significantly influenced by the Islam that is being promulgated and practised there.

Within Pakistan, like India, various Sufi tariqas have flourished with many pirs operating *khanqah* which are associated with the numerous Sufi shrines scattered throughout the country. Some date back to the early appearance of Islam in the Indus valley while the Data Ghanj Buksh, located in Lahore and associated with the Chishti tariqa, is possibly one of the most famous. It too has been violently targeted by those opposed to its presence.[37] While the Barelwi are more sympathetic towards Sufi practices and represent a large section of the Pakistani population, these practices incur the ire of the Ahl-e-Hadith and Deobandi, who express their displeasure in violent attacks, particularly at times of special celebrations.[38] So, the Barelwi respond in kind. On the other side of the equation, political leaders often turn to these pirs or 'saints' for their blessing not only for their political career but also for themselves and their families. In addition, many of these pirs (saints) also adopt political roles as elected members of Government, naturally supported by their clientele.

Politically motivated students with their own religio-political organisations, usually associated with one of the religious parties also play significant roles in Pakistan politics: usually through their agitation and protests. Within Pakistan, the Islami Jami'at-l Tulaba was founded in Lahore in 1947 as a wing of the Jama'at-I Islami whose founder was Mualana Abu'l-A A'la Maududi, provides an excellent example.[39] Originally established for *dawah* it developed study circles to promote its understanding of Islam and the associated practice, which later gave rise to pronounced political activity. The

---

[37] One such attack was in July 2010 by the Pakistani Taliban, cf. Willox. There were also several attacks on the shrine during my time in Pakistan.

[38] https://www.thenews.com.pk/print/186913-Sufi-shrines-under-attack-in-Paki stan-a-chronology, cited August 11, 2020.

[39] Cf. Seyyed Vali Reza Nasr, "Students, Islam and Politics: Jania'at-I Tulba in Pakistan," *Middle East Journal* 46, no. 1 (1992): 59–76.

rise of the madrassas have also increased the politicio-religious perceptions of their students, often encouraging them to action, including the formation of religio-political groups espousing violence. Those belonging to the Deobandi have not only been developing a conservative Islamic awareness and understanding but are also strongly anti Barelwi, which strikes at the heart of much of Pakistan's form of Islam. Often, whether Deobandi or Barelwi these madrassas provide free education for young males who otherwise would not have educational opportunity. These madrassas have strongly scouted for students in the northern tribal areas and amongst the poor and disadvantaged.

Since Pakistan's creation in 1947 there has been a constantly growing thrust to make Pakistan a truly Islamic political identity.[40] Jinnah's speech in which he is said to have invited anyone to make Pakistan their home, providing a 'safe' place for religious minorities, (theoretically demonstrated by the white band on the Pakistani flag) has been rigorously denied by some.[41] Liaqat Khan, a graduate of Aligarh University, the first Prime Minister of Pakistan (1947-1951), and one of the members of the All India Muslim League was a strong defender of Muslim rights. Following Jinnah's death in 1948, he was able to exert considerable influence, giving a 'stronger' lead towards Islamic principles. This was evidenced in the Objectives Resolution which was supported by Maududi's understanding of the Islamic state. Since then, various political leaders – Ayub Khan, Zulifkar Ali Bhutto, Zia, Nawaz Sharif, Musharraf, have used 'Islam' to either strengthen or gain support for their government, while also trying to curb some of the power of the various religious parties. Indeed, dedication to Islam was one of Imran Khan's election campaign strategies. Although Bhutto's orientation was towards the Left he gained the support of the religious parties who from 1973 onward were given a voice in the elections. It was also about that time that Islam was declared the state religion. Religious schools, *madrassa,*

---

[40] In the 1950's, Maulana Shabbir Ahmad Usmani, President of the Jamiat Ulema Islam (JUI) and *pir* of Manki Sharif from the North West Frontier Province (now Khyber Pakhtunkhwa), and Maulana Akram Khan, President of the East Pakistan Provincial Muslim League, actively campaigned for an Islamic state. See Farahnaz Ispahani, "The cleansing of Pakistan's minorities," https://www.hudson .org/research/9781-cleansing-pakistan-of-minorities, cited August 29, 2020.
[41] An October 2017 letter in *History Today* claims that Jinnah pledged to make Pakistan "a truly great Islamic state." The letter also claims that a "Pakistan divorced from faith would have no basis for existence."

grew in number, though subsequently governments have had difficulty in regularising them or their curriculum. Arabic was introduced as a compulsory subject in middle and secondary schools and the teaching of *Islamiat* was also extended into various other subject areas. During this period Saudi Arabia was injecting funds into the country and the town in which I lived was a recipient of this money and its name changed to reflect that of the Saudi giver.

When Zia ul-Haq came to power with his programme of Islamization, he introduced a number of 'shar'ia' laws such as the Hadood ordinance and further extended the existing blasphemy laws which Bhutto had already strengthened. The Hadood ordinance is particularly discriminatory against women who have been raped, especially since their word is considered 'half' that of a male's. Many of those who it is claimed are guilty of 'blasphemy' are killed before their case gets to court.[42] High ranking officials who even dare to question the 'blasphemy' laws have suffered a violent end. Judges who declare the 'accused' not guilty have also been killed. Usually the perpetrators of the violence, even if brought to court and sentenced, manage to escape any punishment: the religious nature of their action the justification. For the religious minorities, the blasphemy law is often used as an excuse to inflict injustice.

Another player in the politics of Islam is the Army which appears to lean towards a conservative religious bias. Indeed, a number of generals have instigated a coup d'état, taking over the controls of government. Meyers analysed a book written by Brigadier S.K. Malik of the Pakistan Army entitled *The Quranic Concept of War*, available from the bazaars of Pakistan and India, which enunciates the Islamic principles of war. It also includes a foreward by Zia ul-Haq reminding the readers that *jihad* is every Muslim's responsibility. Such a publication, with its focus on Islamic principles, no doubt, reflects the ethos of at least the Generals in the Army, and one suspects, shapes the teaching offered to the soldiers.

---

[42] The 'gossip' surrounding most of the blasphemy accusations is that they are unfounded. Those who make the accusation do so for some personal gain or because they have a personal vendetta against the accused. It was known that the person who accused the Christian lecturer in Faisalabad of blasphemy did so because he wanted the lectureship. In another case it was because the accuser wanted the land. By killing the accused before the case reaches court (if indeed it does) the truth is 'hidden' but the attacker (often the accuser) is seen to be 'righteous' and 'obeying Allah's will.' Therefore, they are exonerated.

When Zia ul-Haq took control, possibly the only one to do so with a strong personal religious conviction, he represented the conservative element of Pakistan's vocal Muslim society.[43] Ul-Haq was also influenced by the conservative Maulana Abul Ala Maududi, an advocate of an Islamic state. He was also influenced by the wider Muslim world to make Pakistan a truly Islamic.

Salzman's anthropological analysis of 'balanced opposition' operates at every level of society. The question of 'honour' and 'shame' is more easily understood: 'us' against 'a perceived perpetrator of shame'. The significant presence of non-Muslims in the community, especially Ahmadiyya and Christians, though Hindus are not exempt, is a constant reminder of the distinction between believers and the infidel. For many, this becomes the basis of an underlying and often fermented religious demand to 'make converts to Islam' either by 'fear tactics' and/or 'violence.' A further Islamic principle which is very evident within Pakistani society it the 'right of Muslims to plunder the infidel'' (cf. Sura 2:212) with the aggrieved individual having no means of redress for both the police and the courts are in tacit agreement with the process. Besides, the 'infidel' only has limited rights within the Islamic system being subject to *dhimmi* status.

This 'us' and 'them' dichotomy is also, I suspect, one of the reasons for the constant splitting of groups, compounded by the belief 'that my particular understanding of Islam is the correct one and yours is wrong' which not only reinforces the 'us' and 'them' mentality but also provides a reason to act violently against the 'other' usually citing cases of *bida* or *sherk*.

Conclusion

Pakistan faces two major problems: one is the instability and insecurity that is caused by the constant infighting of the Islamic sects with their propensity to force and violence. This is also reflected in an inability to seek some common ground on which they can live and work with a degree of unity and harmony. This will continue as long as those within Islam terrorise and fight against those who also call themselves Muslims.

---

[43] According to Fair, "Islam and Politics in Pakistan," 261, Zia ul-Haq cultivated the Deobandi mullahs both to gain a degree of religio-political authority and to legitimize his dictatorship.

The other issue is establishing what is an acceptable form of Islamic government by defining what is an Islamic Republic, given the nature and character of Pakistan with its ethnic, linguistic and economic diversity. Both of these require the religious factions within Islam to come to an agreed position as to what constitutes an Islamic republic – that is what is an acceptable Islamic form of not only government but also an Islamic form of life as defined by the shari'a. It also needs to decide if that Republic can include religious diversity, whether that be within Islam and whether it is willing to include the non-Muslim religious minorities giving them rights and privileges, without subjecting them to dhimmi status. Given the 'us' and 'them' orientation inherent in Islam's foundation, the constant accusations of 'bida' and 'sherk, the challenge is enormous and I suspect a solution, virtually impossible.

Bibliography

Ayoob, Mohammad.
"Political Islam: Image and Reality." *World Policy Journal* 21, no. 3 (2004): 1–14.

Ahmed, Akbar.
"Jinnah and the Quest for Muslim Identity," *History Today* 44, no. 9 (1994): 34–40.

Bowering, G., Patricia Crone, Wadad Kadi, Devin Stewart, and M. Qazim Zaman, eds.
The Princeton Encyclopaedia of Islamic Political Thought. Princeton NK: Princeton University Press, 2013.

Das Durga.
India from Curzon to Nehru and After. New York: The John Day Co., 1970.

Devji, Faisal.
"Secular Islam." *Political Theology* 19, no. 8 (2018): 704–718.

Esposito, John L., ed.
The Oxford Encyclopedia of the Modern Islamic World. 2 vols. Oxford: Oxford University Press, 1995.

Fair, C. Christine.
"Islam and Politics in Pakistan." In *The Muslim World After 9/11*, ed. Angel M. Rabasa, Cheryl Benard, Peter Chalk, C. Christine Fair, Theodore Karasik, Rollie Lal, Ian Lesser, and David Thaler, 247–296. Santa Monica, CA: Rand Corporation, 2004.

Feyyaz, Mohammad.
"Facets of Religious Violence in Pakistan." *Counter Terrorist Trends and Analyses* 5, no. 2 (2013): 9–13.

Ispahani, Farahnaz.
"The cleansing of Pakistan's Minorities." *Current Trends in Islamist Ideology*, Hudson Institute, published July 31, 2013.

Jamal, Umair.
"The Politics of Religious Exclusion in Pakistan." *The Diplomat*, published October 18, 2017.
——— "Amid a Pandemic, Pakistan Focuses on a Baloch Insurgency." *The Diplomat*, published June 16, 2020.

Kalin Michael and Niloufer Siddiqui.
Religious Authority and the Promotion of Sectarian Tolerance in Pakistan. Washington, DC: United States Institute of Peace, 2014.

Kamran, Tahir.
"Pakistan: A Failed State?" *History Today* 67, no. 9 (2017): 24–35.

Nasr, Syyed Vali Reza.
"Students, Islam, and Politics: Jami'at -l Tulaba in Pakistan." *Middle East Journal* 46, no. 1 (1992): 59–76.

Neufeldt, Ronald W.
"Religion and Politics in the Thought of Muhammad Iqbal." *Journal of Religious Thought* 34, no. 1 (1997): 35–39.

Reynolds, Nathelene.
"Hindu Nationalism and the Muslim Minority in India." In *Corridors of Knowledge for Peace and Development*, edited by Sarah S. Aneel, Uzma T. Haroon, and Imrana Niazi, 279–

303. Islamabad: Sustainable Development Policy Institute, 2020.

Rizvi, S. A. A.
"Muslim India." In *The World of Islam, Faith, People, Culture*, edited by Bernard Lewis, 301–320. London, Thames and Hudson, 1976.

Salem, Elie.
"Nationalism and Islam," *The Muslim World* 52, no. 4 (1962): 227–287.

Shumack, Richard.
The Wisdom of Islam and the Foolishness of Christianity: A Christian Response to Nine Objections to Christianity by Muslim Philosophers. Sydney: Island View Publishing, 2014.

Siddiqi, Zahoor.
"Gandhi-Jinnah Equation." *Proceedings of the Indian History Congress* 74 (2013): 629–639.

Skelly, Joseph Morrison, ed.
Political Islam from Mohammad to Ahmadinejab, Defenders, Detractors and Definitions. Santa Barbara, CA: ABC-CLIO, 2010.

Spear, Percival.
A History of India. Vol. 2 of 2. London: Penguin, 1984.

Sweetman, J. Windrow.
"Viewpoints in Pakistan II." *The Muslim World* 47, no. 3 (1957): 224–238.

Templin, James D.
"Religious Education of Pakistan's Deobandi Madaris and Radicalisation." *Counter Terrorist Trends and Analyses* 7, no. 5 (2015): 15–21.

Thapar, Romila.
A History of India. Vol. 1 of 2. London: Penguin, 1966.

Tibi, Bassam.

Islam between Culture and Politics. 2nd ed. New York, Palgrave Macmillan, 2005.

Wheeler, Richard S.
"The Individual and Action in the Thought of Iqbal." *The Muslim World* 52, no. 3 (1962): 197–206.

Willox, Alexander.
"Voices of Political Islam in Pakistan," *Australian Institute for International Affairs,* published May 26, 2014, http://www.internationalaffairs.org.au/news-item/ voices-of-political-islam-in-pakistan.

Chapter 11

ISLAM and POLITICS in MALAYSIA:
the First 60 years of Statehood

Peter G. Riddell[1]

Malaysia has a lot going for it. It represents the meeting place of three of the world's greatest civilisations: the Malays, the Chinese and the Indians. Such ethnic plurality is mirrored in religious demographics as well. Muslims constitute just over 60% of the population, with the remaining almost 40% divided among Buddhists, Hindus, Christians, various Chinese religions and other minor religious groupings. As such, Malaysia could be a dynamic laboratory for Islamic religious pluralism.

In fact, Malaysia is a country in ferment. To the casual observer it looks like a prosperous, modern, stable 21st-century state. However, in 2020 the country was tottering on the brink of unrest, facing a range of challenges which had very deep roots.

From independence to the new millennium

Since independence, first as the Federation of Malaya in 1957 then as the enlarged Malaysia in 1963, the country witnessed a tussle between two political parties which vied for the support of the majority race, the Malays, who are all Muslim. The United Malays National Organisation, or UMNO, was the key player in the ruling coalition for the first 60 years following Malayan independence. It originally represented a more modernising approach to Islam while its principal rival for Malay support, the Islamic Party of Malaysia

[1] Peter G. Riddell (PhD, ANU, 1984) is Senior Research Fellow of the Australian College of Theology at Melbourne School of Theology and Professorial Research Associate in History at SOAS University of London. His last book examines Qur'anic interpretation in the Malay world and he is currently preparing a book on the history of Christian-Muslim relations in Southeast Asia.

(known by its Malay acronym of PAS) was conservative traditionalist.

For the first decade of its existence Malaysia flourished as a multicultural, multifaith state. But bitter race riots in 1969 left a legacy of fear among the majority Malay race that their position of predominance was under threat. Malay identity is tied up very much with the Muslim faith: Islam represents the religious default, a fact reflected in the 1963 Constitution which states in Article 3.1 that "Islam is the religion of the Federation; but other religions may be practised in peace and harmony" (The Commissioner of Law revision, Malaysia 2010). Therefore attempts to shore up Malay identity inevitably assumed a religious dimension.

The rise of Islamic revivalism in Malaysia from the 1970s resulted in the emergence of a number of radical Islamic movements which called Malaysian Muslims to be more devout in the practice of their faith. In response, fearful of a surge of support for its PAS rivals, the UMNO-led Malaysian coalition Government, or Barisan Nasional (BN), sought to consolidate its position among its Malay constituency by launching its own Islamisation drive.

Under the leadership of Prime Minister Mahathir Mohamad during the 1980s and 1990s, the Barisan coalition government sought to entrench Malay power and predominance by strengthening Islam in the fabric of the state. The Mahathir government introduced a raft of Islamic legislation and established a diverse set of Islamic institutions, such as an Islamic Economic Foundation and an Islamic foundation for social welfare. In 1992 the Institute of Islamic Understanding was inaugurated by Dr Mahathir "to conceptualise, design and provide the required inputs of Islam" (Institute of Islamic Understanding Malaysia 2001) to the development of society. A compulsory course at university in Islamic Civilisation was introduced for Muslim students, and in 1997 the Government extended this requirement to cover all students, both Muslim and non-Muslim. An Islamic Bank was set up, as well as the Department of Islamic Development under the Prime Minister's Department. All these initiatives resulted in the creation of a powerful Islamic bureaucracy at both federal and state levels by the turn of the 21st century.

The Government's principal opponents, the Islamic Party of Malaysia (PAS), encountered success at the level of state politics, with the Barisan governing coalition losing much support in the 1999 elections, while still retaining power at a federal level. For the first time, PAS won power in the state of Terengganu, supplementing its hold in neighbouring Kelantan since 1990. The PAS state governments moved to institute Islamic penal codes in their respective states. The entertainment industry was dramatically reduced, dress codes for women in government offices were implemented, separate queues for men and women at supermarket check-outs were required and hotels in the two states were prohibited from selling alcohol. The Terengganu government also announced soon after its victory that it would impose the old Islamic tax of *kharaj* on non-Muslim run businesses.

Protests at such measures by non-Muslims and some Muslims were muted compared with the howls of concern when the PAS state government in Terengganu announced its intention to implement strict Islamic codes of punishment for serious crimes. This followed PAS efforts to do the same in Kelantan in 1993 (Kamali 1995).

Stern opposition to these PAS initiatives came from the UMNO-led Barisan federal government. The Muslim modernist UMNO has always been willing to support a measured implementation of Islamic law in the private domain for Muslims, such as concerning marriage, divorce and inheritance. However, UMNO opposed the introduction of Islamic codes of crime and punishment. The party was successful in blocking these PAS efforts, as responsibility for this area of law lay within federal, not state jurisdiction.

In short, the Barisan governments spoke the language of promoting "Islamic values" such as Trust, Responsibility, Sincerity, Diligence, Cooperation and Integrity; their rivals in the Islamic Party responded that values weren't enough; Islamic Shari'a laws were required. The country witnessed a spiral of Islamisation as the competing Malay-based political groups struggled to win the hearts and minds of the majority Malays.

The early years of the 21st century to the 2004 elections

The stakes were raised considerably as the new century dawned when in October 2001, Malaysian Prime Minister Mahathir Mohamad declared, in response to repeated calls from PAS for the establishment of an Islamic State, that Malaysia was already one. PAS was unimpressed by the Prime Minister's declaration. In July 2002 the Party proceeded with presenting a parliamentary bill in the state of Terengganu designed to implement harsh Shari'a Islamic laws relating to crime and punishment.

Fragmentation among Malaysia's 60% Muslim majority increased. It was not simply a case of the UMNO modernisers and the Islamic Party hard-liners being locked in political combat. Many Muslims spoke out increasingly against the pervasive Islamising rhetoric from both sides. Malaysian political scientist Farish Noor lamented the "use of religious vocabulary as the ideological weapon of first resort." He warned that the outcome would be "a new generation of activists and ideologues who will undoubtedly take up the Islamist cause if and when they are able to" (Noor 2000). In other words, the ongoing struggle for supremacy among competing Muslim groups was all grist to the mill of Islamic radicalism.

The 1999 elections had proved to be a watershed for UMNO. The significant loss of support for the party among the Muslim Malay population precipitated an internal process of change in the lead-up to the March 2004 elections.

Dr Mahathir retired as Prime Minister in October 2003, after twenty-two years at the helm of Malaysia. He was replaced by Abdullah Badawi, who came to the position with significant credentials as an Islamic scholar. However, he was something of an unknown quantity as a national leader. Many commentators questioned his ability to stem the seemingly irresistible surge of support for PAS among the Malays.

In his first three months as Prime Minister, Abdullah prioritised policy in both secular and religious matters. He first launched a campaign against corruption, authorising the arrest of several leading public figures, including a former minister in the Mahathir cabinet. He also scaled back several grandiose building projects which had been conceived under the previous administration. These measures served as a shot across the bows for those within UMNO who expected Abdullah to be simply a clone of Mahathir.

Abdullah's attention was also directed to religious affairs. He led mass prayers during the fasting month of Ramadan, thereby signalling his intention to challenge the claims of PAS leaders to speak for Malay Muslims in spiritual matters.

When federal and state elections were announced for 21 March 2004, leaders of the Islamic Party declared that those who voted for PAS would earn a place in heaven. Abdullah responded sardonically: "We can't promise heaven. It is up to God. We can only work to become good Muslims" (Ahmad 2004).

At the same time, Abdullah launched his vision of "Islam Hadhari" as a counter to the PAS dream of an Islamic state. For Abdullah, Islam would be equated with forward-looking development and progress, rather than a backward-looking Shari'a state. Furthermore, he preached a vision of Malaysia for all Malaysians, regardless of race or religion.

As a step in this direction, his administration introduced a new national service programme designed to gather 85,000 young Malay, Chinese and Indian citizens for a three-month training programme intended to lead to greater inter-ethnic and inter-religious harmony.

So the choice was left to Malaysia's ten million voters to determine whether the surge in support for PAS's purist vision seen in 1999 would be carried further. International interest in the elections was intense, given the prominence of radical Islamic conservatism in the context of the 9/11 attacks, the War on Terror, and bombings in Bali and Madrid in previous years.

In the event, the PAS engine ran dramatically out of steam. The State of Terengganu was swept from their grasp, with the party only retaining four of the 32 state parliamentary seats. Even in Kelantan, considered safe for PAS, the Barisan coalition almost won, with a desperate PAS victory being declared by the barest of margins only after a recount.

Nationally, the governing coalition won 198 of the 219 seats. This was a sweet victory for both Abdullah Badawi as Prime Minister and for his Barisan Nasional coalition government, which had been so shaken after the 1999 results. It also brought considerable relief to Malaysia's non-Muslim minority.

Political Islam shocks in 2008: From Abdullah Badawi to Najib Razak

The setback experienced by PAS in the 2004 federal and state polls caused much soul-searching. In the lead-up to the 2008 federal and state elections, PAS played its cards differently. Rather than calling for an Islamic state, which had previously alienated non-Muslim voters, PAS focused on issues of social welfare and advocacy, even fielding some women and non-Muslim candidates. The change in strategy paid handsome dividends as its share of the federal parliament increased from 7 to 23 seats. This was in spite of efforts by the Barisan Government to marginalise PAS among Muslim Malays during the previous four years. In the state of Terengganu, for example, 62 mosques were built by the government during the life of the previous parliament in an attempt to persuade Muslim voters that it, not PAS, represented the voice of Muslim Malays.

The stocks of the ruling UMNO-led Barisan coalition dramatically deteriorated in the election. In the previous parliament, the Barisan had a 177 seat majority; in the new parliament that majority was reduced to 58 seats. Furthermore, it previously controlled 12 of Malaysia's 13 states, but in state elections held concurrently with the 2008 national vote, the Barisan was thrown out of power in four additional states.

Discontent with Barisan policies was felt by many sectors of Malaysia's multi-racial and multi-faith society. Religious minorities, constituting 40% of Muslim-majority Malaysia, felt particularly aggrieved at the policies of the government. The 9% Christian community was alienated by a range of issues, not least of which was the continuing rhetoric about Malaysia being an Islamic state, declared by Deputy Prime Minister Datuk Seri Najib Tun Razak after several previous such statements by leading government figures.

Topping off the Islamic state issue were other factors. English language Christian children's books were confiscated in several bookshops in three states because they supposedly contained offensive caricatures of prophets, according to the Islamic authorities

(The Voice of the Martyrs Canada 2008). Furthermore, the attempt by Islamic authorities to ban the use of the word "Allah" by non-Muslims in their worship and in their publications, discussed in more detail below, raised Christian voices in protest.

Joining Christians in protest were Hindus and Buddhists. The former witnessed demolition of a number of temples, and considered that due consultation with local communities was not carried out by government officials. Thousands of Hindus took to the streets in the national capital in November 2007, claiming discrimination in government policies and economic exclusion.

But public discontent with the government of Prime Minister Abdullah went beyond issues of religious division. In Malaysia race and religion are closely intertwined, so issues of religious discrimination have a knock-on effect on racial tensions. In the words of Malaysian Christian academic, Dr Albert Walters:

> The alarming slide in race relations continues, along with the rising influence of Islam thus giving rise to racial and religious polarisation in Malaysian society. Some of the most racially charged rhetoric seems to be coming from the ruling party itself (Riddell 2008).

Of even greater significance in the 2008 election outcome was the rise of another opposition party, the PKR Justice Party. Its principal spokesman was the charismatic Anwar Ibrahim, former Barisan Deputy Prime Minister who had fallen foul of Prime Minister Abdullah's predecessor, Mahathir Mohamad. Anwar and his Party were able to tear from the Barisan's grasp the mantle of Muslim moderation, previously claimed by the Barisan's major member party, the United Malays National Organisation. At the same time, the Justice party, through skilful candidate selection, succeeded in appealing to Malaysia's non-Muslim minority. Net result: Justice Party representation in the national parliament increased from one seat to 31, and it became the senior partner in the new coalition governments in three of the five states not controlled by the Barisan.

Many of Malaysia's racial and religious minorities were rejoicing, with good reason. First, the traditional more-Islamic-than-thou struggle between UMNO and PAS had been pushed off centre stage. It was replaced by a competition pitting the Barisan, which

261

claimed to be pluralist yet Islam-friendly, with a loosely allied opposition, now led by the Justice Party, which spoke the language of multi-ethnic and multi-religious equality. In the wake of the election result, Justice Party icon Anwar Ibrahim said,

> The people have voted decisively for a new era where the government must be truly inclusive and recognise that all Malaysians, regardless of race, culture or religion are a nation of one (Ting 2008).

Even the PAS Islamist old guard, represented by its spiritual leader Haji Nik Abdul Aziz Nik Mat, was forced to speak in similar terms, declaring that

> We will approach this victory from an Islamic point of view and this means everyone is equal... All are brothers and sisters. There should be no more dividing people along racial lines (Riddell 2008).

2010: Copyrighting 'Allah' in Malaysia Stirs Strife

As we have seen in the previous discussion, the worldwide resurgence in Islamic consciousness since the 1970s had a profound impact on Malaysian Muslims, especially during the Prime Ministership of Mahathir Mohamad (1981–2003). As one aspect of the goal to purify Islamic practice, the government of Dr. Mahathir sought to protect certain religious terms considered to be the preserve of Islam.

On December 5, 1986, four terms—*Allah*, *Baitullah* (house of God/worship), *Solat* (prayer), and *Kaabah* (direction of prayer)— were gazetted as exclusive to Muslims under a Malaysian government circular. In time *Allah* proved to be the main sticking point. In 1988, the Non-Islamic Religions Enactment affirmed the restriction on non-Muslim use, either verbally or in print, of the term *Allah*, with this ban reaffirmed by the Cabinet on October 18 and November 1, 2006.

Allah was used for one of the deities, probably the supreme deity, in pre-Islamic Arabia some 1,500 years ago. In today's Arab world, *Allah* is the standard term for God among Arabic-speaking Christians of different denominations. The Catholic Maltese, whose language is related to Arabic, refer to God as *Alla*. In Indonesia, *Allah* is commonly used by Christians; the 1974 New Translation of the

Bible in Indonesian renders the Old Testament Hebrew terms for God with *Allah*. These usages occur in their different locations without objection from local Muslims.

The Malaysian and Indonesian national languages are related dialects, much like American and British English, so Indonesian books regularly circulate in Malaysia. In June 1993, authorities temporarily withheld a shipment of almost 1,500 imported Indonesian-language Christian books, claiming they included the "forbidden" words. Four years later, 230 Christian books imported into Malaysia from Singapore and Indonesia were similarly confiscated.

The challenge against the ban on non-Muslim use of *Allah* was led by the Malaysian Catholic newspaper, the *Herald,* which from time to time used *Allah* in its Malaysian-language edition. The editor, Fr. Lawrence Andrew, argued that the case concerned religious and cultural freedom for all of Malaysia's minorities, not simply the use of one term. The simmering dispute heated up in 2007 when the Home Ministry invoked the 1986 Cabinet directive in temporarily refusing to renew the publication permit of the *Herald.*

Matters came to a head in 2008. On January 3 of that year, the Malaysian Cabinet reaffirmed the restriction against non-Muslim use of "Allah." In May, the Catholic *Herald* petitioned the High Court for judicial review, seeking permission to use *Allah* in its Malay-language edition. When the High Court ruled on December 31, 2009, that Catholics were allowed to use *Allah* to describe the Christian God in the national language, the decision triggered a storm among Malaysia's Muslim population. Within days, there were street protests against the ruling, and attempts were made to hack into the online version of the *Herald.* A campaign against the ruling on the social networking website Facebook attracted hundreds of thousands of supporters. And a coalition of 27 Muslim organisations petitioned the nine Malay sultans, each the head of Islam in his respective state, to help overturn the verdict. Most significantly, a string of churches of various denominations, a convent school, and a Sikh temple were firebombed in Malaysia in the wake of the ruling.

The 2008 elections had revealed Malay political allegiances as being in a state of flux. The opposition alliance was posing a real challenge to the UMNO-dominated Barisan coalition for the first time since independence. Seeing the *Allah* debate as one way of connecting with the more conservative PAS constituency, new Prime Minister Najib Razak, who had stepped up from his Deputy Prime Minister position to replace Abdullah Badawi in April 2009, declared that the Home Ministry would appeal against the High Court's ruling. But in doing so Najib risked alienating Malaysia's minorities and threatening the "One Malaysia" slogan that he was promoting as a hallmark of his new prime ministership.

Unexpected Support

Paradoxically, the dispute at one level affirmed Christian-Muslim cooperation. The arson attacks on churches were widely condemned, with Abdul Hadi Awang, the President of PAS, describing them as "un-Islamic," because

> Islam respects the rights of others to practise their own religion [and] have their own places of worship, including churches (Spykerman 2010).

Prime Minister Najib announced a government allocation of 500,000 Malaysian dollars to rebuild the Metro Tabernacle, the church most damaged in the attacks.

Some Muslims disassociated themselves not only from the attacks on churches but also from the ban on non-Muslim use of *Allah*. In a stinging critique of government policy, Ustaz Maszlee Malik and Dr. Musa Mohd Nordin warned that the dispute "brought up the dark side within us," and they asserted that Muslim secularists, religious zealots, and Muslim NGOs joined together to "form a lethal concoction of religious intolerance" (Malik and Nordin 2010).

Ida Bakar, a Muslim contributor to an online chat forum, noted that the *Allah* debate was a non-issue in other Muslim countries:

> Arabs—Christian and Muslims—are probably laughing their head-gears off at the sheer stupidity. I am cringing with utter embarrassment (Riddell 2010).

Nevertheless, the determination of many activist Muslims was still clearly in evidence. Mohd Aizam Masod, spokesman for the Islamic

Development Department, argued somewhat loosely that the Christian use of *Allah* would confuse Muslims:

> Imagine if Jesus Christ, which under the Unitarian concept is considered as God to the Christians, be called *Allah,* wouldn't it be confusing? *Allah* is by definition a description of a singular Muslim God, but non-Muslims' usage will pluralize it (Riddell 2010).

Shock for political Islam in 2018: from Najib Razak to Mahathir Mohamad

In May 2018, Malaysia was seemingly on the cusp of an exciting new era. Pakatan Harapan (PH), a dynamic, emerging political coalition of moderate Muslim, Chinese, and other ethnic parties, won the fourteenth national elections in a landslide, almost doubling its representation in parliament by winning 121 of 222 seats in the lower house and garnering 48.3 percent of the national vote.

The losing Barisan Nasional coalition was reduced to 79 seats, down from 133 in the 2013 elections. As we have seen, under the leadership of its long-serving prime minister, Mahathir Mohamad, who led the country from 1981–2003, successive Barisan governments had pursued a top-down programme of Islamisation of the bureaucracy. The aim was to instil and reinforce Islamic values throughout the government, at both federal and state levels, as well as across Malaysia's multicultural and multi-faith society.

When the PH coalition won power in 2018, non-Muslims and many of the more liberal Muslims anticipated and celebrated an end to the relentless Islamising drive of the previous Barisan governments. But some of the more conservative Muslims were dismayed by the prospect of greater power-sharing with non-Muslim minorities and were fearful of a more secularised society in which the dominance of Islam-friendly policies would be eroded. By a strange twist of fate, the new PH government was led by none other than Mahathir Mohamad, by then a nonagenarian, as Prime Minister. He had switched his party allegiances after becoming disenchanted with successive BN governments led by his successors.

Islamist Opposition to Racial Equality

Following the 2018 general election, Malaysia's hardline Islamist groups triggered ongoing protests against the new government. Their aim was to undermine the nation's stability and to re-establish the Islamisation process that had been underway since the early 1980s.

Concerned that the new Malaysian government might ratify the International Convention on the Elimination of All Forms of Racial Discrimination (ICERD)—a UN policy dating from the 1960s, which has received widespread support from world governments—Islamist lobby groups organised a massive protest rally against the ICERD on December 8, 2018 in the nation's capital of Kuala Lumpur. They feared that ratification might undermine the special privileges enjoyed by the all-Muslim Malay race in multi-racial Malaysia.

The Islamist protests were widely criticised both within and outside Malaysia. Prominent Turkish scholar and activist Mustafa Akyol commented:

> I would recommend that all those in Malaysia who oppose the ICERD on Islamic grounds read the Ottoman Constitution of 1876...

which, in his view, accorded with ICERD principles (Koya 2018). Pro-ICERD Malaysian Muslim lawyer Latheefa Koya observed that a large number of Muslim nations had already ratified ICERD. Nevertheless, under pressure, Prime Minister Mahathir announced that Malaysia would not ratify the UN convention. This climb-down on his part resulted in the menacing anti-ICERD rally passing off on December 8 without incident. Islamist pressure had paid off for the hardliners.

Islamist Championing of Special Privileges for Malays

In the midst of the ICERD dispute, some Malays found another creative way to swim against the world tide of racial equality. In November, some 53 Malay Muslim NGOs (non-governmental organisations) formed the G3 group, a "third force alliance" designed to champion special rights for the Malay race in Malaysia. Some G3 spokespeople expressed a longing for "the spirit of May 13"—an ominous reference to the 1969 riots by Malays against ethnic Chinese Malaysians, which was triggered by a controversial result in the national elections that year. Many were killed in those riots, a fact alluded to in expressions of "longing for blood" by G3 spokespeople

(Riddell 2019). Islamist pressure was thus adopting a more menacing tone.

Anti-Christian Sentiments

Although most of the increasing Malay Islamist rhetoric targeted the Chinese, some was aimed at Christianity and Christians (many of whom are Malaysian Chinese). On December 23 2018, the youth chief of the opposition Islamic Party of Malaysia (PAS), Muhammad Khalil Abdul Hadi, cautioned Muslims not to celebrate Christmas, claiming that the Christian festival was against the teachings of Islam. In a lecture in the PAS heartland of Kuala Terengganu, Muhammad Khalil reportedly declared,

> Christmas has an element of syirik (idolatry) which is against Islam's teaching. They claim that God had a child, which is against our beliefs as Muslims. They celebrate Christmas with such elements and claim that Prophet Isa (Jesus) is the son of God (Prakash 2018).

Such anti-Christian sentiments evoked a sharp rebuke from Dr. Ahmad Farouk Musa, a faculty member of Monash University's Malaysia campus and founder of the modernist Islamic Renaissance Front (IRF). He questioned the Islamist party's understanding of Islamic teachings and multiculturalism, adding,

> Perhaps it is time for PAS to think whether they should buy an island and proclaim it as an Islamic State and live exclusively with their own kind with the same mentality (FMT Reporters 2018).

An Islamic State?

Just after Christmas 2018, the Islamist group Ikatan Muslimin Malaysia (ISMA) launched a campaign for Malaysia to be recognised as an "Islamic state." This attracted howls of protest from diverse quarters, Muslim voices among them. Majidah Hashim of the Sisters in Islam lobby group declared:

> Why can't we just be good Muslims in a progressive country that embraces modernity and is friendly with all nations East and West? Because if we can do it here, we can do it anywhere, and seriously, isn't that what we want? For Malaysians to be globally savvy instead of a Malaysia that is paranoid and suspicious of everything that comes from outside our borders? I wonder about the fragility of the faith of an ummah [Muslim

community] that is built upon the fear of humans and not love for God. I wonder how they would fare on the stage of the great wide world out there (Hashim 2019).

The Malaysian scene was heating up, as Muslim groups manoeuvred to shape the Malaysia of the future. That future hung in the balance, as was seen in a decision of the Kuching Sessions Court to sentence 22-year-old Alister Cogia from Sarawak to ten years in jail for posting insults against Islam and Muhammad on his Facebook page. PAS, Malaysia's Islamic party, continued to seek greater influence and drew ever closer to UMNO, which was still smarting from losing the 2018 elections and finding itself in the unaccustomed position of being in political opposition. Professor Ahmad Fauzi Abdul Hamid of Universiti Sains Malaysia warned that Muslims in Malaysia were "slowly but surely becoming radicalized," pointing out that classes in Islam, taught in government schools since the early 1990s, had shifted their manner of teaching from a traditional Malay style to one derived from the Middle East, especially from Saudi Arabia (Abdul Hamid 2016).

All this raised concerns among Christians and other religious minorities. Christian civil rights activist and lawyer Eugene Yapp commented:

> PAS is now seen as the frontline in defending Malay Muslim rights. The religious community is badly polarized even further now. It's now a bi-polar relationship; between non-Muslim and Muslim. ... This is going to be the key social and religious driver in the days ahead that will influence the political scenario (Riddell 2019).

Political Islam and Religious Minorities Face Off in Malaysia

In the face of the decades-long tide of Islamisation in Malaysia, the country's almost 40% non-Muslim minority was increasingly galvanised into action. The government-controlled media was awash with Islamic programming, with no time allocated to the beliefs and practices of other faiths. Malaysia's Buddhists, Hindus, Christians, and other religious minorities realised at an early point of the Islamisation process that organised resistance was called for.

In 1983, Malaysia's four main religious minorities joined forces to form a lobby group, the Malaysian Consultative Council of Buddhism, Christianity, Hinduism and Sikhism, and were later joined by the country's Taoists (MCCBCHST – the Council). Muslim authorities declined the invitation to partner in this interfaith initiative. This body became increasingly adept at taking up the challenge facing the minorities. In subsequent decades the Council issued many press statements and bombarded the government with memoranda and requests addressing minority concerns.

For example, the Council issued a Press Release on 20 July 2002 in response to the PAS Terengganu state government's Hudud Bill, stating that "the Bill is an alarming attempt by the State to change the character of our country, which is multiracial, multi religious and constitutionally secular."

This followed an earlier Council Memorandum to the Government Commission on Human Rights (SUHAKAM), entitled "Problems faced by Non-Muslims in Freely Professing and Practising their Respective Religions." This memorandum called for Interreligious Councils to be established by statute at both State and Federal levels and to include Muslim representatives.

Many of these petitions fell on deaf ears. But there have been some notable successes since the Council's formation. For example, as the 21st century approached, Council representatives lobbied government authorities in the Malaysian state of Perak about plans to demolish 45 houses of non-Muslim worship. The plans were stopped as a result.

There was also a surge in ecumenical activity among diverse Christian groups. Christians constitute about nine percent of Malaysia's population, or around two million people. Christianity's roots date back to the 7th century, when Persian traders established a settlement on the west coast of the Malay peninsula near present-day Kedah. Although these early Christians merged with the local population over time, the sign of the cross reappeared in the region in 1511 with the Portuguese conquest of the trading city of Malacca. The Catholic community which they established represents the oldest church in Malaysia. It was joined by various Protestant groups, brought to the region by Dutch and English colonial authorities in subsequent centuries.

In 1986 the National Evangelical Christian Fellowship joined the Catholic Church and the original Council of Churches of Malaysia to form the Christian Federation of Malaysia. This body, representing 90% of Christians in Malaysia, stated its mission as to preserve

> the interests of the Christian community as a whole with particular reference to religious freedom and rights enshrined in the Federal Constitution.

Yet the Malaysian Constitution itself contains elements which work against religious tolerance. Article 11.4 specifies that

> State law and ... federal law may control or restrict the propagation of any religious doctrine or belief among persons professing the religion of Islam (The Commissioner of Law revision, Malaysia 2010).

Thus several bills were brought by PAS members before Federal Parliament since independence seeking to outlaw conversion by Muslims to other faiths. Though the Federal Government resisted such legislation, it has nevertheless allocated considerable public funds to the propagation of Islam among non-Muslims.

This inequitable situation is reflected in statistics on religious conversion. For example, between 1994 and May 1997 519 Muslims, of whom only 55 were Malaysian citizens, applied to change their religion. In the same period, over 11,000 people converted to Islam in Malaysia. This was testimony to the efficacy of the Malaysian Government's generously-funded Islamisation programme.

The various Barisan Governments provided ongoing support to Muslim services, such as the media, which were actively involved in proselytising other religious groups for Islam. This intensified in the wake of the 1988 Government announcement that religious programming on Radio and TV Malaysia would be devoted to Islam alone.

Legislation disadvantaging religious minorities was passed by successive Barisan governments. Distribution of Malay and Indonesian translations of the Bible were subject to certain restrictions. Muslims were entitled to a tax rebate on charitable *zakat*

270

contributions, but Christians were not entitled to such a rebate on church contributions. Government construction quotas defined the ratio of mosques to Muslims as 1:800, but this ratio increased to 1:4000 for churches and temples for non-Muslims.

Malaysia: a promise unfulfilled

In the midst of the intra-Muslim struggle for control of the Malay masses, the 40% non-Malay religious minority felt more and more marginalised as institutions assumed an increasingly Islamic hue. One key area affected was education, as explained by Tan Kong Beng, Executive Secretary of the Christian Federation of Malaysia, who commented in a 2016 interview that "creeping Islamization in Malaysia's schools has been going on for over 20 years" (Riddell 2017). This was reflected in many ways, including the favouring of Muslims in teacher recruitment and the curriculum, with the study of Islam being enhanced in government schools and the study of other faiths being excluded, replaced by ethics.

While the Islamisation of institutions is tangible, what is even more debilitating for inter-religious harmony is the subtle humiliation of non-Muslims that sometimes accompanied Malaysia's Islamisation process. This was seen at times in interfaith events. Rev Dr Hermen Shastri, General Secretary of the Council of Churches of Malaysia, described an event held in 2016 under government auspices to commemorate World Interfaith Harmony Week.

> Prime Minister [Najib Razak] came and the ceremony began with a long Muslim prayer, first in Arabic, then in Malay, after which there was a speech by the Chairman who is a Muslim. I'm Deputy Chair because I represent the non-Muslim section, but I was not asked to speak. The Prime Minister spoke and he also began with the usual Islamic statements. It came across to me as a purely Government function showcasing plurality and interfaith in Malaysia but there was no respect given to the fact that we were gathered there as different religions (Riddell 2017).

Accompanying such processes of foregrounding Islam and backgrounding other faiths was a level of deference that non-Muslims were increasingly expected to show in engaging with Muslim interlocutors. Tan Kong Beng explained: "We have to be over-courteous in formal meetings. The forms of courtesy: 'Pardon my ignorance, I would like to ask a question.'" Dr Shastri concurred in saying that in inter-religious meetings with Government "there is this constant permeation of a culture of fear. Somehow you cannot be open about taking a different stand" (Riddell 2017).

Hudud won't affect non-Muslims. Really?

Anxious about the continued yearning among some Malay Muslims for the introduction of harsh Islamic criminal codes, religious minorities found small comfort in the assurances by the authorities promoting this development that it would only apply to Muslims. Throughout the second decade of the 21st century, cases of non-Muslims having to comply with Islamic regulations abounded in Malaysia. Several examples will suffice.

In 2016, two young Chinese non-Muslims were charged in the City Hall magistrate's court with hugging and kissing in a park. On another occasion, a middle-aged Chinese lady was refused service in a Department of Transport office until she covered her bare lower legs with a sarong, an ankle-length item of Malay apparel. Food items popular among non-Muslim (and many Muslim) Malaysians which carried names considered offensive to Muslims (such as "ginger beer" and "hot dog") had to change their names in order to receive halal certification. Chinese shops in several Malay cities were raided in 2016 for selling paintbrushes that were suspected of containing pig bristles. As an example of bottom-up pressure, a group of Muslims demanded the removal of the cross from a church in a public square in Selangor.

With such cases abounding of regulations made by an increasingly Shari'a-sensitive Muslim bureaucracy impacting on religious minorities, assurances that non-Muslims would not be affected by proposed hudud criminal codes had a very hollow ring. Eugene Yapp, Executive Director of the Kairos Dialogue Network, an NGO dedicated to dialogue on issues affecting Christian-Muslim relation, commented that,

> ...as for the religious bureaucracy, its aim is to widen the powers of the Shari'a courts to facilitate the implementations of Hudud laws. It is part of its plan to review the entire Shari'a judicial system, which includes upgrading the levels of Shari'a court and the harmonization of Shari'a and civil laws, as part of the Islamization agenda (Riddell 2017).

This constantly creeping Shari'a is not good news for Malaysia's 40% religious minority population.

Conclusion: Where to from here?

As the third decade of the 21st century dawned, a virtual political coup-d'état took place in Malaysian politics. Malay fears of losing their dominant political position triggered a previously-unlikely partnership between UMNO and PAS in the federal parliament. When Prime Minister Mahathir Mohamad unexpectedly resigned in February 2020, the UMNO-PAS alliance was joined by representatives from several other political groupings to constitute a slim majority in parliament. The government that had been elected in 2018 fell from power and was replaced by a mainly Malay coalition of parties under the leadership of new Prime Minister Muhyiddin bin Haji Muhammad Yassin, who had served as Deputy Prime Minister under former Prime Ministers Najib Razak and Mahathir Mohamad. In this new scenario, according to columnist Amy Chew writing for the Lowy Institute,

> [W]ith an Islamist party now in government agitating for social curbs, the way of life in a secular nation is at stake... The tone of the demands sounded like a playbook straight out of Afghanistan under the Taliban (Chew 2020).

In this new context, the 2016 comment by Dr Ng Kam Weng about the push for greater powers for Shari'a courts seemed prophetic. He pointed out that the Islamic bureaucracy

> talks about implementing Shari'a in phases. Whatever they say, we know that their ultimate goal is hudud. Even without present attempts to enhance Shari'a courts (Ting 2016), they are already infringing our rights. What more when Shari'a courts are enhanced further and other steps embolden them. The record shows that they have no respect for my constitutional rights even within the present constitutional system. So we have no reason to believe that they would do any better [with enhanced Shari'a courts] and probably would do worse.

Despite the turn of events in February 2020, there are some hopeful signs on the horizon. For one, Malaysia's two eastern states on the island of Borneo, Sarawak and Sabah, have substantial Christian populations and have always stood strongly against expanding Islamization and enhanced Shari'a powers. The votes of their representatives in the federal parliament will be key as Malaysia charts its future. Tan Kong Beng pointed out that

The East Malaysians are unhappy with wasted oil money. They pump so much oil and gas and only get 5%. While there is great progress and expenditure in West Malaysia, the East Malaysian states lack in electricity, water, schools. The East Malaysian are also unhappy about the large number of West Malaysian teachers sent over – all Muslim, mostly with non-science qualifications and Islamic education (Riddell 2017).

Another positive sign is the support the religious minorities have received in some issues from progressive Muslim groups. Hermen Shastri comments that,

The Council of Churches of Malaysia interacts with Malay NGOs on a regular basis. The ones we find most helpful are those who have made up their mind that Malaysia is secular and there is nothing unIslamic about that. Malaysia was never meant to be an Islamic state. This has only come to excess because of having one government rule for so long (Riddell 2017).

Malaysia represents an unfulfilled promise, a country that could blaze an exciting trail of progressive Islamic pluralism but has so far disappointed in many respects. It will take a strong leader, and probably a further change of government, to turn the ship of state away from the drift towards political Islam so that it is facing towards, rather than away from, the 21st century. It seems that Malaysia's experiment in religious pluralism, which is a pioneering venture in the Islamic world, needs further thought.

Bibliography

Abdul Hamid, Ahmad Fauzi. "The Extensive Salafization of Malaysian Islam." *Trends in Southeast Asia* (ISEAS – Yusof Ishak Institute) 9 (2016).

Ahmad, Reme. "Abdullah's Tactics Confound Opposition." *The Straits Times*, published March 9 2004.

Chew, Amy. "Malaysia is now in uncharted waters." *The Interpreter*, published March 5, 2020.

FMT Reporters. "Buy an island and live there, Muslim activist tells PAS over Christmas greetings." *Free Malaysia Today*, published December 24, 2018.

Hashim, Madjidah. "Devastating for Malaysia." *The Star*, published January 4, 2019.

Institute of Islamic Understanding Malaysia (June, 2001), www.ikim.gov.my/s301-1.htm.

Kamali, Mohammad Hashim. *Punishment in Islamic Law: An Enquiry into the Hudud Bill of Kelantan.* Kuala Lumpur: Ilmiah Publishers, 1995.

Koya, Abdar Rahman. "The caliphate had ICERD too, Turkish scholar reminds Malaysian Muslim groups." *Free Malaysia Today*, published November 16, 2018.

Malik, Maszlee, and Musa Mohd.Nordin. "Love and Intellect in Absentia." *Der Reisende*, published February 2, 2010, http://maszleemalik.blogspot.com/2010/02/my-join-written-article-with-dato-dr.html.

Noor, Farish A. "Islamization on Campus: One academic's personal viewpoint." *Asiaweek.com*, published June 16, 2000, http://edition.cnn.com/ASIANOW/asiaweek/ma gazine/2000/0616/sr.academic.html.

Prakash, G. "PAS Youth chief warns Muslims not to celebrate Christmas." *The Malay Mail*, published December 24, 2018.

Riddell, Peter G. "A Watershed for Malaysia." *Church Times*, published March 12, 2008, https://www.churchtimes. co.uk/articles/2008/14-march/comment/a-watershed-for-malaysia.
_____. "Churches at risk in 'Allah' debate." *The Church Times*, published January 13, 2010, https://www.churchtimes. co.uk/articles/2010/15-january/comment/churches-at-risk-in-allah-debate.
_____. "Malaysia's progressive Muslims want a secular future." *Lapidomedia: Centre for Religious Literacy in Journalism*, published March 1, 2017. http://religiousliteracyinstitute .org/battle-secular-malaysia.
_____. "Malaise in Malaysia." *Touchstone*, July/August, 2019.

Spykerman, Neville. "Hadi flays church arson, says dialogue key to 'Allah' issue." *Badan Perhubungan PAS Negeri Sabah*, published Janurary 9, 2010, https://pasabah.wordpress.com/tag/church.

The Commissioner of Law Revision, Malaysia. "Federal Constitution." *Government of Malaysia*, November 1, 2010. http://www.agc.gov.my/agcportal/uploads/files/Publications/FC/Federal%20Consti%20(BI%20text).pdf, accessed August 30, 2020.

The Voice of the Martyrs Canada. *Christian Children Books Seized*, https://www.vomcanada.com/my-2008-01-16.htm, accessed August 30, 2020.

Ting, Helen. "Anwar may not be Malaysia's political messiah." *Eureka Street*, published April 15, 2008, https://eurekastreet.com.au/article/anwar-may-not-be-malaysia-s-political-messiah.
. _____ "The Politics of Hudud Law Implementation in Malaysia." *ISEAS Working Papers* 4 (2016): 5.

www.ingramcontent.com/pod-product-compliance
Lightning Source LLC
Chambersburg PA
CBHW060313030426
42336CB00011B/1026